The Opera Gazetteer

Maria Callas in Lisbon

The Opera Gazetteer

Robert Turnbull

RIZZOLI
NEW YORK

First published in the United States of America in 1988 by RIZZOLI INTERNATIONAL
PUBLICATIONS, INC. 597 Fifth Avenue, New York, NY 10017

ISBN 0-8478-0727-4
LC 86-42738

Typeset in Linotype Plantin by Goodfellow and Egan Ltd, Cambridge.

Printed on Matrice Matt paper supplied by Lynton Paper and Board Ltd by R.J. Acford,
Chichester.

To my parents and R.E.N.C.

Contents

Introduction

The doors of the world's opera houses are open wider than they have ever been before. Opera now reaches a large audience through broadcasts, recordings and videos, and the growing number of people travelling abroad for business and pleasure has increased interest in foreign opera houses and festivals. Opera-going is no longer the exclusive and financially prohibitive pursuit it once was; many regional companies flourishing all over the world offer excellent productions for little more than the price of a cinema ticket, and even the most grandiose establishments make provision for the less wealthy opera lover.

This book is intended both as a practical guide and a general reference work. It gives information on the best way to obtain tickets to well over one hundred opera houses and festivals in the hope that it will encourage those who might previously have been put off booking abroad by language barriers or unfamiliarity. Current information on repertoire, directors and musical directors, dates of seasons and prices has also been included, although it will obviously be subject to fluctuation, to give the reader a reasonable idea about the nature of each operatic venue, its size, the scope of its ambitions and its musical preferences. In most cases, booking information has been restricted to ways of obtaining tickets directly from the opera house in question, but it should also be borne in mind that it may be also be possible to book through international agencies such as American Express, or through theatrical ticket agents in the town concerned.

I also hope that the book will be enjoyed at home by everyone interested in the story of opera. Opera houses often have fascinating histories; they have all at one time or another been affected by the social and political upheavals surrounding them, as well as arbitrary factors such as earthquakes, floods and fires – in the age of gas and candle light opera houses burned down with astonishing regularity. They have also witnessed murders, political demonstrations and revolutionary tribunals, and have at various times been turned into gambling dens and military arsenals. Operatic companies, too, have often had checkered and unpredictable careers, with famous singers, composers and conductors all contributing to their evolution.

Space has not allowed for the inclusion of every operatic establishment in the world, and selection has been made according to the musical, theatrical or historical importance of each venue, so that as well as large, well-established opera houses such as La Scala in Milan, lesser-known but interesting festivals like those held at Orange and Wexford are covered. Some theatres of historical interest have been included as much for the excellence of their architecture as for their operatic performances. It would require an entirely different type of book to cover the idiosyncratic but equally intriguing venues I have come across during my researches, such as Adelina Patti's opera house at her home in Craig y nos in Wales, or the Amargosa Opera House in Death Valley Junction in California, where Marta Beckett and her assistant Tom Willet perform melodramas to a permanent audience of sixteenth-century Spanish royalty painted on the walls.

My choice of English or foreign language in the naming of operas and operatic venues has been governed by the form that I feel will be most familiar to an English-speaking readership. Thus Mozart's Zauberflöte is rendered in its better-known translation The Magic Flute, whereas Die Entführung is kept in the original language. A short glossary explains unfamiliar foreign operatic expressions, although technical terms have deliberately been kept to a minimum.

Robert Turnbull

Acknowledgements

I would like to thank the following people, who have all helped in various ways:
Hugh Canning, Rupert Christiansen, Mel Cooper, Jean-Jacques Gabas, Gary Michalek and Don Sparling

The 1985 Ludwigsburg Festival production of 'Semele'

Santa Fe Opera House

UNITED STATES
AND CANADA

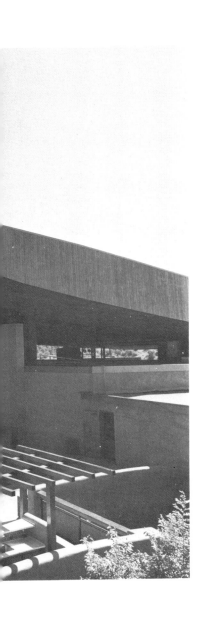

Boston Opera Company
539 Washington Street, Boston, Massachusetts 02111

Director: Robert Canon
Artistic Director: Sarah Caldwell
Season: December–May
Productions: 4
Performances: 3–4 of each
Capacity: 2,500

Box Office: (617) 426 3626
Box open: Mon–Fri 10.00a.m.–6.00p.m.
Postal: PO Box 50, Boston, Mass, MA 02112
Prices: $12–$50
Concessions: For students and senior citizens

Boston's flourishing musical life predates that of most other cities in the USA. The Symphony Orchestra alone was one of the first to be founded (in 1888) and the presence of some of the greatest musicians from Europe, some associated with nearby Harvard University, has, over a long period, contributed to a generally high standard of instrumental playing as well as scholastic achievements in musicology.

The first opera to be heard in Boston was *Love in a Village* given as a concert performance in 1769 – public stagings of drama and opera were banned at the time, although there were a few performances of ballad operas staged towards the end of the century. During the nineteenth century the most famous opera companies came to Boston: in 1855 Mario and Grisi appeared for the first time and Adelina Patti, who had lived in New York since early childhood, tried out Rosina for the first time in Boston. The Mapleson Company began visiting the city in 1878. They introduced Lillian Nordica as Violetta in 1884, and the French company of Maurice Grau was active in Boston from 1879. At the same time, the first attempts to form a company from local talent resulted in the Boston Ideal Opera and the Castle Square Company, giving seasons during the 1880s and 1890s.

The enormous popularity of opera along the Eastern seaboard at this time was quick to infect Boston, and the decision was taken around the turn of the century to build the city's first and only opera house. The move had been inspired by the formation three years earlier of the Boston Opera Company, which began its short and spectacular life with Lillian Nordica returning to sing the title role in *La Gioconda*. For five years the company managed ninety performances a year and attracted well-established singers such as Bori, Destinn and Garden. Felix Weingartner made his US debut conducting the company in *Tristan*. Despite having an excellent manager in Henry Russell, the company sadly lost money through over ambition; there wasn't sufficient demand to make the opera house pay for itself, and after a disastrous European tour in 1914 the company folded.

Visiting troupes resumed their appearances, including one from Chicago, and from 1934 the Metropolitan Company from New York. Both visits were organised by the Boston Opera Association, which was set up with government help to maintain operatic life in the city. a considerably shortened version of *Les Troyens* was put together by another short-lived group which was started by Boris Goldovsky in 1946 – the New England Opera Theatre. This was the first US performance of the opera, but its failure was catastrophic for the company, and three years later, the Opera House itself was demolished amongst protests.

Just when the situation looked especially bleak for opera lovers in Boston, with the only available space being the Orpheum Theater, an old cinema which had been turned into a Vaudeville House, Sarah Caldwell arrived from Missouri to form, in 1957, the Opera Company of Boston, and has been its director ever since. Caldwell achieved a miracle with this company. Having won considerable respect as a conductor and producer she began a policy of adventurous productions, often of US premières, with the stress being laid firmly on teamwork and brought many important singers to the city eager to assist her. She managed to instill a sense of discipline and co-operation which is maintained to this day. She was furthermore the only woman to have achieved any degree of fame as a conductor let alone as a producer and general manager. The first US performances of *Moses and Aron* (1968), Nono's *Intolleranza* (1966), *Benvenuto Cellini* (1975), *The Icebreak* (1979), Zimmermann's *Die Soldaten*, and Peter Maxwell Davies's *Taverner* (1986) were all produced and directed by her. Sutherland, Tebaldi and Sills have all sung with the company, Sills giving her first Norma and Lucia in Boston. Other notable productions have included Prokofiev's *War and Peace* (1914) and Massenet's *Don Quichotte* (1976) and Handel's *Giulio Cesare* (1987) by innovative producers such as Peter Sellars and Frank Corsaro. Since 1979 the company has been based at the old Keith Memorial Theater, now known as The Opera House.

Adelina Patti as Violetta in 'La Traviata'
(photo: BBC Hulton Picture Library)

Lyric Opera, Chicago
20 North Wacker Drive, Chicago, Illinois 60606

Director: Ardis Krainik
Artistic Director: Bruno Bartoletti
Season: September–February
Productions: 9, 4 new
Performances: Approx. 14 of each
Capacity: 3,636

Box Office: (312) 332 2244
Telex: 190252/253550
Box open: Mon–Fri 9.00a.m.–8.00p.m.; during season Sat and Sun 10.00a.m.–5.00p.m.
Postal: As above
Prices: $10.75–$71.50
Cards: VISA, Mastercharge, American Express, Diners

Video: Eugene Onegin

A resident opera company did not exist in Chicago until 1910 when the impressario Harold McCormack formed the Chicago Grand Opera company. The company got off to a propitious start. Many of its members were recruited from the recently disbanded Hammerstein company which had so successfully competed with the Metropolitan Company in New York. The choice of Cleofonte Campanini as musical director proved to be a good one: for the first season he invited Mary Garden, the Scottish soprano who had studied singing in Chicago to repeat Mélisande, a role she had created, and later Thaïs and the highly controversial role of Salome. So great was her popularity at this time that in 1919 she became director of the company but resigned after only one season after running up an enormous deficit of one million dollars. Her lasting contribution to the company was the commissioning of Prokofief's *The Love of Three Oranges* in 1920, which was conducted a year later by the composer himself.

When Samuel Insull took over as director a potentially profitable era began: he had the excellent idea of moving the opera into the basement of a sky-scraper and making the offices above pay for its general expenses. In 1929 the company moved in (with a performance of *Aida*) and there they remain. In the years to come Insull made Chicago the leading house for Wagner in the United States, importing famous Europeans such as Lotte Lehmann, Frida Leider, Alexander Kipnis and Eva Turner, and it remained so until the Flagstad Melchoir seasons at the Met during the thirties. The house also had a strong Italian repertoire, with two of its most exciting interpreters appearing regularly – Rosa Raisa and Claudio Muzio – and for a time was considered by many to be a superior company to the Met. Unfortunately, unlike its great rival in New York, the Grand Opera never survived the depression and was dissolved in 1932.

Various attempts were made to present opera in Chicago from 1933 to the end of the war, most relying heavily on singers from New York companies. But thanks to the impresario Paul Logone, foreign singers continued to be invited – many, like Björling and Tagliavini making their US débuts. The tenor Martinelli acted briefly as musical director of an improvised company between 1941 and 1942 having successfully sung his first ever Otello and his only Tristan in Chicago in 1936 and 1939 respectively.

Finally, in 1954 Carol Fox, Lawrence Kelly and Nicola Rescigno formed the Lyric Opera of Chicago, with Fox as the general manager. From the outset she went for the big names, establishing a policy of depending on singers to draw revenue. For the first season Maria Callas made her US début with Violetta and Lucia, returning the following year for *I Puritani* and *Madame Butterfly*. In 1958 Callas and Tebaldi appeared during the same season, the latter becoming a firm favourite as was Tito Gobbi who sang for twenty years for the company. The stream of stars continued unabated: Birgit Nilsson, Boris Christoff, Giulietta Simionato, Mario del Monaco, Luciano Pavarotti, Jon Vickers, Mirella Freni and Placido Domingo represent a fraction of the eminent names associated with the Lyric.

The company is unashamedly biased towards Italian opera prompting the nick-name 'La Scala West' and there are glaring omissions in its French and German repertoire. Furthermore, the company became the recipient of the first every grant made to a foreign company by the Italian government in 1958, and hosted the Verdi Congress in 1974.

Bruno Bartoletti, the Lyric's artistic director since 1964 has introduced some important twentieth-century works into the repertoire to prevent the company becoming a museum piece, and has made the radical step of commissioning an opera from Krystoff Penderecki (*Paradise Lost*, 1978) and giving the first US performance of Berio's *La Vera Storia* in 1986. Since the death of Carol Fox in 1981, the new general manager Ardis Krainik has continued essentially the same policies and maintained standards. Chicago has introduced some of the highest ticket prices of any leading opera house in an attempt to cover its mounting deficit.

The 1982 Lyric Opera production of 'Madame Butterfly'

Cincinnati Opera Association
1241 Elm Street – Music Hall, Cincinnati, Ohio 45210

Director: James de Blasis
Season: June and July
Productions: 4
Performances: 2 of each
Capacity: 3,632

Box Office: (513) 721 8222
Box open: Mon–Fri 10.00a.m.–6.00p.m.; Sat 12.00p.m.–5.00p.m.
Postal: As above
Prices: $6–$30
Cards: Visa, Mastercharge, American Express

Open-air operas were held at the local zoo in Cincinnati from 1920 to 1974. Notable early performances from the second oldest opera company in America include the world première of *The Music Robber* by Isaac Van Grove in 1927, and the first all-American cast of *Die Meistersinger* in 1928. By 1933 audiences were down to just six hundred, with the seasons cut from eight to six weeks. In 1934 the company temporarily parted from its backdrop of elephants, gazelles and baboons to move into the local football stadium for a year. By the late 1930s it was attracting better artists and improved seating conditions, but it was not until 1959, under the general managership of John Magro, that Cincinnati began to attract significantly larger audiences and adopt a much more professional approach.

In 1961 Teresa Stratas sang Mimi and Musetta in two different performances of *La Bohème*, in 1964 Sherrill Milnes played Il Conte di Luna in *Il Trovatore*, and in 1965 he sang Scarpia in *Tosca*. They were followed by Placido Domingo and Monserrat Caballe in 1966 and 1967 before the company at last left the zoo for the renovated Music Hall. The Hall was opened in 1878 and was built in just twelve months to house the local symphony orchestra. It has three main sections, one devoted to music, the other two to trade shows, all contained within a marvellous piece of architectural eccentricity. Nearly four million red bricks were used to create this Gothic/Byzantine fantasy with its turrets, garrets and gables.

The Hall was modernised in 1927, and again in 1955, and now provides exceptional acoustics and first-rate conditions for performers and singers alike. The company has displayed a notable preference for French works and has recently staged works both in and out of the main repertoire. In 1983 *Attila, La Favorite, Boris Godunov, The Pearl Fishers, Die Entführung aus dem Serail*, and *La Rondine* were all performed. Cincinnati is now essentially a debut house, sometimes referred to as 'the cradle of American opera singers'. Singers who have made their first appearances here include James Melta, Jan Pierce and Dorothy Kirsten. From 1985 Italian operas appear to have been favoured, making up half the productions in 1985 and 1986, and four out of five in 1987. Subtitles are used when operas are sung in their original language. Two recent achievements have been the US premières of Alfano's *Resurrection* (1983) presented in a new English translation by Andrew Porter and a revival of Leoncavallo's *Zaza* in 1985.

Dallas Opera House

1925 Elm Street, Suite 400, Dallas, Texas 75201

Director: Plato Karayanis
Artistic Director: Nicola Rescigno
Season: November–December; additional
spring programme
Productions: 7, average of 2 new
Performances: 7 of each
Capacity: 3,420 (at the Music Hall, Fair Park)

Box Office: (214) 8710090
Box open: Mon–Fri 9.00a.m.–5.00p.m.; also
on Sat during season
Postal: As above
Prices: $4–$60
Concessions: Available for senior citizens,
students, disabled

Dallas opera means big names, lavish productions, and big business. Yet for the first seventy years or so, following the opening of the Dallas Opera House in 1883, opera in Dallas was a relatively humble affair. Initial performances were given by travelling musicians and opera companies, followed by regular visits from the Chicago Opera, and in the early 1940s the Metropolitan stepped in to give six performances each spring. Dallas took over in 1957 when the Civic Opera Company was set up by Lawrence Kelly.

High standards were set right from the opening productions. The inaugural *L'Italiana in Algeri* was designed and directed by Franco Zeffirelli, and was his American début. The following year Maria Callas sang Violetta in *La Traviata* and appeared alongside Jon Vickers and Teresa Berganza, also making their American débuts, in *Medea*. Other highlights have included the stage première of Handel's *Giulio Cesare* in 1965 and Alfredo Kraus taking the leading role in *Werther* in 1972, which was to be the first of his eleven star roles with Dallas. Jon Vickers returned in the lead role in the first American staging of Handel's *Samson* in 1976, and the first US staging of *Orlando Furioso* with Marilyn Horne took place in 1980. One year later Wagner's *Ring* cycle was performed, and the spring season of 1984 was inaugurated with Gian Carlo Menotti's *Amelia Goes to the Ball*.

By 1981 sixteen productions were being staged each year, rising to twenty-nine over the next five years. By 1995 it is hoped that the total number of performances will have reached seventy. Dallas opera-goers' taste is very pro-Italian, favouring Verdi, Puccini, Donizetti and Bellini. The 1987 thirtieth anniversary celebrations included two Puccini operas and one Rossini, as well as Massenet's *Werther*. Leading roles went to Alfredo Kraus, Johanna Meier, Marilyn Horne and Maria Slatinaru.

The rapid growth of Dallas Opera, with its ability to attract the top singers and conductors, is rooted in its exorbitantly wealthy community. Unfortunately though, despite the ability to raise finances, Dallas Opera, once the vanguard of companies in the United States, has recently been beset by ill-fated productions, cancellations and inadequate planning. The drive to purchase land for a new opera house has thus far produced $2 million of the $3½ million required, and the company plan to move in the late 1990s.

Fort Worth Opera

3505 West Lancaster, Fort Worth, Texas 76107

Director: Mario Ramos
Season: November–April
Productions: 3
Performances: 2 of each
Capacity: 3,054

Box Office: (817) 737 0775. Single tickets also available at Central Ticket Office (817) 429 1181 two weeks before performance.
Box open: Mon–Fri 9.00a.m.–5.00p.m. The Convention Center Box Office, 1111 Houston Street, Forth Worth, tel. (817) 332 9222 opens Fri 7.00p.m. and Sun 1.00p.m. before performance
Postal: As above
Prices: $5–$35

The Fort Worth Opera Association was founded in 1946 by the ex-singers Mrs. F. L. Snyder and Mr August Spain, and opened in November of that year with *La Traviata*. Although the type of operas produced in the first period were fairly standard, including *Madame Butterfly*, *Aida* and *Die Fledermaus*, the idea was to nurture American talent and create in-house productions regardless of the star system. It was Rudolf Kruger who was responsible for the initial successes, which included, in 1962, Placido Domingo's first major role in America, as Edgar in *Lucia di Lammermoor* when he sang opposite Lily Pons in her last performance on stage, and two years later its first production of Wagner's *Lohengrin*. Attracting a growing number of grants from various sources, the largest coming from the Ford Foundation (over one hundred thousand dollars over a period of five years), the Association managed to increase the number of annual productions from four to five and started a more adventurous policy of giving more unfamiliar works such as Suppé's *Die Schöne Galatea* in 1966, and *The Shepherdess and the Chimneysweep* by Julia Smith in 1967.

Kruger's tenure lasted for twenty-eight years until 1982, and although there were high points, including a successful *Cavalleria Rusticana* and *Pagliacci* with Beverly Sills, a slow decline set in towards the end. It was up to Dwight Bowes, general director until 1985, and his successor Mario Ramos, to improve standards and keep individual donations coming in. At present the Association is reforming its entire structure with a plan to renovate two old theatres, one seating two thousand, the other one thousand one hundred, for the production of two Grand Operas per season in the larger theatre and four chamber operas in the smaller one. It also intends to expand its repertoire to introduce more Baroque and twentieth-century works, as well as to undertake some commissions.

At the time of writing the company is still using the vast Tarrant Convention Center which may look like an aircraft hanger from the outside but has adequate facilities for opera production.

Houston Grand Opera

615 Louisiana Street, Houston, Texas 77002

Director: David Gockley
Musical Director: John Demain
Season: Mid Oct–Nov, Jan–Feb, April–May
Productions: 7, 3 new
Performances: 6–8 of each
Capacity: John & Alice Wortham Theater
2200; Cullen Theater 1100

Box Office: (713) 227 2787
Telex: 546 0200
Box open: Mon–Fri 9.30a.m.–5.30p.m., Sat–Sun 10a.m.–5p.m.
Postal: Houston Grand Opera, c/o Houston Ticket Centre, 615 Louisiana Street, Houston Texas 77002
Prices: $9.50–$85, some tickets for sale on day of performance at half price
Cards: Mastercards, Visa, American Express, Diners Club
Concessions: For disabled people; for group concessions, ring (713) 546 0236

Recordings: Treemonisha (PG), Porgy and Bess (RCA)

Operatic history in Texas can be measured in terms of decades. Certainly the oil-rich, cowboy state was not entirely innocent of opera in the wild days of the nineteenth century, but it consisted primarily of the itinerant kind, touring Italian singers and companies bent on making a fortune in the Golden West. Houston was always one of the best touring venues for the established companies, the New York Met, the Chicago Lyric or the Boston Opera, but not until 1955 did the State's most popular town acquire its own Grand Opera.

The company was founded by Walter Herbert, an emigré from Frankfurt. German-born and Vienna-trained, he was principal conductor of the Volksoper in Vienna until Hitler's Anschluss in 1933, when he left for the USA. He opened his Houston company adventurously in January 1956 with Richard Strauss's *Salome* (conducted by himself and with a largely American cast including Frederick Jagel as Herod) and, more conventionally, with *Madame Butterfly*.

During Houston Grand Opera's early years, financial constraints tended to limit the scope of performances, but Herbert scored a notable success with his first attempt at Strauss's *Elektra* for which he secured the services of a reigning exponent of the title role, the Munich-born Norwegian singer Inge Borkh and the celebrated American Klytemnestra Regina Resnick. Otherwise the repertory consisted of staple fare, cast predominantly from local strength.

The early 1960s saw a move towards more lavish and adventurous staging, as in *Turandot* with Richard Tucker and Lucille Udovick, and the encouragement of young singers, soon to be stars of international standing: Cornell MacNeil, Placido Domingo, Beverley Sills and Sherill Milnes. One of Herbert's great achievements in the late sixties was the American première of Hans Werner Henze's *The Young Lord* given in Houston only a year after its Berlin première in 1967. But this isolated example of progressive programming did not pass without controversy. The conservative taste of Houston opera-goers has determined the artistic policy of the Grand Opera and still influences the highly enterprising regime of Herbert's successor, David Gockley. Even in 1985,

Gockley demurred at importing Ruth Berghaus's surrealist production of *Don Giovanni* – an announced collaboration between Houston and Welsh National Opera – and substituted instead a 'safer' version by the young Swedish producer, Göran Järvefelt.

Since Gockley's appointment in 1972, nevertheless, Houston's image as a serious centre of high musical and theatrical standards has gained ground. The young General Director has striven for a balance between old-fashioned star nights with conventional stagings, vehicles for the *prime donne* Sutherland, Sills and Horne, and music-theatre productions with integrated young ensembles of American soloists. He has maintained Herbert's tradition of matinée performances given by up-and-coming singers at popular prices. Gockley has also championed the cause of American composers in the opera house to a greater degree than perhaps any other of the USA's opera directors. True, these have tended to be of the musical rearguard: Thomas Pasatieri's *The Seagull*, Dominic Argento's *Postcard from Morocco* and several operas by Carlisle Floyd. More recently, Houston Grand Opera gave the world première of Leonard Bernstein's *A Quiet Place*, sequel to *Trouble in Tahiti*, and the first American production of Philip Glass's *Akhnaten*. Gockley has also consistently programmed the popular classics of the American musical tradition, among them Romberg's *Student Prince*, Jerome Kern's *Showboat*, Scott Joplin's *Treemonisha*, Berstein's *Candide* and Steven Sondheim's *Sweeny Todd*. A rare example of an opera company succeeding in a difficult popular medium.

Houston has had its share of successes in the classical repertoire too. Its production of *Der Rosenkavalier* with Evelyn Lear, Frederica von Stade (her first Oktavian) and Michael Langdon attracted worldwide attention as did a subsequent staging of Strauss and Hoffmannsthal's Viennese opera *Arabella* in 1977 with Kiri te Kanawa and Ashley Putnam. The company has continued to discover its own home-grown stars; in addition to Putnam, Houston gave early opportunities to Neil Shicoff, Catherine Malfitano and Faye Robinson.

Houston Grand Opera has always lived a hermit-crab existence, performing in its first years in the city's Music Hall, later, in October 1966, moving to the better equipped Jesse H. Jones Hall for the Performing Arts for a spectacular new production of *Aida* starring Tucker, Gabriella Tucci and Giorgio Tozzi. In the autumn of 1987 the Grand Opera moved again, this time to the purpose-built Wortham Theater Center, an arts complex incorporating two adjacent auditoria, the larger John and Alice Wortham Theater for major presentations of Houston's ballet as well as the Grand Opera, and the smaller Lillie Cullen Theater to be the venue for chamber concerts and small-scale theatre productions. Houston Grand Opera's new home, with splendid rehearsal facilities opened in October 1987, with a new production of *Aida*, starring Domingo and Freui. For the same season the HGO commissioned the avant-garde San Fransisco-based composer John Adams to write the satirical opera *Nixon in China*.

Los Angeles Opera

The Music Center, 135 North Grand Avenue, Los Angeles, California, 90012

Director: Peter Hemmings
Season: September–March
Productions: 7, 4 new
Performances: Varies
Capacity: Wiltern 2,300; Dorothy Chandler 3,197

Box Office: (213) 972 7211
Telex: 650 290 9442
Box open: Daily 10.00a.m.–6.00p.m.
Postal: As above
Prices: $10–$70

Los Angeles has only just surpassed the touring company stage. From the 1880s almost right up to the present they have been the source of the city's opera life, the principal companies being the Del Conti, the Metropolitan, the San Carlo, the Chicago Opera, and the San Francisco Opera.

In the past twenty years there have been two significant events. First, the opening of the Dorothy Chandler Pavilion in 1964, a theatre seating just over three thousand and the home of the LA Philharmonic, which also provides a regular stage for touring productions. The second, in 1986, was the opening of Los Angeles' first resident opera company. The directors were actually considering two possibilities, continuing to bring in outside productions or produce works themselves. Peter Hemmings, fresh from his managing directorship of the London Symphony Orchestra and previously in charge of the Scottish Opera, propelled them towards the latter. Since then, in just three years, the company has achieved what many older and distinguished companies have not, and is clearly going to be one of America's foremost companies. The première season began with Placidio Domingo in *Otello*, *Salome* (with $130,000 worth of scenery), *Madame Butterfly* and *Alcina*, and top singers Sherrill Milnes, Leona Mitchell, Maria Ewing and Arleen Auger. The season concluded with a sold-out ten-performance run of *Porgy and Bess*. The season was an instant artistic and financial success, with tickets a revenue of a quarter of a million dollars in excess of projections.

In 1987 there were three new productions. These were *Macbeth* conducted by Domingo, and the much-awaited co-productions with Los Angeles Philharmonic, *Tristan und Isolde*, conducted by Zubin Mehta, designed by David Hockney, and produced by Jonathan Miller. Hemmings has also held well over eight hundred auditions for local singers. Eventually ten were chosen, being given three-month contracts.

The 1988 season offers five works at the Dorothy Chandler. *La Bohème*, with Domingo and Dessi in the title roles, *The Fiery Angel*, a new production starring Marilyn Zschau, *La Cenerentola*, a new production, conducted by Sir Neville Marriner, a revival of *Tristan und Isolde*, and *Macbeth* conducted by Domingo, starring Justino Diaz. The Wiltern Theatre (re-opened 1985) offers *A Midsummer's Night Dream* and *The Mikado* directed by Jonathan Miller, with Dudley Moore as Ko-Ko.

Montreal Opera House

1157 St Catherine Street East, Montreal, Quebec H2L 2G8

Director: Bernard Creighton
Artistic Director: Jean-Paul Jeannotte
Season: September–June
Productions: 4
Performances: Approx. 7 of each
Capacity: 3000

Box Office: (514) 842 2112
Telex: 05561201
Box open: Mon–Sat 12.00–9.00p.m.
Prices: $14–$45

Opera in Montreal has had a chequered history. The earliest performances were in the late eighteenth century, with touring companies taking centre stage in the nineteenth, performing the standard repertoire, notably Bellini, Donizetti and Rossini. In 1910 Montreal gained its own one-hundred strong company which relied heavily on famous guest singers, but it could find few theatres large enough to handle its huge cast. Despite some critical successes the company faced financial disaster and came to an end after just four years. In 1913 the National Opera Company of Canada was founded, but it too was short lived, and in the twenty-five years before resident opera returned, Montreal relied on touring productions, principally from the Met in New York. Les Variétés Lyriques was founded in 1936 and ran for nineteen years at the Monument National, during which time it built up a following of over seventeen thousand subscribers for its programme of popular opera, including over a thousand performances of eighty-three operas.

From 1936 to 1966 the Montreal Summer Festival presented one opera a year. It catered much more for opera lovers, providing Canadian premières of *Pelléas et Mélisande, Ariadne auf Naxos,* and Thomas Beecham was guest conductor for the 1942 to 1943 season, giving *Figaro, Roméo et Juliette* and *Tristan and Isolde.*

In 1941 the Opera Guild of Montreal was set up under the directorship of Pauline Donalda, who had previously been a top European singer and teacher. The Guild ran for twenty-seven years, until Donalda died, during which time it adopted a low key policy, initially staging just four performances a year, though adventurously selecting works such as *Louise* and *The Love of Three Oranges.*

In 1964 the Montreal Symphony Orchestra under Zubin Mehta staged two to three operas a year at the Place des Arts. This venture was followed by the short-lived L'Opéra du Quebec, which disbanded in 1975. Five years later matters considerably improved and opera gained what should certainly be a permanent footing in the city when the Montreal Opera was founded. The Montreal Opera perform a small number of works each year at the Salle Wilfrid Pelletier; the 1986 to 1987 season included an exceptional *Roméo et Juliette,* and a *Magic Flute,* produced by Frank Corsaro and designed by Maurice Sendak. The 1987 to 1988 season, under the artistic directorship of Jean-Paul Jeannotte, offers *Otello, La Cenerentola, Carmen, Don Giovanni* and *Madame Butterfly.*

New Orleans Opera

333 St Charles Avenue, Suite 907, New Orleans, LA 70130

Director: Arthur G. Cosenza
Season: October–March
Productions: 4
Capacity: 2,300

Box Office: (504) 529 2278
Box open: Mon–Fri 9.00a.m.–5.00p.m.;
During performance week Sat 9.00a.m.–
1.00p.m.
Postal: As above
Prices: $14–$60
Concessions: for students; season tickets
available
Cards: VISA, MasterCard

French touring companies gave New Orleans its first taste of opera in the late eighteenth century. During the time of Louis Tabery's management from 1806–10, there were some three hundred and fifty performances of seventy-six operas. At this time there were two opera houses, the Rue St. Pierre, 1791, and Rue St. Philippe, 1808, with the Théâtre d'Orléans opening a year later with the unusual feature of latticed boxes for those in mourning or preferring an evening's anonymity. The Théâtre was destroyed by fire in 1813 and rebuilt on the same site. Drama struck again in 1859 when Charles Boudousquie, the manager, set up his own opera company, but this burned down after just seven years. During that time it gave many American firsts, including Herold's *Zampa* in 1833, Donizetti's *Lucrezia Borgia* in 1837, Meyerbeer's *Les Huguenots* in 1839 and Adam's *Le Chalet* in 1839. Excitement was generated by the appearance of Adelina Patti between 1860 and 1861. Aged only seventeen prior to her debut on the international scene, she first appeared as Lucia and for the rest of the season as Gilda Valentine and Dinorah in *Le Pardon du Ploermel*. From the 1870s onwards she appeared in the States in operas by Thomas, Lalo, Gounod and Massenet. New Orleans was slow to respond to Wagner until Damrosch's travelling company performed in one week the whole of *Ring* plus *Tannhäuser*, *Tristan* and *Die Meistersinger*. Touring companies included San Carlo who gave the first US production of Cilea's *Adriana Lecouvreur*.

The fourth opera house in New Orleans was built in 1859. This was one of the greatest operatic American centres and featured famous singers such as Adelina Patti, and Mme St. Urban. In December 1919 fire struck yet again, taking with it a unique collection of props, costumes, scores and documents. It was not until 1943 that the city gained another opera house, relying in the meantime on touring companies. The founder of the New Orleans Opera Association was Walter Loubart, and the venue for the next thirty years was the Municipal Auditorium where there were three music directors, Walter Herbert, Renato Cellini, and Knud Andersson. The Opera Association badly needed better facilities, and found them in the new Theatre for the Performing Arts.

New Orleans sees itself as the primary venue for French opera, producing revivals of totally neglected operas such as Halévey's *La Juive*, Meyerbeer's *Les Huguenots*, Donizetti's *La Favorite* and Massenet's *Hérodiade*, as well as staging the ever popular works of Mozart, Wagner and Strauss, all attracting the world's top singers.

Vinay, Treigle and Placido Domingo have all made US debuts here. Native born singer Norman Treigle created the title role in the world première of Carlisle Floyd's *Markheim* in 1966, and Richard Tucker sang his only stage performance of Eleazor in Halévy's *La Juive* in 1973. Other celebrated appearances include *Carmen* with Verrett in 1980, Nilsson in *Turandot* in 1966, *Un Ballo in Maschera* with Bergonzi in 1981, Siegfried Jerusalem as Lohengrin in 1985 and June Anderson as Rosina in 1983.

The 1983 New Orleans Opera production of 'Pagliacci'

New York City Opera
Lincoln Center, NY 10023

Director: Beverly Sills
Season: July–November, March–April
Productions: 19, 4 new
Performances: Varies
Capacity: 2,779, 30 standing
Ballet: 120 per season

Box Office: (212) 870 5570
Box open: Mon 10.00a.m.–8.00p.m., Tues–Sat 10.00a.m.–9.00p.m., Sun 11.30a.m.–7.30p.m.
Postal: As above
Prices: $5–$42
Cards: Diners, American Express, MasterCard, VISA
Concessions: 50% discount for students and senior citizens ½ hour before performance

New York's 'other' opera house, originally at the City Center on West 57th Street, midtown Manhattan, was founded in 1943 by two politicians, Mayor La Guardia, former President of the New York City Council, and a successful businessman named Newbold Morris. Their express aim was to 'present opera with the highest artistic standards, while maintaining the democratic ideas of moderate prices, practical business planning and modern methods.' The City Opera has thus provided a much-needed venue for low-income opera lovers and has for at least twenty years outshone the Metropolitan Opera in the quality of its productions, all created at relatively low cost. Unlike the Oscar Hammerstein company, however, which during the thirties made life very uncomfortable for the Met, it has never attempted to provide serious competition for the two companies, but rather to provide a popular alternative.

The original company was made up of fifteen singers, two conductors and one stage director with short seasons, and sets usually borrowed from the Saint Louis Opera from which its first artistic director came, the Hungarian-born László Halász. Halász had held important conducting posts in Prague, Salzburg and Vienna, and his insistence on defining the production policy himself led him into direct conflict with the board of directors. He was dismissed for 'bad conduct' in 1951 and despite winning the ensuing lawsuit which made him substantially richer, he was not rehired. His legacy, however, included the opening production *Tosca* (1944), the two remaining works of the season Flotow's *Martha* and Bizet's *Carmen* all warmly received, and the first production to be mounted by the new company, the US première of *Ariadne auf Naxos* (1946). The success of the latter led to an extension of the season to twelve weeks and this increased further to between two and three months a year in 1958 when the company began to tour the Midwest and Atlantic Coastline.

Halász's successor Joseph Rosenstock's principal accomplishment was to introduce *Wozzeck* into the repertoire in 1952 when the opera was still highly controversial and a pet hate amongst critics, and in the same year give US première of Bartok's *Bluebeard's Castle*. Next came Eric Leinsdorf who stayed for only a season and then Julius Rudel, originally a conductor from Vienna who had joined the City Center as a repetiteur in 1943. Rudel stayed as musical director for twenty-two years until 1979 and changed the face of the entire institution over that period. Realizing the monopoly the Metropolitan had on the star system, he set about creating an alternative by introducing more unfamiliar operas, including many commissions, with the stress firmly inclined towards ensemble and innovative stagings. He was responsible for many premières of US operas, when the Met. showed little interest in such things and these included Kurka's *The Good Soldier Schweik* (1958), Weisgall's *Six Characters in Search of an Author* (1959), Floyd's *The Passion of Jonathan Wade* (1962), Ward's *The Crucible* (1961), Rorem's *Miss Julie* (1965) and Menotti's *The Most Important Man* (1971). With a keen eye to what was going on in Europe, he introduced many works to the US such as Wolf-Ferrari's *I Quattro Rusteghi* (1951), Von Einem's *Der Prozess* (1953), Orff's *Der Mond* (1956), Strauss's *Die Schweigsame Frau* (1958) and Prokofiev's *The Fiery Angel* (1965).

On 22nd February, 1966, the company moved to the State Theater, Lincoln Center with the first performance in the US of Ginastera's *Don Rodrigo* with a cast that included the young Mexican tenor Placido Domingo. The auditorium which seats two thousand eight hundred, has been criticized for its faulty acoustics, arising from the fact that it was never intended for opera but rather as a home for Balanchine's New York City Ballet. Despite this inconvenience, an ongoing policy of putting ensemble above individual prestige and the mounting of imaginative productions as a result of having to be economical (enabling more conceptual interpretations of standard works) have been the company's greatest achievements. In 1979 the soprano Beverley Sills took over as director and led the New York City Opera into its finest period. Having joined the company in 1955, she became specially associated with a variety of roles that showed off her powers as an actress. Feeling unappreciated by Rudolf Bing, the general manager of the Met, she defiantly became the star of the City Opera by giving a series of great performances of Italian Romantic roles including the three Tudor queens of Donizetti. Sills's populist ideas were highly influential in the United States because they appeared to point to available alternatives for opera production and her example gave great hope to smaller companies wanting to avoid the star system. In 1980 she cut subscription prices by 20% and the box office takings increased by 25%, a highly unusual step to be taken by a major opera company. At the same time she expanded the number of musicals and operetta in the repertoire to include what became a series of legendary productions – of Bernstein's *Candide* (1975), Weill's *Der Silbersee* (1980), Sondheim's *Sweeney Todd* (1984), Gilbert and Sullivan's *Mikado* (1985) and Romberg's *Desert Song* (1987). The less orthodox producers to have worked with the ensemble have included Frank Corsaro, Tito Capobianco, Sarah Caldwell and Harold Prince while many outstanding singers have begun their careers at the City Opera, some going on to become major attractions at the Met.

A warehouse fire in 1986 destroyed the vast majority of costumes and with them many productions have been virtually lost. The repertoire has had to be less adventurous owing to this destruction but plans are still going ahead for the production of a new specially commissioned opera *Rasputin* by Jay Reise in 1988, and a new production of *Moses and Aron*.

The principal company tours to various festivals around the States, including Orange County, Saratoga Springs, Wolftrap and Tampa Bay, while a national company of younger singers goes on tour to thirty states.

Metropolitan Opera, New York
Lincoln Center, NY 10023

Director: Bruce Crawford
Artistic Director: James Levine
Season: September–April
Productions: 22, 4 new
Performances: Varies
Capacity: 4,000, 265 standing

Box Office: (212) 362 6000
Box open: Mon–Sat 10.00a.m.–8.00p.m.;
Sun 12.00p.m.–6.00p.m.
Postal: As above
Prices: $15–$80; most tickets sold through subscription
Cards: All major cards
Concessions: Score desks for students

Recordings: 13 disc recordings including Madame Butterfly (Columbia); Tosca and Così fan Tutti (Columbia); Barber of Seville (RCA) and 46 videos.

Italian opera first reached New York in November 1825 at the Park Theatre where an Italian company led by Manuel Garcia, the celebrated Spanish singer and teacher, made its début. The opera was Rossini's *Barber of Seville*, with Garcia himself playing Count Almaviva and his daughter (later famous as Maria Malibran) and two other members of his family in the cast. Encouraged by Lorenzo da Ponte, Mozart's librettist who happened to be teaching Italian at Columbia College, the New York vintner Dominick Lynch took Garcia's company to New York for a season of seventy-nine performances of operas by Rossini, Mozart, Zingarelli and others.

The first opera house, situated on Church and Leonard Streets, only lasted two seasons. Opening in 1833 with Rossini's *La Gazza Ladra,* it burned down six years later. Following this another attempt to set up an opera was made by a group of businessmen who created the Astor Place Opera House, which opened with a performance of Verdi's *Ernani* in 1847 but crashed ten years later. In 1854 came the immediate forerunner to the Met. – the Academy of Music at 14th Street and Irving Place – which opened in 1854 with Giulia Grisi and Mario as *Norma,* and continued with regular seasons until 1886. It was built at a cost of $335,000, had a capacity of four thousand six hundred and contained the largest stage in the world. A series of impresarios directed operatic activities during this period, including Max Maretzek who was responsible for the first American *Rigoletto* (1855) and *La Traviata* (1856); the brothers Maurice and Max Strakosch; and more importantly the British Colonel James Henry Mapleson, who signed a five-year contract to provide four months of opera a year. Mapleson first of all became the proprietor of the soprano Adelina Patti and went on to manage Mario and Grisi in New York and on tour. Some home-bred singers also sang for Mapleson at the Academy before 1884, the greatest being Lillian Nordica, Minnie Hauk and Clara Kellogg.

Dissatisfaction with the Academy intensified as it became evident that its limited number of boxes could not accommodate all its shareholders: the growing class of rich businessmen were determined to be seen to have 'arrived'. As money was then plentiful, it did not take long for the Morgans, Vanderbilts and representatives of the landed gentry to find the necessary $800,000 to create 'a new opera house which should compete in costliness and splendour with those of the great European capitals'. Boxes were sold at $100 and represented one hundred shares. The hope was that the new theatre would be self-supporting from rentals of the auditorium and the shops built along the perimeter of the house. The architect Josiah Cadey proposed an acceptable design at the relatively low cost of $430,000, which contained one hundred and seventeen boxes and had a capacity of three thousand two hundred. Every box was to have its own anteroom, in the style of La Scala where, in the words of the architect 'the wealthy fashionable classes, who even if not caring especially for, nor appreciating deeply the music, find it a peculiar and valuable social feature'.

In 1880 the new Metropolitan Opera House Company signed up the theatre producer Henry E. Abbey to deliver opera to the new stage and three and a half years later on 22nd October 1883 the curtain rose to Gounod's *Faust*, with Kristina Nilsson as Marguerite. The first season was financially disastrous, largely owing to Abbey's policy of paying unprecedented amounts to singers (Nilsson received $1,000 for the opening night's performance; more than ten times what the average orchestral player earned in a month) and the company sustained a loss of half a million dollars.

The following year, the conductor Leopold Damrosch succeeded in persuading the shareholders to allow only German opera to be given at the Met, partly for the growing numbers of German immigrants to New York. His sudden death brought his son Walther to replace him who for the third season enlisted Anton Seidl, an experienced conductor and protegé of Richard Wagner. Until 1891 German singers were imported for the American premières of most of Wagner's operas – Albert Niemann, Max Alvary and Lilli Lehmann were all singing at Bayreuth at that time. Judging from Lehmann's account of the reception for *Tristan und Isolde*, where 'the audience sat still for minutes, silent and motionless in their places, as though drunk or in a transport, without being conscious that the opera was over', it would seem that New Yorkers were not necessarily opposed to novelty.

When in 1892 their patience eventually ran out, Abbey was returned as manager, the German policy was abandoned, and the star principle came into play. This was based on the belief that people attended opera primarily to hear fine singing; a policy that was maintained at the Met, until the 1950's. The intense enthusiasm for great singers under Abbey and later Maurice Grau initiated New York's golden age of singing with performers such as Melba, Plançon, Nordica, Sembrich, Schumann-Heink and the de Reszke brothers making up the body of the company. But the declining production standards prompted justified criticism. In 1900 *the Times* critic Richard Aldrich grumbled:

'Habitués of the Metropolitan Opera House have been called upon to suffer many things to compensate for the privilege of listening to their great singers – incompetent and inane stage management, miserable and inappropriate scenery and costumes, a chorus wretched in vocal equipment and squalid in appearance.'

Grau had to withdraw with poor health in 1903 and Heinrich Conried was awarded the lease for five seasons starting in 1903. A new re-organization of the company took place with his arrival and since the box-holding system had become outdated, twelve directors were appointed to oversee finances and recruit company shareholders. The Conried regime installed the singers Caruso (who made his debut in 1903) as well as Olive Fremstad, Geraldine Farrar and Shalyapin (who appeared in Boito's *Mefistofele*,

1907), and the conductors Gustav Mahler and Felix Mottl during one of the Met's most productive periods. Two premières caused considerable controversy: Conried was the first person to defy Cosima Wagner by attempting to stage *Parsifal* outside Bayreuth. When the dispute went to court, New York split into two camps, one siding with Cosima and the other with Conried, who eventually won. The production of *Salome* in 1907 with Fremstad in the title-role outraged righteous-minded citizens who joined forces to have it banned, and this time Conried had to accede. Other notable events during his tenure included invitations to Puccini and Humperdinck to attend performances of their works *(Hansel und Gretel* and *Manon Lescaut)*, the attention given to operetta (lavish productions of *Die Fledermaus* and *The Gypsy Baron)* and the first strike in a US opera house when the entire chorus walked out just before a performance of *Faust*.

In 1908 the company was re-organized again under the leadership of the German-Jewish banker Otto Kahn, who payed off the Met's debts and attempted to turn it into a non-profit making organization. It was largely due to him that the engagements of Toscanini and Gatti Casazza came about. Both men came to the Met at the same time making their debut with *Aida*, and Gatti Casazza remained general manager there for a quarter of a century. Under him the policy of giving opera in the original language was established and repertory was expanded to include as many as forty-eight different operas in a twenty-four week season. American opera appeared for the first time at the Met with Frederick Converse's *The Pipe of Desire* (1909) and a ten thousand dollar prize for another home-grown opera was won by Horatio Parker's *Mona*, premièred in 1911. The first seven of his seasons were distinguished by Toscanini's presence, after which a posse of important conductors including Bodansky and Serafin, eagerly took up the baton. There were world premières of Puccini's *La Fanciulla del West* (1910) and *Il Trittico* (1918) Humperdinck's *Königskinder* (1910) and Giordano's *Madame Sans-Gêne* (1916) as well as the first American productions of *The Queen of Spades*, *Boris Godunov* and *Der Rosenkavalier*. The quality of the singing was further enhanced by the débuts of Galli-Curci, de Luca, Gigli, Lauri-Volpi, Muzio, Jeritza and the revolutionary presence of Rosa Ponselle who dominated during the twenties.

In 1935, rendered powerless by the depression, Gatti retired and was succeeded briefly by the American singer Herbert Witherspoon, whose sudden death in turn led to the appointment of Edward Johnson as manager. Johnson inaugurated the special popular priced spring season and encouraged the foundation in 1935 of the Metropolitan Opera Guild, a supporting organization which attracted sponsorship for educational programmes and special performances for school children. He was also responsible for consummating a deal with Columbia Records for the recording of performances at the Met and promoting the careers of young singers through the Metropolitan Opera Auditions. By this time Met productions were being broadcast into the home via Texaco-sponsored Saturday matinees.

The outstanding Wagnerian team of Kirsten Flagstad and Lauritz Melchior were the greatest moneyspinners of the following seasons. Their presence supplemented by that of Lotte Lehmann kept the Met afloat after a period of falling business. Box office receipts almost doubled during the 1938/9 season when Lehmann's *Isolde* captivated audiences and it is tragic to think that after the war she was not asked back since her

Enrico Caruso in the 1910 Metropolitan world première of 'La Fanciulla del West'

husband was briefly associated with the Nazis. In July 1939 the Metropolitan Opera Association decided to raise money to buy the theatre, a move heavily opposed by box-owners, some of whom brought lawsuits. One million dollars was raised from one hundred and sixty-six thousand donors and the following year the grand tier boxes were converted into ordinary balcony seats. The controversy took its toll on all concerned and the Met's war years were difficult. During the petrol shortage Sir Thomas Beecham asked a taxi driver to take him to the Met. He was refused this request on the grounds that the destination was a place of entertainment. Beecham is known to have replied: 'the Met is not a place of entertainment, but a place of penance.'

Johnson was succeeded in 1950 by Rudolf Bing, the Viennese impresario and ex-manager of both the Glyndebourne and Edinburgh Festivals. Bing was essentially conservative in both his personal tastes and in his methods, although several new operas were commissioned by him, notably Barber's *Vanessa* (1958), Menotti's *The Last Savage* (1964) and Levy's *Mourning becomes Electra* (1967). His decree that 'the function of the Metropolitan Opera House is not to become a home for contemporary opera but to preserve the great works of the literature in excellent modern frames' was attacked as antiquated and the Met was often compared to a museum. Under Bing's direction the company became more disciplined and individual whims were not pandered to as they had been; he actually had the nerve to sack Maria Callas in 1958. Furthermore, almost every performance was a sell-out. Essentially the policy stayed the same as before: the Met aimed primarily to satisfy the public's craving for singing stars and the rest came second. In keeping with this populist philosophy, Italian opera enjoyed something of a

The Metropolitan Opera during the daytime

come-back and floods of international singers established themselves overnight: Bjorling, Los Angeles, Callas, Tebaldi, Milanov, di Stefano, Bergonzi and Siepi during the fifties; Caballe, Price, Sutherland, Pavarotti, Nilsson and Scotto in the sixties. In 1955 he broke the colour bar by inviting the negress Marion Anderson to take a principal role in *Un Ballo in Maschera*. Other achievements include the preparation of TV broadcasts to theatres throughout the country, (the first operas to be televised were *Die Fledermaus* and *La Bohème*), and the introduction of some operas in English translation.

Several attempts were made to escape the confines of 39th street, where inadequate staging facilities were causing persistent problems. Eventually the Metropolitan Opera Association, with the help of John Rockefeller III, raised forty-six million dollars and found a new site at the Lincoln Centre. The new house, designed by Wallace K. Harriman, was generally considered to be a great success. The auditorium is simple in style but supplemented by crystal-like chandeliers that are suspended in mid-air until the lights dim when they rise to the roof. The lighting and backstage facilities have been conceived scientifically, the dressing rooms and orchestra pit have been designed for convenience and comfort. There are three stages, one on top of another which rise and fall by hydraulics; an innovation that gives particular excitement to some Met productions.

The New Metropolitan Opera House opened in 1966 with the world première of Barber's *Antony and Cleopatra*, with Leontyne Price and Justino Diaz in the title-roles in a production by Franco Zeffirelli. It was not a success and turned briefly into farce when stage machinery left Cleopatra stuck in her tomb.

In 1972 the Swede Göran Gentele was to replace Bing but was killed in a car crash before the first season. Three years later Anthony Bliss assumed the directorship and appointed James Levine as Music Director.

The Met has only once in its history been threatened by direct competition: in 1906 the impresario Oscar Hammerstein, established the Manhattan Opera Company and managed to secure the services of Calvé, Melba, and Mary Garden for a programme of mostly French Opera, including the US premières of *Thaïs, Louise* and *Pelléas et Mélisande* (1907/8). This created an opera war which lasted for four years, fuelled by the press who adored Hammerstein, seeing him as an underdog and challenger, despite his already established fortune. The 1908/9 season put the Met. two hundred and five thousand dollars in debt, while the Manhattan Company raked in a profit of a similar amount. Finally the Met conceded defeat and paid Hammerstein one million two hundred thousand dollars to agree to refrain from giving opera in New York for ten years.

The Met is still considered by many to be a museum; it hardly ever commissions new works and its total dependence on subscribers approval has been a disincentive to experiment. The attraction of the Met lies in the high musical standards maintained by the pervasive influence of James Levine in the pit and the profusion of great singers on stage. There are always regulars and favourites with Caballé, Freni and Scotto, Bumbry, Verrett, Troyanos, Pavarotti, Domingo, all at some stage having taken the limelight. Newcomers, however, are just as much in evidence, often coming out of the country's great Academies of Music. Recent discoveries include Kathleen Battle, Samuel Ramey and Aprile Millo.

Opera Company of Philadelphia

1500 Walnut Street, Suite 700, Philadelphia, Pennsylvania 19102

Director: Margaret Everitt
Season: October–May
Productions: 4 new
Performances: 2 of each
Capacity: 2,800

Box Office: (215) 732 5813; advance booking 3 weeks before performance from Academy of Music Box Office (215) 893 1930, or by calling CHARGIT (215) 665 8051, or long distance TOLL FREE CHARGIT, 1 (800) 223 1814
Box open: Mon–Sat 9.00a.m.–1.00p.m.; 2.00p.m.–5.00p.m.
Postal: As above or from Academy of Music, Broad and Locust Street, Philadelphia 19102
Prices: $12–$58
Concessions: Half price for students ½ hour before performance

Recordings: Telecasts of La Bohème, The Queen of Spades, Faust

Philadelphia's first opera production was in 1754, at Plumsted's warehouse, which usually staged rather light, frivolous pieces. By the next century the city had acquired three more opera venues, the most important being the Academy, the oldest American opera house in continuous use. Despite the lack of one main opera centre, the city's production list was impressive, with American premières of *Faust* (in German), *Norma*, *The Flying Dutchman* (in Italian), *Cavalleria Rusticana* and *Manon Lescaut*, which attracted some of the world's top singers, including Lilli Lehmann and Jenny Lind. More and more companies were founded in the nineteenth and twentieth centuries, until in 1975 the Philadelphia Lyric and the Grand Opera Company put an end to the city's fragmented operatic life by merging to form the Opera Company of Philadelphia. Since then the quality of Philadelphia Opera has improved enormously.

The company's working principle has always been informed by a mixture of caution and innovation; They have opted for both new works and classics, featuring international stars and young talent. Highlights have included Gian Carlo Menotti's new work *The Hero*, written to launch the company and given its world première in 1970, the American première of the original version of Bizet's *The Pearl Fishers*, and the revival of John Sousa's *The Free Lance*.

In 1981–82 the company began concentrating on new productions. This policy yielded some exciting performances, notably Joseph Baber's *Rumpelstiltskin* with words by the novelist John Gardner; Puccini's *La Rondine*, in 1982, and a surprising double bill featuring Stravinsky's *Oedipus Rex* and Purcell's *Dido and Aeneas*, with Jessye Norman taking the lead in both. The most talked about production was a bold and provocative interpretation of Bizet's *Carmen* set in fascist Spain.

In 1982 the company broke new ground staging operas for PBS television. The first broadcast was a guaranteed success from the moment it was announced that Pavarotti was to star in *La Bohème*. The second was Tchaikovsky's *The Queen of Spades*. Since the opera was sung in Russian, another first for American television, the producers brought in a cast of Eastern Europeans, including the then recent Russian emigré Vladimir

Popov, the Bulgarian soprano Stefka Evstatieva, and the Hungarian baritone Lajos Miller. The same year the company tackled the Faust legend, with James Morris linking the series with his performance as the devil in Gounod's *Faust* in 1983 Berlioz's *La Damnation de Faust* in 1985 and Bioto's *Mefistofele* (1988). Operas staged recently include *Aida* and *Carmen*.

The 1982 Opera Company of Philadelphia production of 'Dido and Aeneas'

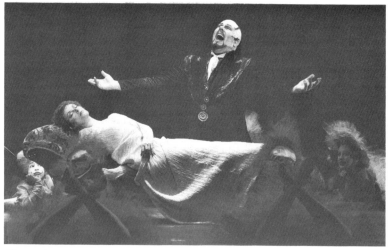

The 1985 Opera Company of Philadelphia production of 'La Damnation de Faust'

Pittsburgh Opera

711 Penn Avenue, Pennsylvania 15222

Director: Tito Capobianco
Season: June–October
Productions: 5, 1 new
Performances: 3–4 of each
Capacity: 2,770

Box Office: (412) 281 5000
Box open: Mon–Sat 10.00a.m.–6.00p.m.
Postal: As above
Prices: $12–$55
Concessions: Half price for senior citizens and students 2 hours before performance

Touring companies provided the only form of opera in Pittsburgh from 1838 to 1939 when the Pittsburgh Opera Society opened at the Carnegie Music Hall. *Eugene Onegin*, *The Marriage of Figaro* and *The Tales of Hoffman* were among the original productions and are still popular today. After six years the company moved into the Syria Mosque, where Dr. Richard Karp, the artistic music director until 1977, improved standards by introducing international stars to take on leading roles. At the same time the orchestra was considerably expanded, then, as now, being made up of members of the Pittsburgh Symphony Orchestra.

In 1971 the opera company took over the Heinz Hall, where it will be based until the autumn of 1987. The fine building boasts two spectacular fifteen foot chandeliers in the main entrance, and as further two hundred and sixty four smaller, newer ones, specially designed in Vienna. In 1984 Pittsburgh gained its third artistic director, Tito Capobianco, a Verdi specialist. Not surprisingly, the repertoire consists largely of widely-known Italian operas, as well as some Mozart. The company's conservative outlook is confirmed by a forty-six year production record in which, among others, *Carmen* has been staged fifteen times, *La Bohème* fourteen, *La Traviata* twelve, and *Madame Butterfly* ten. Capobianco has increased the number of performances for each production from two to three. In 1985 he oversaw the introduction of 'Optrans' screen mounted high above the stage on which a translation of the dialogue was projected. It was clearly favoured by the audience whose numbers notably increased in the following season. The translations were never intended to provide a full literary interpretation of the original; more a kind of précis and general guide for the audience.

Good though the Heinz Hall is, the company is to be housed in the renovated Benedum Center from October 1987, where Capobianco intends to develop two seasons a year, one from October to November, and one in the spring from March to April, both with three productions. One of the main reasons for moving is that the new opera house more closely conforms to other great opera centres by being short and wide, allowing more of the audience to be closer to the stage. Seventy-five per cent of the orchestra is hidden beneath the stage in Heinz Hall; the Benedum Center provides more room and so the accoustics should significantly improve.

San Diego Opera

P.O. Box 988, San Diego, California 92112

Director: Ian Campbell
Season: January–April
Productions: 4, 1 new
Performances: 4 of each
Capacity: 3,000

Box Office: (619) 236 6510
Telex: 278 TIXS
Box open: Mon–Fri 8.30a.m.–4.30p.m.
Postal: As above
Prices: $10–$50, $6 standing on day of performance
Cards: VISA, Mastercharge

Regular opera first came to San Diego in 1952 with the formation of an Opera Guild. The Guild lasted fifteen years, during which time it managed to afford some of the greatest voices – Giuseppe di Stefano and the young Jon Vickers; Jerome Hines; Salvatore Baccaloni, Elisabeth Schwarzkopf, and the young Joan Sutherland. The repertoire at this time largely centred around Mozart, Verdi, Bellini and Puccini. In 1965 the current opera company was formed, opening to *La Bohème*, San Diego's most frequently performed work. The first director/principal conductor was Walter Herbert who did much to assist the company at this time in lobbying for grants, and staging the American premières of Henze's *Der Junge Lord* (1967) and Alva Henderson's *Medea* (1972). By the time of his death in 1975 the Opera's season of five operas were nearly sold out at the box office. His successor Tito Capobianco raised the stakes and transformed a national reputation into an international one. He extended the number of operas to eight or nine, and in addition to *Otello, La Traviata, Rigoletto* and *Pagliacci*, brought in modern works such as *The Saint of Bleecker Street*, Menotti's *The Medium, Cendrillon, Manon Lescaut, Mefistofele*, and *Don Pasquale*. Some of his greatest successes included the 1977–78 season opener *The Merry Widow*, with Beverly Sills, *La Traviata* (1977) later staged in Washington and televised, the first summer Verdi festival (1978), and *Die Fledermaus* (1980), starring two of the then greatest divas, Sutherland and Sills.

But Capobianco's trail-blazing style and dominance never really blended with San Diego's more sober approach, and it was no real surprise when, after eight years, he suddenly departed. Ian Campbell stepped in, and took over where Walter Herbert had left off, developing the company's marketing side and initially concentrating on increasing membership and subscriptions. Since then the number of productions off season has been reduced to five or six operas, while the selection of standard repertoire has been maintained.

San Francisco Opera
301 Van Ness Avenue, San Francisco, California 94102–4509

Director: Terence A McEwan
Season: September–December
Productions: 10, 3 new
Performances: Varies
Capacity: 3,252

Box Office: (415) 864 3330
Box open: Mon–Sat 10.00a.m.–6.00p.m.
Postal: As above
Prices: $9–$75
Cards: VISA, MasterCard

The earliest operatic performances in San Francisco were organized by the French bass and impressario Alfred Roncovieri who founded the Pellegrini company to perform the standard French and Italian repertoire. The first recorded operatic performance, Bellini's *La Sonnambula*, was given on February 12th 1851 at the Adelphi Theatre, Bellini's *Norma* and Verdi's *Ernani* followed, and by 1889 over one thousand performances had taken place in over eleven different theatres. These included the Tivoli Theatre, a former beer garden which stayed open for ten years, presenting grand opera in winter and the lighter repertoire in summer; the Grand Opera House, built by a dentist on Mission Street in 1873; and the Auditorium and the Civic Opera House which received Jenny Lind during the 1870s. A press description from 1872 gives an idea of a typical audience at the San Francisco Opera: 'In the stalls . . . the Germans and Italians who know their opera . . . in the dress circle the elite resplendent in silks, laces and diamonds . . . in the pit the Dutchmen. . . . up in the galleries the red-shirted, black-bearded Italian fishermen.'

In 1884, Adelina Patti, the much-loved Italian coloratura, appeared with a company formed by James Mapleson and caused a sensation, returning in 1889 to appear in Gounod's *Romeo and Juliet*. Similar smaller companies occupied the stages of San Francisco until 1890 when the New York Metropolitan company made its début appearance, bringing the tenor Francesco Tamagno in Verdi's *Otello*, Meyerbeer's *L'Africaine* and Verdi's *Il Travatore*. Wagner's *Ring* was eventually given by this company in 1900.

The entrepreneurial Italian Merola came to the city, which had been devastated by earthquake three years earlier, for the first time in 1909 as accompanist to the mezzo Eugenia Mantelli. He returned three years later as conductor of W.A. Edwards International Opera Company and came again in 1919 as director of the touring San Carlo company. Merola's aim was to import the best singers of the day from New York and Chicago rather than try to encourage local talent. He knew that San Franciscans were prepared to pay a lot of money to hear the most important singers, as evident from the fact that in 1921 six thousand, three hundred and thirteen people paid over thirty thousand dollars to hear Geraldine Ferrar in *Madame Butterfly*; a box office record.

The San Francisco Opera Company was founded in 1923, with the help of fellow Italian workers and businessmen, and a year later was turned into a non-profit organization with Merola as the general director and Robert I Bentley as President. The first season took place at the stadium at Stanford University and included three operas all starring the great tenor Giovanni Martinelli – *Pagliacci*, *Carmen* and *Faust*, drawing crowds of up to ten thousand.

Until 1932 the annual autumn seasons continued at the Civic Auditorium – where San Franciscans were given a diet of nineteenth century Italian opera, sprinkled with a few French offerings. The *verismo* style particularly attracted Merola and Giordano's music is extremely well represented. German opera came comparatively late: a *Tristan* in 1923 and *Salome* in 1931 were greeted with indifference, prompting the conductor Bodansky to describe the audience as 'unsophisticated'.

With no really satisfying opera house for the company, in 1918 a small group of San Franciscans renewed efforts to erect one, obtaining funds from selling subscriptions and gaining pledges from various institutions. The plan envisaged was a building based loosely on the Paris Opéra with a grand staircase leading to the auditorium, although it was a technical expert from Milan's La Scala who was asked to assist the architects on the matter of design. The opera house is essentially classical in ideas and harmonizes with a group of buildings, including the San Francisco Museum of Modern Art, to form the Civic Centre Complex. The foyer and international staircases are predominantly marble, leading to a large auditorium that can seat almost three and a half thousand people. The stage at eighty-five by one hundred and thirty one feet is the second largest in the country.

The Memorial Opera House finally opened on October 15th, 1932. For that night Merola chose his favourite singer, Claudio Muzio to give his favourite opera, Puccini's *Tosca*. The first act was broadcast nationally over NBC's Red Network. For the rest of his directorship, Merola continued to work within the existing framework, with the production budget heavily compromised in order to pay out generously for star talent. After his death in 1953, his assistant Kurt Herbert Adler took over immediately as general director. Under his regime, more interesting productions were encouraged and principal artists were drawn from Europe as well as the States. Many great singers sang roles for the first time in San Francisco, including Martinelli as Otello, Tibett as Iago, Horne as Eboli and Gwyneth Jones as Isolde.

He was responsible for the US débuts of Rysanek, Nilsson, Schwarzkopf, Margaret Price and Sena Jurinak and for the premières of Strauss's *Die Frau ohne Schatten*, Walton's *Troilus and Cressida*, Poulenc's *Dialogues of the Carmelites* and Orff's *Carmina Burana*. Other changes included putting a halt to touring and thereby doubling the season, reviving forgotten operas of value, such as those of Berlioz, Spontini, Cherubini and Meyerbeer and expanding the repertoire to include modern operas by Berg, Janáček and Shostakovich.

In 1960 he established Spring Opera, with the aim of giving intimate performances by younger, less established singers. It fulfilled a need for more adventurous productions of contemporary American opera and staged *Of Mice and Men* by Carlisle Floyd and Viktor Ullman's *The Emperor of Atlantis* were during the 1976–77 season, and has also put on some unusual revivals including Donizetti's *La Convenienze de Inconvenienze Teatrali*, renamed *Viva La Mamma* and Offenbach's *La Perichole*. Finally, Spring Opera has also staged some important modern European works such as Henze's *Elegy for Young Lovers* and Britten's *Death in Venice*. Western Opera, begun in 1967, is a training school for audience and singers alike, and takes small productions to other towns on the Pacific coast.

Meanwhile, the main troupe of the San Francisco Opera has stuck to a more conventional policy although many consider its productions to be second only to the New York City Opera for interest. The complete *Ring* cycle of 1985, conducted by Edo de Waart and designed by John Conklin brought the major interpreters of Wagner to appear in what was a huge popular and critical success. The house has also become associated with some sensitive productions of Mozart, featuring some outstanding singers such as Baltsa, Te Kanawa and Geraint Evans. Since 1980 productions have been broadcast live to various states in the US, including *Aida*, *Samson and Delilah* and *La Gioconda*.

Geraldine Farrar as Cio-Cio-San in 'Madame Butterfly'

Opera Theater of St Louis
1 Kirthom, St Louis 63119

Director: Charles MacKay
Season: May–June
Productions: 4 new
Performances: Approx. 8 of each
Capacity: 954

Box Office: (314) 961 0171
Box open: Daily 10.00a.m.–5.00p.m.
Postal: P.O. Box 13148, St Louis 63119
Prices: $6–$40
Cards: VISA, MasterCard, American Express

In 1976 the first director of the Opera Theater of Saint Louis wrote:
'As I'm sure you know there has been no permanent opera company for many years now . . . My plan is to present a season using the best young singers and with a strong emphasis on the theatrical aspect in addition to the musical one.' Looking back on the company's past eleven years it certainly looks as though Richard Gaddes's ambitions have been successful.

Even though the St Louis Symphony Orchestra was founded as early as 1880 making it one of the oldest in the country, opera until 1976 was an extremely checkered affair. The great touring companies passed through, including Mapleson and the Metropolitan group who came regularly but from 1968 there was literally nothing going on in the city and local born singers like Helen Traubel, Grace Bumbry and Richard Stilwell began their careers elsewhere.

Opera now takes place in the Loretto-Hilton Theater of Webster College about eight miles from the city centre. The theatre itself is situated in the most charming cluster of freshly-mown lawns and deciduous trees and there are more than superficial resemblances to Glyndebourne as people gather in the garden to chat and mingle with the crew or cast. Gaddes himself would admit to borrowing or at least adapting ideas from Glyndebourne as well as possibly Santa Fe (where he was director) and Wexford. The policy of giving more chamber-like operas, stressing the importance of ensemble, and not enlisting major stars may be more familiar to opera goers in Britain than in the United States, but herein lies St Louis' great success. With a smallish stage and enough room for only nine hundred, productions are economical but intimate.

The first season began with *Don Pasquale*, *Albert Herring*, and a double bill of Mozart's *Der Schauspieldirektor* and Menotti's *The Medium* with a cast of virtually unknown singers, two of whom have since made their names at home and abroad, Ashley Putnam and Stephen Dickson-Gaddes. The following year's group of operas was similarly unusual and provocative and featured Rameau's *Pygmalion* and Rossini's *Le Comte Ory*. In a few years the repertoire settled down to a pattern of four productions, including a Mozart, standard Italian work, a new work or revival, and a double-bill. Of the new operas Stephen Paulus's *The Postman Always Knocks Twice* commissioned by the company was a popular success and was taken on tour to opera festivals throughout Europe in 1975. There have been a number of US premières including Weber's *Der Drei Pintos*, Delius's *Fennimore and Gerda* and Prokofiev's *Maddelena*. A general sense of innovation has extended to the producers, with Jonathan Miller arriving in 1972 for *Così fan Tutte*, Colin Graham for *Béatrice and Bénédict* 1983, and Frank Corsaro for the staging of Delius's *Margot la Rouge*, also in 1983.

Santa Fe Opera

P.O. Box 2508, Santa Fe, New Mexico, 87501

Director: John Crosby
Season: July–August
Productions: 5
Performances: Varies
Capacity: 1,773

Box Office: (050) 982 3855
Box open: Mon–Fri 9.00a.m.–5.00p.m.; Sat 9.00a.m.–5.00p.m. during season. Standing tickets available at $3 one hour before performance
Postal: As above
Prices: $10–$55
Cards: VISA, Mastercharge, American Express

There are many unlikely settings for opera companies, and the foothills of the Sangre de Cristo Mountains with their magnificent panoramic views, are one of the most unlikely of all.

Santa Fe's open-air theatre was built in 1968 and like most daring examples of modern architecture tends to attract fiercely opposing views. It was built to replace the theatre destroyed by fire in 1967, just hours after the first US performance of Hindemith's *Cardillac:* the season had been forced to continue at the local high school. A six-foot-thick wedge in the theatre forms an acoustic ceiling and contains most of the lighting, as well as part-sheltering the singers and audience, but it does not entirely circumvent the recurrent problem of summer shows and productions are frequently abandoned due to rainfall. A lift varies the orchestra level by up to eight-and-a-half feet.

Santa Fe's trademark is contemporary opera. The nine-week summer season consists of five operas including rarely performed as well as popular works, one Mozart piece and a contemporary opera. The thirty-four American premières include Villa-Lobos' *Yerma* in 1971, Berio's *Opera* in 1970 and Carlisle Floyd's *Wuthering Heights* in 1958, while works by Henze, Hindemith, Schönberg and Shostakovich are amongst the world premières. The house is also noted for its adventurous style. Here the first performance since the eighteenth century of Cavalli's *L'Egisto* was given, initiating a revival of Venetian opera in America. Kiri te Kanawa, Frederica von Stade and Marilyn Horne, all began their careers here.

Strong links with England are provided by Raymond Leppard, the conductor, and John Lot, the producer. Director and founder John Crosby ensures that the company is a blend of established figures and new talent, with auditions held throughout the country from December to February. The necessity for a strong sense of ensemble is also taken seriously. Santa Fe is run by a non-profit-making organization which provides a budget of four and a half million dollars, half of which is returned through ticket sales, half through subsidies.

Seattle Opera Association

305 Harrison Street, Seattle

Director: Speight Jenkins
Production Director: Colleen Armstrong
Season: September–May
Productions: 5, the complete Ring is performed every year
Performances: 5 of each, 8 of the Ring
Capacity: 3,000

Box Office: (206) 443 4711
Subscription Bookings: (206) 443 3299
Telex: 160595 EOPRA UT
Box open: Daily 9.00a.m.–5.00p.m.
Postal: As above
Prices: $9–$110
Cards: VISA, MasterCard, American Express
Concessions: Limited 50% discount for senior citizens and students

Opera did not reach Seattle until the 1950s, with the foundation of Northwest Grand Opera, apart from the usual touring companies which had travelled extensively throughout the US for several decades. Although some progress was made, it was the formation of Seattle Opera in 1964 that gave the city its first taste of regular, first-rate opera.

In its opening season, under artistic director Glynn Ross, the strategy was very conservative. Initial productions were of proven favourites, such as *Carmen* and *Tosca*, later *La Bohème*, *Madame Butterfly* and *Rigoletto*. Within three seasons, four operas were being produced each season to audiences of fifty thousand.

In 1965 the Seattle Opera Guild was formed to provide some financial support, and it enabled the company to become the first opera house to present a series of productions in English and to become the first house other than the Metropolitan to keep a nucleus of singers on contract. Other innovations included the scenery exchange system with Vancouver, Portland and British Columbia, which helps to keep production costs to a minimum. High standards and an innovative, go-ahead policy have lost Seattle the reputation given to it by Thomas Beecham of being no more than a 'cultural dustbin'. In 1969 the company produced *Turandot*, starring Birgit Nilsson, using filmed scenery. Then followed Stravinsky's *L'Histoire du Soldat*, conducted by Stravinsky himself, *The Eggs*, with kinetic sculpture, and *Mantra*, described by Seattle as a 'multi-media' event. Other firsts include Carlisle Floyd's *Of Mice and Men*, Thomas Pasatieri's *Black Widow*, and the professional stage première of the rock opera *Tommy*.

In 1967 Joan Sutherland gave her American debut in *Lakmé*, and in 1970 she played four heroines in *The Tales of Hoffman*. Other international stars who have appeared here are Jon Vickers, Sherrill Milnes, Eileen Farrell and Anna Moffo. Seattle is also famous for its annual *Ring* cycle performed in English and German for two weeks each summer.

The Canadian Opera Company

227 Front Street East, Toronto, Ontario

General/Artistic Director: Lotfi Mansouri
Season: September–June (excluding November and December)
Productions: 7, 1 new
Performances: 7 of each
Capacity: O'Keefe Center 3,200

Box Office: (416) 872 2262
Box open: Mon–Fri 11.00a.m.–4.00p.m.
Postal: As above
Prices: $16–$65
Cards: VISA, MasterCard, American Express
Concessions: 1 hour before performance at $10

In one vital respect Toronto opera is still in its infancy. The city has no acceptable opera house, and moves have only just begun to remedy the situation. There was no real resident company in Toronto until 1867 when the English opera troupe rented the Lyceum. Their stay lasted for thirteen years, and they staged nearly forty different productions. The Grand Opera House was open from 1874 to 1893, but for the next seventy years the city relied on visiting companies or short-lived resident companies, such as the 1929 Conservatory which lasted for about four months. The Royal Conservatory Opera Company was formed in 1950, and so successfully that it led to the Opera Festival Association and to the now flourishing Canadian Opera Company.

Canadian Opera's principal policy is to use Canadian singers and players, and to stage Canadian works whenever possible. To date there have been four such operas; *Dierdre*, *The Luck of Ginger Coffey*, *Louis Riel*, and *Heloise and Abelard*. The company has benefitted enormously from its opera school, which has produced some fine singers, notably Jon Vickers and Teresa Stratas.

In 1976 Lotfi Mansouri took charge of the company, and up to 1986 has presided over thirty-nine productions. The highlights include Berg's *Lulu*, the Canadian première of *Death in Venice*, *Wozzeck*, *Norma*, *Tristan und Isolde*, *Elektra*, and most recently *Boris Godunov*.

A lack of adequate facilities has caused problems. The opera company shares the modern multi-purpose O'Keefe Center with the National Ballet, but both have way outgrown what it has to offer. The accoustics and sightlines are poor, with one thousand three hundred members of the three thousand two hundred capacity audiences having restricted views. Consequently, the company loses thousands of potential subscriptions annually. The conditions for the performers are equally unsophisticated, with the orchestra pit, in the words of Mansouri, 'being the worst I have ever known.' He adds, 'Accoustically, it's the only place I have worked in the world where you have to use amplification. When you bring in people like Sutherland and Troyanos you don't get the true value of their voices.'

There is now a project to build a new one hundred and twenty one million dollar opera and ballet hall, which should be completed in the 1990s.

Vancouver Opera

1132 Hamilton Street, Vancouver BC V6B 2S2

Director: Beverly Trifonidis
Artistic Director: Brian McMaster
Season: October–May
Productions: 4, 2 new
Performances: 4 of each
Capacity: 2,800

Box Office: (604) 683 0222
Telex: 04 352848 VCR
Box open: Mon–Sat 9.00a.m.–5.00p.m.
Postal: Vancouver Ticket Center, 765 Pacific Blvd. South, Vancouver B.C., V6B, tel. (604) 682 4444 or (604) 682 3311
Prices: $17–$50
Cards: VISA, MasterCard, American Express
Concessions: Students and senior citizens; $6 on evening of performance, $7 rush seats

Opera came to Vancouver in the late nineteenth century with a gala performance of *Lohengrin* given by a touring American company, but it was a long time before it became a regular part of city life. The theatres put on as many recitals, minstrel and local shows as they did opera. The high cost of mounting a performance ruled out a resident company, with the spotlight falling, in the early twentieth century, on San Fransisco Opera, who performed *Fantana*, *Olivette* and *The Toymakers*; and the International Grand Opera who gave *Aida*, *Carmen*, *Cavalleria Rusticana*, *Pagliacci*, and *Lucia di*

The 1986 Vancouver Opera production of 'The Barber of Seville'

44

Lammermoor. They provided a kind of operatic feast, with a number of works being crammed into a very brief season of just a few days.

World War I put a brief halt to opera, afterwards revived through the visiting New York-based San Carlo Company. During the thirties, there was a growing serious interest in opera which was also sustained by the Salzburg Opera Guild. After the end of World War II the number of productions by visiting companies diminished, and the onus fell on Theatre Under the Stars, which, from 1940 to 1963, performed at Malkin Bowl in Stanley Park.

From the 1950s until the 1980s opera was also performed by the Greater Vancouver Operatic Society and, from 1955, the Opera Society of British Columbia. More significantly, in 1958 the Vancouver International Festival was set up by Nicholas Goldshmidt who brought in Joan Sutherland for *Don Giovanni*, the Peking Opera in 1960, and the North American première of *A Midsummer's Night Dream* in 1961. In 1965 the festival changed its name to The Vancouver Association, but three years later it folded through lack of finances.

Two years after the festival had opened, the Vancouver Opera Association was founded, playing in the newly opened Queen Elizabeth Theatre. It staged from three to six operas a year under its artistic directors Irving Guttman (1960 to 1974 and 1982 to 1984), who brought a number of important singers to Vancouver including Joan Sutherland for *Lucrezia Borgia* (1962) and for *Norma* (1963) with Marilyn Horne; Richard Bonynge (1974 to 1979); Hamilton McClymont (1980) and Anton Guadagno (1980 to 1982). While most of the major productions have been drawn from the standard repertoire, there have also been performances of Massenet's *Le Roi de Lahore* in 1977, and Leigh's *Man of La Mancha*, which ran for eleven performances in 1982. The 1987 to 1988 season offers *La Bohème, The Turn of the Screw, The Cunning Little Vixen,* and *Die Fledermaus.*

The new artistic director, Brian McMaster, was invited to Vancouver to share productions with the Welsh National Opera where he has held the same position since 1973. This gave the Vancouver Opera a chance to hire ready-made productions and the Welsh Opera to gain an important source of revenue. Several operas including *From the House of the Dead* (produced by David Pountney), *Eugene Onegin* and *I Puritani,* (both produced by Andrei Serban), were extremely popular although David Pountney's feminist interpretation of *Carmen,* which was televised, drew angry reactions from a conservative audience. One very recent shared production, *Barber of Seville* began life in Vancouver.

The Washington Opera

The Kennedy Center, Washington DC 20566

Director: Martin Feinstein
Artistic Director: Francis Rizzo
Season: November–March
Productions: 8, 5 new
Performances: Varies
Capacity: Kennedy Center 2,200; Eisenhower Theater 1,100

Box Office: (020) 822 4757
Telex: 904163
Box open: Mon–Sat 10.00a.m.–5.00p.m.
Postal: As above
Prices: $15–$65

Recordings: Stravinsky's Le Rossignol and Oedipus Rex; Schoenberg's Erwartung; Ginastera's Bomarzo; Menotti's The Medium. All on CBS Masterwork series.

Opera in Washington D.C. dates back to the late nineteenth century when a black company was established in 1872. For the next ninety years or so the city had to rely on touring companies, but in 1956 the Opera Society was set up with the express purpose of producing lesser known operas.

The founding force was the music critic Day Thorpe who presided over the National Symphony Orchestra and employed Paul Calloway of the Washington Cathedral as musical director. The opening performance was *Die Entführung aus dem Serail*, which established strong musical links with Mozart that have lasted to the present. The company at this time was based at the Lisner Auditorium in the local university, but there were major drawbacks. The stage was too shallow, the orchestra pit too small, and rehearsals had to be held in New York. Props were never ready to hand, and each production had to be individually conceived and financed. Despite this, Washington quickly made its name with an offbeat programme featuring, amongst others, *The Old Maid and the Thief*, and *The Unicorn, The Gorgon and the Manticore*, both 1956–1957, produced in close collaboration with the Italian American composer and producer, Gian Carlo Menotti. Also during the 1950s Stravinsky conducted his own *Oedipus Rex*. It wasn't until the fifth season, in 1960–1961, that more familiar works, including Bizet's *Carmen*, became part of the repertoire. Nonetheless, the policy aimed at the unfamiliar remained, with performances of Strauss' *Ariadne auf Naxos*, Monteverdi's *Orfeo*, Debussy's *Pelléas et Mélisande*, a double bill of Schönberg, and Stravinsky's *Le Rossignol*, conducted by the composer. Two of the most notable productions were Ginastera's *Bomarzo* (1967) and Delius' *Koanga*, sung by an all-black cast, against a backdrop of colour projections of South American forests and swamps. Washington also gained a reputation for boosting the careers of previously unrecognized singers, such as Shirley Verrett, Donald Gramm and John Reardon.

Between 1967–68 there were no performances while the company sorted out its financial and managerial problems. By 1971 all was well and the company moved to the Kennedy Center, with its infinitely better facilities, opening to Ginastera's *Beatrix Cenci*. Since then, a string of notable performances has included Tchaikovsky's *Queen of Spades* and Monteverdi's *Il Ritorno d'Ulisse in Patria*.

Washington is also growing in international stature and recently initiated a three-year co-production project with L'Orchestra de Paris, cellist Daniel Barenboim directing *Così fan Tutte*, *The Marriage of Figaro* and *Don Giovanni*. Other outstanding events include the world première of Ginastera's *Bomarzo* and US premières of Berlioz's *Béatrice and Bénédict*, Cavalli's *L'Ormindo*, Delius's *Koanga* and *A Village Romeo and Juliet*, and Verdi's *Attila*. Rostropovitch and his wife Vishnevskaya have conducted and directed some recent productions.

The Kennedy Center, Washington DC (photo: Carl Purcell/Colorific)

One of David Hockney's set designs for the Glyndebourne production of 'The Rake's Progress'

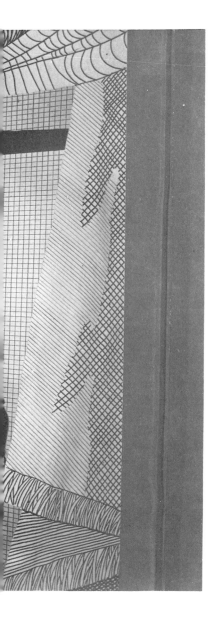

THE UNITED KINGDOM

Aldeburgh Festival
The Maltings, Snape, Suffolk

Director: Kenneth Baird
Season: June
Productions: 1 new each June
Performances: 4
Capacity: Snape 840; Jubilee Hall 300;
Blythburgh Church 700; Orford Church 475
Ballet: None
Bookings: Advance Booking from March

Box Office: (072885) 3543/2935
Box open: From May Tues–Sat 10.00a.m.–
1.00p.m., 2.15–4.00p.m.
Postal: Festival Office, High Street,
Aldeburgh
Prices: £5.50 – £12.50; 48 hour standby
system: £2 for under 26
Cards: All major credit cards

Although this small and sleepy East Anglian fishing village may at first sight seem an unlikely venue for a music festival, the event has become one of the most creative focuses of operatic activity in the world. The Festival was set up in 1948 by Benjamin Britten – a native of the area – with the help of the tenor Peter Pears and librettist Eric Crozier, and its flavour has been decisively influenced by the music and tastes of the composer himself. Only two years earlier, Britten had helped form the English Opera Group following the first performance at Glyndebourne of his chamber opera *The Rape of Lucretia*. The Group, based in Aldeburgh, was conceived as a means of encouraging the creation of new British operas using only small to medium scale resources.

The initial problem that the Festival and the company faced was the lack of suitable performing space. Except for the badly-equipped local Jubilee Hall which seated only three hundred, there were no facilities for giving opera in the area. The only option, therefore, was to use available neighbourhood resources to maximum advantage: thus, the Britten 'parable' operas, *Curlew River* (1964), *The Burning Fiery Furnace* (1966), and *The Prodigal Son* (1968), were written specifically with the local parish church of Orford in mind.

The situation improved in the 1960s when the disused Maltings in the village of Snape, a few miles inland, became free. The Maltings was part of a rambling complex of buildings which had previously been used to store grain and convert it into beer, and the architect Ove Arup successfully maintained the building's rustic character – keeping the bare brick walls and strictly functional roof – while transforming it into a sophisticated opera house and concert hall. The acoustics are magnificent, while the lack of a proscenium arch and minimal lighting facilities enhance rather than detract from Britten's artistic aims, given his distaste for unnecessary elaboration.

The Maltings was opened by the Queen in 1967 with a performance of Britten's *Midsummer Night's Dream* given by the English Opera Group. The following year the Sadler's Wells Opera arrived with their own production of Britten's *Gloriana*, and there was also a concert performance of Handel's then rarely heard *Hercules*. Yet tragedy struck only two years after the opening when the Maltings auditorium was burned down: a planned production of Mozarts's *Idomeneo* was speedily transferred to a nearby church in true Aldeburgh spirit. However, the Maltings was restored within two years, and during the 1970s gave outstanding presentations of *The Rape of Lucretia*, Purcell's *King Arthur* and, in 1973, the world première of Britten's last major work, *Death in Venice*.

50

The concert hall at Snape Maltings

The programme at Aldeburgh has tended to favour early music and modern British opera; between 1954 and 1975 there were premières of new works every year. These included Berkeley's *A Dinner Engagement* (1954), Williamson's *English Eccentrics* (1964), Birtwhistle's *Punch and Judy* (1968), Crosses's *The Grace of Todd* (1969), and Gardner's *The Visitors* (1972)

Britten formed close links with many internationally distinguished singers, and during his lifetime artistes such as Janet Baker, Dietrich Fischer-Dieskau and Galina Vishnevskaya regularly visited Aldeburgh to enjoy the intimate and informal music-making provided by the Festival. Since the deaths of both Britten and Pears, the directorship of the Festival has undergone various changes, and opera does not play such a large part in the schedule, more emphasis being given to concerts and recitals. A new feature, however, is the annual production given by the post-graduate students at the Britten-Pears Music School at Snape Maltings.

Buxton Festival

1 Crescent View, Hall Bank, Buxton, Derbyshire SK17

Artistic Director: Malcolm Fraser
Musical Director: Anthony Hose
Season: 19 July–10 August
Productions: 2 new
Performances: Average 5 of each
Capacity: 1000

Box Office: (0298) 71010
Box open: Mon–Sat 10.00a.m.–8.00p.m.
Postal: Festival Box Office, above address
Prices: £5.50–£20.00
Cards: Access, VISA, American Express

Situated high in the magnificent Peak District, the Georgian spa town of Buxton provides an excellent setting for the annual summer festival. In 1903 Frank Marcham, acclaimed architect of opera houses, designed an exquisite Edwardian theatre which was fully restored in 1979 for the opening of the festival. Each year a specific theme is tackled and the most prominent aspect of Buxton's policy is to stage long neglected operas, often giving them their first performance in Great Britain. In 1980, the theme was Shakespeare, with performances of Thomas' *Hamlet* and Berlioz's long neglected comedy based on *Much Ado About Nothing; Béatrice et Bénédict.* Kodaly provided the theme for 1982, with British premières of *Hary Janos* and *The Spinning Room.* The theme of Boccaccio in 1983 saw the professional British première of Vivaldi's *Griselda* and the first British performance for a hundred and twenty years of Gounod's *La Colombe.* Cherubini's *Medea,* which drew great attention to its principal singer Rosalind Plowright, and the professional British première of Cavalli's *Jason* were staged for the Greek Revival theme of 1984. Commedia dell'Arte was used in 1985, with performances of Piccinni's *La Buona Figluiola* and Galuppi's *Il Filosofa di Campagna,* and in 1986 Purcell's *King Arthur* and Handel's *Ariodante* were staged for the theme of King Arthur. For 1987, with Spain as the theme, Rossini's *L'Occasione fa il Ladro* and the British première of Donizetti's *Il Pigmalione* were staged.

Other operatic events at the Buxton Arts Festival include opera workshops, talks by leading opera producers such as Jonathan Miller and children's opera. Talks, films, light entertainment, literary luncheons, jazz, folk and classical music concerts also take place. Buxton relies heavily on business sponsorship, and unlike most other festivals receives very little government subsidy.

Kent Opera

Pembles Cross, Egerton, Ashford, Kent TN27 9EN

President: Sir Michael Tippett
Musical Director: Ivan Fisher
Artistic Director: Norman Platt
Season: March–April, October–November

Box Office: No central box office, booking through individual theatres
Information: From the company on 023 376 406/7
Touring schedule: The Marlowe, Canterbury; Theatre Royal, Norwich; The Orchard, Dartford; King's Theatre, Southsea; Theatre Royal, Plymouth; Congress Theatre, Eastbourne; Assembly Hall, Tunbridge Wells; Theatre Royal, Bath; Derngate, Northampton; Arts Theatre, Cambridge.
Prices: Varies according to venue

The company, founded in 1969 to give three performances of Monteverdi's *The Coronation of Poppea* has flourished in the succeeding years to the extent that it now represents the regional opera provision for a number of British towns in the south-east of England which had no 'live' professional opera before Kent Opera's artistic director, Norman Platt, persuaded five hundred friends and well-wishers to donate £1.10s each towards the inaugural production. Today, the company tours sixty-five performances of two or three operas around the smaller theatres to packed and enthusiastic audiences.

The secret of Platt's success is that Kent Opera is the antithesis of 'international' opera, having set its sights from the beginning on a policy of taking thoroughly rehearsed, musical stagings – almost invariably in English – to a largely new audience. It has never understood the need for great vocal stars, but instead has assembled ensembles of singers, unaltered for every performance barring accidents, dedicated to discovering the musical and dramatic truth of a work. Initially under the controversial direction of Roger Norrington, musical performances were meticulously prepared and productions offered uncomplicated views of the opera's dramaturgy.

This, by and large, has remained Kent Opera's watchword: the repertoire is deliberately restricted according to the taste of the artistic director and scale of the company's production – no Puccini, no Strauss and, obviously, no Wagner. Monteverdi, at first in the 'corrupted' Leppard texts, but later in 'authentic' editions, and Mozart have been the mainstays, but the range extends to Handel (*Atlanta and Agrippina*), Tchaikovsky (*Eugene Onegin*), Verdi (*Rigoletto, La Traviata,* and *Falstaff*), Britten (*The Turn of the Screw*) and Tippett (*King Priam*), often in stagings both stimulating and unconventional. Kent Opera was the first British company to lure Jonathan Miller away from the theatre and medicine towards the body operatic – his *Così, Onegin* and *Rigoletto* stand as models of theatrical ingenuity on a microscopic budget – and Nicholas Hytner's production of the Tippett opera won widespread recognition as the highlight of the composer's eightieth birthday year in Britain.

Standards have been sustained by coherent and cost-effective planning masterminded by a compact administration from an oast-house in the artistic director's garden. In general each production remains in the repertoire for two consecutive tours at either end of the year – spring or autumn – and is then revived two or three years later, as far as possible with the same cast, before it disappears from the programme. Many of the singers are closely associated with the company but occasionally guest artists of the quality of Felicity Palmer, Sarah Walker and Jonathan Summers have brought their special talents to such roles as Agrippina, Penelope and Rigoletto. The emphasis, however, remains firmly on team-work.

Kent Opera's greatest contribution to opera has been the remarkable series of Monteverdi performances using period instruments. Roger Norrington blazed the trail for a historical, and musically truthful, approach to such works and the tradition continues under the present musical director, Ivan Fischer. At its best, Kent Opera offers some of the most satisfying examples of ensemble opera in Britain.

The 1987 Kent Opera production of 'A Night at the Chinese Opera'

Welsh National Opera

John Street, Cardiff, CF1 4SP

Director: Brian McMaster
Musical Director: Sir Charles Mackerras
Season: September–July
Productions: Average 12, 4 new
Performances: Varies
Capacity: 1,168
Touring Venues: Hippodrome Theatre, Birmingham; Gaumont Theatre, Southampton; Hippodrome Theatre, Bristol; Apollo Theatre, Oxford; Dominion Theatre; Grand Theatre, Swansea

Box Office: (0222) 394232
Telex: 464666
Box open: Daily 10.00a.m.–6.00p.m. (8.00p.m. if performance)
Postal: Theatre Box Office, New Theatre, Park Place, Cardiff CF1 3LN
Prices: £4.00–£17.50
Cards: Access, VISA, American Express

Recordings: Parsifal (EMI); Tristan and Isolde (Decca)

Given the great Welsh musical traditions, especially the Welsh love of choral singing, it is hardly surprising that the country should have its own opera company. In 1946, the Welsh National Opera was launched by the baritone John Morgan, local choral conductor Idloes Owen, and a businessman Bill Smith, who had all been discussing the idea since 1943. Opening at the Empire Theatre, Cardiff with a selection of arias followed by *Cavalleria Rusticana*, the company went on to give *Faust* and *Pagliacci* in a first season that a local newspaper proudly described as 'as important to the art of singing as the national Eisteddfod itself.'

In its early years the company scored a particular hit with Verdi's *Nabucco*, in which the great Welsh choral tradition was spectacularly exploited. A first visit to Sadler's Wells Theatre in London came in 1955, and in the following year the company settled in Cardiff's New Theatre, where it has subsequently been based.

By 1966 the company had staged thirty-four operas, including ten by Verdi and the world première of Arwel Hughes' *Menna*, an opera with a strongly Welsh flavour. Over the years it had gradually become increasingly professional in personnel, and by 1970 it had its own full-time orchestra and chorus, under the overall musical direction of James Lockhart. With the appointment of Michael Geliot as director of productions, the company began on a remarkable policy which involved the engagement of some of the most adventurous and radical opera producers in Europe. The general administrator Brian MacMaster consolidated these experiments after Geliot's and Lockhart's departure by importing Harry Kupfer for *Elektra* (1978), Ruth Berghaus for *Don Giovanni* (1984), Andrei Serban most notably for *Norma* (1985), Peter Stein for *Otello* (1986), and Tim Albery for *Les Troyens* (1987).

Other achievements have been the exploration of the otherwise neglected Eastern European repertoire (Janáček, Dvořák, Martinů); the first staging by a British company of Berg's *Lulu* in 1971; and some impressive Wagner productions (*Tristan* (1979) and *Parsifal* (1983) under Reginald Goodall, a *Ring* (1983–5) conducted by the company's musical director until 1986 Richard Armstrong). However, despite some fine productions of Britten's works, the company has been relatively weak in the field of modern opera, and none of the works it has commissioned from Welsh composers has had more than a most modest success.

Welsh-born singers who have appeared with the company include Margaret Price, Gwyneth Jones, Stuart Burrows and Geraint Evans; and guest artists have included Elisabeth Söderström (in Janáček operas) and Josephine Barstow (*Traviata, Peter Grimes*). But the company has also nurtured a large number of its younger members over the years and turned them into stars: Helen Field, Suzanne Murphy, Arthur Davies, Anne Evans and Dennis O'Neill among them.

During 1987–8 the New Theatre was in process of renovation, and the company took longer seasons in its other two major Welsh bases in Grand Theatre, Swansea and Theatre Clwyd, Mold. It tours regularly to London, Oxford, Liverpool, Birmingham and Bristol and has had great success on its trips abroad.

The 1986 Welsh National Opera production of 'Otello'

The Edinburgh Festival

21 Market Street, Edinburgh EH1 1BW

Director: Frank Dunlop
Season: July–August
Productions: Varies
Performances: Varies
Ballet: Varies
Information: Can be obtained from the
Festival Information Centre at the Mound

Box Office: (031) 226 4001 (main festival);
(031) 226 5138 (fringe)
Box open: 23–28 June Mon–Fri 10.00a.m.–
4.30p.m., Saturdays 10.00a.m.–12.00p.m.,
30 June–1 August Mon–Fri 10.00a.m.–
6.00p.m., Saturdays 10.00a.m.–12.00p.m., 2
August–30 August Mon–Fri 9.00a.m.–
6.00p.m.
Postal: As above
Credit Cards: (01) 246 7200 All major cards
Prices: £4.00–£16.50

What the Washington Post called 'the greatest arts festival in the world' fills Scotland's capital city with three action-packed weeks of music, theatre, dance and art exhibitions, as well as an enormous number of fringe events, including opera. It all began in 1946 when the Viennese impresario and then artistic director of Glyndebourne, Rudolf Bing and the company's founder Audrey Christie, were discussing the possibility of finding additional outlets for their productions which had hitherto been restricted to a short festival season in Sussex. What Bing suggested was to turn Edinburgh into a second Salzburg. He pointed out the similarities between both cities: both had considerable scenic and picturesque appeal and contained a sufficient number of theatres, concert-halls and open spaces for a large variety of events. At the same time Bing could guarantee the festival the highest standards of opera production which would bring international attention.

A committee was set up, the plans were accepted, and preparations were made for a first festival to take place the following year, in 1947. Not surprisingly it was a great success and featured two events that drew the crowds – Glyndebourne's *Macbeth*, produced by Carl Ebert and the legendary performance of Mahler's *Das Lied von der Erde* which brought together Bruno Walter, Kathleen Ferrier and the Vienna Philharmonic. Ferrier was moved to write of the first festival: 'it was unforgettable . . . opera and ballet by the finest artists were being performed literally morning noon and night and hospitality was being showered upon guests and visitors by the so-called dour Scots . . . what a misnomer!'

The Glyndebourne Festival Opera dominated the Edinburgh Festival until 1955 as there was really no other company in Britain at that time capable of achieving the standard required for an international festival. In 1953 the first UK production of *The Rake's Progress*, with Wallenstein conducting, was a major success and it was followed soon after by the famous Beecham *Ariadne auf Naxos* and the UK première of Hindemith's *Mathis der Maler* conducted by Leopold Ludwig. Eventually the decision was made to import foreign companies and in a post-war gesture of reconciliation the Hamburg State Opera was invited in 1952 to give six German operas including an important *Salome* with Helga Pilarczyk which was sensational. Four years later they returned to further approval and then again in 1968 with *Elektra* and *The Flying Dutchman*. But it was the appearance of Maria Callas in *La Sonnambula* in 1957, given by the Scala company that, according to the music critics of *The Scotsman* 'inflamed the audience to a fever of enthusiasm without parallel in the history of the festival's operatic annals'. Unfortunately Madame Callas wasn't quite so happy and having initially taken the festival by storm she left the event without completing her engagements. For the final performance she was replaced by the young Renata Scotto, an evening which actually launched her career, at least as far as the critics were concerned.

During the sixties and seventies large established companies visited Edinburgh bringing with them a gallery of stars. Covent Garden's contribution of *Lucia di Lammermoor* with Joan Sutherland in 1961 and the Stockholm Opera's *Jenůfa* and *Elektra* with Elisabeth Söderström and Birgit Nilsson in 1974 may be considered fine examples. Other visiting foreign companies included those from Belgrade, Naples, Prague and Munich. More recently the festival has favoured smaller unconventional groups such as the Stockholm Folk Opera (whose *Aida* in 1986 featured a chorus of twelve!) and the Opera Theatre of St. Louis, largely because of the inadequate facilities of the two major venues, the King's and Lyceum theatres.

Since 1973 the festival has mounted its own productions; a *Don Giovanni* and a *Marriage of Figaro* conducted by Daniel Barenboim and, in 1977, the Faggioni production of *Carmen* with Domingo and Berganza started a *Carmen* epidemic which has continued unabated. Otherwise the policy has remained virtually the same under a series of excellent directors that include Robert Ponsonby (1956–1966), Peter Diamand (1966–1979), John Drummond (1980–1984) and most recently Frank Dunlop. An average of three foreign companies are invited to give between three and seven performances of one production. Occasionally the festival also produces its own opera.

There have been plans to build an opera house which would act as a necessary alternative to the present cramped circumstances. Unfortunately the government withdrew its support during the strained economic period of 1975 but the controversy continues and a gaping hole in the ground testifies to a once ambitious plan. Frank Dunlop's new idea is to buy the Playhouse which has the largest auditorium in Europe, seating over four thousand, and to spend nine million pounds to install proper backstage facilities. If this money can be raised from the private sector, it would presumably encourage the return of large-scale opera production and make Edinburgh the rival of Salzburg in this field.

A separate festival of fringe events takes place every year and usually anything between five and ten operas by small companies are given in a variety of different venues from churches to hotels. For postal booking there is an official form and tickets can be ordered by cheque or by credit card.

Scottish Opera

Theatre Royal, Hope Street, Glasgow G3

Director: Richard Mantle
Musical Director: John Mauceri
Season: September–June
Productions: 6 new
Performances: 5 of each
Capacity: 1,560
Ballet: 3 (Scottish Ballet)
Main Touring Venues: Theatre Royal, Newcastle; His Majesty's Theatre, Aberdeen; Empire Theatre, Liverpool; King's Theatre, Edinburgh

Box Office: (041) 331 1234
Telex: 776264
Box open: During season: Mon–Sat 10.00a.m.–7.30p.m.
Postal: As above
Prices: £3–£21
Cards: Access, Barclaycard, American Express, Diners
Concessions: ½ price seats for children, standby tickets one hour before performance at £3.00 for senior citizens, students and unwaged

Since the Carl Rosa company came to Glasgow in 1877, the city has taken a lively interest in opera. In 1905 the amateur Glasgow Grand Opera Company was formed by Eric Chisholm (1904–65) and it gave several important UK premières including *Idomeneo* (1933), the first part of *Les Troyens* (1935) and *Béatrice et Bénédict* (1936), setting a precedent for future companies based in the city. It also mounted noteworthy productions of neglected Italian and French works such as *Mefistofele* and *Le Roi d'Ys*.

Home-based professional opera was started up by Alexander Gibson, an enterprising Glaswegian, largely under the inspiration of another provincial company, the Welsh National Opera, which made annual visits to Sadlers Wells Opera House in London when Gibson was musical director there. Leaving the post for home in 1957 to take up the baton for the Scottish National Orchestra, Gibson set about creating Scottish Opera, encouraged by a political climate that seemed to support regional arts. The first season consisted of just two operas Puccini's *Madame Butterfly* and Debussy's *Pelléas and Mélisande* but under Peter Hemmings' general administration, the company managed to mount eight hundred performances of over fifty operas by the end of the 1974/75 season. Part of Gibson's great achievement was to sign up major singers, many of whom were at the time unknown to British audiences: Helga Dernesch and Elizabeth Harwood were more than instrumental in two of the company's most memorable productions – *Der Rosenkavalier* in 1968 and the *Ring* in 1970 – the first production in German by a provincial company. Gibson also gave Janet Baker an opportunity to sing Dido in *The Trojans* and the success of this production which brought international attention caused a revival of interest in Berlioz's operas. Local taste, meanwhile, was wooed by the commissioning of four full-length operas from Scottish composers.

Until 1975 the company was based at the King's Theatre, Glasgow and toured to the neighbouring cities of Aberdeen and Edinburgh as well as a few cities in the North of England. From 1967 it began to appear at the Edinburgh Festival making an enormous impact with a new production of *The Rake's Progress* described by one critic as 'based on teamwork and communal zest . . . the chorus work was first rate – the orchestral playing crisp and alert'. It also took Henze's *Elegy for Young Lovers* and Britten's *Peter*

Grimes, as well as giving the first performances of three Scottish operas there – Robin Orr's *Full Circle*, Hamilton's *The Catline Conspiracy* and Thea Musgrave's *Mary Queen of Scots*. After 1975 a full annual season became possible after the Theatre Royal became available to the company. This Victorian theatre, elegantly restored by Arup Associates, represented an improvement in facilities and encouraged more ambitious productions. However, the plan to build a new opera house for Scotland set out by the Harold Wilson government was greeted with enthusiasm and relief, although the project was later abandoned. There is, however, still some hope for its realisation.

During the sixties and seventies the company had a reputation like the Welsh National Opera have today: they consistently mounted ambitious and controversial productions with strong emphasis on ensemble. More recently critics and public alike have been less enthusiastic and the company suffered a series of administrative scandals. Recent productions such as Graham Vick's over-domesticated *Don Giovanni*, or Tony Palmer's eccentric *Turandot* were generally considered to be pretentious and in bad taste. In September 1987 John Mauceri, a protégé of Leonard Bernstein, took over as musical director with new productions of *Aida* and *Lulu*. He plans to do for Hindemith what Mackerras did for Janáček by reviving most of his operas in forthcoming seasons.

Glyndebourne Festival Opera
Glyndebourne, Lewes, East Sussex BN 8500

General Administrator: Brian Dickie
Musical Director: Bernard Haitink
Artistic Director: Sir Peter Hall
Season: May–August
Productions: 6, 2 new
Performances: Approx 8–15 of each
Capacity: 830

Box Office: (0273) 541111
Telex: 877862 GLYOP G
Box open: From end April, Mon–Fri
10.00a.m.–5.00p.m.; during Festival
10.00a.m.–7.30p.m., Sundays to 6.30p.m.,
non-performance days 10.00a.m.–5.00p.m.
Postal: As above
Prices: £25–£50
Touring Venues: Apollo Theatre, Oxford;
Palace Theatre, Manchester; Hippodrome,
Birmingham; Gaumont Theatre,
Southampton

Recordings: Don Giovanni, Così fan Tutte, 50th anniversary album, Le Comte Ory (EMI)

Of all British operatic stories, Glyndebourne's is perhaps the strangest. When John Christie unveiled his own opera festival to an unsuspecting public and sceptical critics with performances of Mozart's *Marriage of Figaro* and *Così fan Tutte* in May 1934, few believed it would survive. It must have seemed a mad Citizen Kane-like dream in which a rich British landowner built a small theatre on the grounds of his country house to show off the talents of his young wife. That Glyndebourne proved more than a passing fancy, however, can be credited to Mrs. Christie, the soprano Audrey Mildmay, who had already established herself as a soubrette in the touring Carl Rosa company. It was she who persuaded her husband, a Wagner fanatic, not to create a miniature Bayreuth in the midst of the Sussex countryside – he had planned to open his festival with *Die Walküre* and announced in the press his ambition to stage the complete *Ring* – but to give works appropriate to the modest proportions of his theatre which, at the time, had a capacity of only three hundred.

By good fortune, the birth of Glyndebourne coincided with the flight from their native Germany of two artists, who were to find refuge in the English countryside and establish from the outset musical and theatrical standards of the highest order in this unlikely place. Fritz Busch, musical director of the Dresden State Opera until the Nazis had him removed in 1933, and Carl Ebert, a distinguished actor and theatre director from Berlin, brought with them the virtues of the German ensemble company, and a professionalism and dedication to excellence which took audiences by surprise at the performances of *Figaro* and *Così*. By the end of the 1930s Glyndebourne had added Mozart's great German operas, *Die Entführung aus dem Serail* and *The Magic Flute* to its repertory, fulfilling Audrey Mildmay's practical vision of a Mozart festival in Sussex. Over the succeeding decades the range of repertoire has been opened out to embrace Rossini, Strauss, the early Baroque and a select number of twentieth-century pieces, but Mozart has always remained the favourite.

However Glyndebourne's instant success rested not solely on the musical standards of the performances. Rather, it was the quality of the Glyndebourne experience which made the place unique, and still does today. Curtain-up is early, usually at 5.30 in the afternoon, enabling the audience to dine at leisure in one of the restaurants or to picnic in the lovely grounds of the house. On a fair day, given one of Glyndebourne's vintage productions, there can be no more pleasurable operatic encounter.

Yet, the theatre itself is no architectural masterpiece. From the outside, it looks a crude and clumsy extension to the main body of the mansion; a late Tudor building substantially renovated and recast in the nineteenth century. The original interior of the auditorium, too, was no model of interior good taste, as can be seen from early photographs. Today, with its wood-panelled walls, its bare-boarded floor and its complete lack of decoration, it looks functional and inoffensive, though still surprisingly austere to the first time visitor. Rather more importantly, the stage and back-stage facilities have been constantly improved and extended over the years so that the theatre is now furnished with the most sophisticated flying and lighting equipment. Consequently, Glyndebourne has managed to attract leading directors, not only from the world of opera, but from the theatre as well. Indeed, this might even be regarded as a Glyndebourne tradition. Ebert's association with the festival lasted until his retirement in 1964 and he saw the expansion of the repertory beyond the five most popular Mozart operas. Already in the immediate pre-war years, Donizetti's *Don Pasquale* and, rather less obviously, Verdi's *Macbeth*, had set Glyndebourne on a course of rediscovering, at that time, unfamiliar works. Indeed, Ebert's *Macbeth* production, born of the German Verdi revival of the early thirties, gave British audiences their first opportunity of seeing his early Shakespeare opera.

During the war years, Glyndebourne closed its doors and might never have opened them again but for outside initiatives. The first came from an unexpected source. Although John Christie had never demonstrated much sympathy for modern music – nor did he ever acquire it – he agreed to present the initial performances of Benjamin Britten's newly-founded English Opera Group in 1946. After the huge success of *Peter Grimes* the year before, Britten turned to the more intimate form of chamber opera – a concept he more or less invented for the second half of the present century – with *The Rape of Lucretia*. The world première was given at Glyndebourne with Kathleen Ferrier in the title role, Joan Cross and Peter Pears as the Male and Female Chorus and Otakar Kraus as Tarquinius. Ernest Ansermet conducted in alternation with Reginald Goodall, who recorded excerpts from the opera with Pears and the second Lucretia, Nancy Evans. The following year Glyndebourne hosted the first performances of *Albert Herring* with Pears in the title role, Cross as Lady Billows and Evans as Nancy. A subsequent disagreement between Britten and the Christies brought the artistic association to an abrupt halt and not a note of Britten's music was heard again in the theatre until 1981 when Glyndebourne unveiled Sir Peter Hall's magical staging of *A Midsummer Night's Dream*. Since then, *Albert Herring* has returned to his rightful home in another Hall production; one of the most distinguished events in the festival's recent history.

It was not until 1950, though, that Mozart filled the auditorium again. In the meantime, the Glyndebourne company had toured a version of *The Beggar's Opera* and performed its Mozart and some new Verdi productions at the early Edinburgh Festivals. They returned to Sussex with a new *Figaro* and *Entführung* and a *Così* not yet seen at the company's home theatre. In 1951, the Mozart canon was extended to include

Idomeneo, its first professional British staging, and Fritz Busch's last new production at Glyndebourne. His death in 1951 robbed British opera of a major artistic force, but the musical standards he had set were maintained by the Italian Vittorio Gui, who brought Rossini's comedies into the house; *La Cenerentola* in 1952, *The Barber of Seville* and *Le Comte Ory* in 1954, *L'italiana in Algeri* in 1957 and *La Pietra del Paragone* in 1964. Gui and Ebert together appropriated Verdi's *Falstaff* (with Geraint Evans) and Debussy's *Pelléas et Mélisande* as quintessential 'Glyndebourne' operas in the mid-fifties and early sixties.

Under Gui's successor, John Pritchard, who had been Busch's assistant on *Idomeneo* back in 1951, the Mozart works were renewed, most memorably in the Peter Hall productions of the three Da Ponte operas. A Strauss series, begun in 1950 with *Adriadne auf Naxos* and continued in 1959 with *Der Rosenkavalier* was devised to explore his less familiar stage creations: a memorable *Capriccio* directed by Günther Rennert in 1963 with Elizabeth Söderström as the Countess was updated by John Cox in 1976 for the same soprano. As director of productions, Rennert had staged Glyndebourne's first opera of the early Baroque, Monteverdi's *Coronation of Poppea*, his own version of Rossini's *La Pietra del Paragone*, the British première of Henze's *An Elegy for Young Lovers* – which John Christie is reputed to have loathed – as well as a number of Mozart productions, most notably the 1960 *Don Giovanni*.

In recent years, John Cox and Peter Hall have been responsible for the majority of Glyndebourne productions, both representatives of a conservative style of staging which Glyndebourne's well-heeled audiences tend to prefer, but both at their best intelligent directors who have left their own individual stamp on the house's repertory. Hall began his work at Glyndebourne with Raymond Leppard's realisation of Cavalli's *Calisto;* a vehicle for Janet Baker who proved a memorable interpreter of the dual role of Diana and Jove disguised as his huntress daughter. Later they introduced Monteverdi's *Il Ritorno d'Ulisse in Patria* to the festival and Baker made her operatic farewell at Glyndebourne in a Hall production of Gluck's *Orfeo*.

During the seventies, Glyndebourne indulged a fad for 'designer' opera, although in the fifties the festival had already made progress in that area with the beautiful sets and costumes of Oliver Messel. David Hockney's brilliant and original drawings for *The Rake's Progress* in 1975 (Stravinsky's opera had had its British première at Glyndebourne in 1953 staged by the original producer, Carl Ebert) launched the artist on a brief career as a painter for the stage. He followed his success with beautiful backdrops for John Cox's inevitably anonymous production of *The Magic Flute* in 1978. After a brief dalliance with the French fashion designer, Erté, whose anachronistic, wedding-cake *Rosenkavalier* was liked by the modish if not the Straussian, Glyndebourne 'discovered' the American illustrator, Maurice Sendak, whose designs for Prokofiev's *Love of the Three Oranges*, perversely given in French, and for Oliver Knussen's opera based on his best-selling book *Where the Wild Things are* have proved hits of recent festivals. A 'fantasy opera' series seems to be emerging with this team and the director Frank Corsaro, who staged Ravel's two one-act operas in 1987. Meanwhile, Peter Hall and Bernard Haitink are preoccupied with a Verdi series, *Simon Boccanegra* in 1986, *La Traviata* 1987 with *Falstaff* and *Un Ballo in Maschera* to come.

Glyndebourne is unique among British opera institutions in that it receives no

The opera house at Glyndebourne (photo: Guy Gravett)

subsidy for festival performance. An autumn tour comprising the best of the repertory performed by young British audiences is supported by the Arts Council, but the summer performances are financed purely from box office revenue and private and corporate sponsorship. Tickets are generally hard to come by, but in general they are worth the effort and expense. If you fail however, it is always easier to catch the company on tour.

Opera North

Leeds Grand Theatre and Opera House, 46 New Briggate, Leeds

Director: Nicholas Payne
Artistic Director: David Lloyd-Jones
Season: Mid September–mid October; mid December–mid January; end March–end May
Productions: 9, 6 new
Performances: 4 of each
Capacity: 1,534
Main Touring Venues: Theatre Royal, Nottingham; New Theatre, Hull; Palace Theatre, Manchester; Theatre Royal, York

Box Office: (0532) 459351
Telex: (Gold) 265871 REF 83: BET037
Box open: Mon–Sat 10.00a.m.–7.30p.m.
Postal: As above
Prices: £3.80–£17.80
Concessions: Up to 25% reductions for subscriptions, group bookings; 50% for students, senior citizens and under 18s

Opera North was founded in 1978 with the aim of providing the north of England with its final permanent professional opera company. Modelling itself closely on its elder siblings, the Welsh National and Scottish Operas, it started as a financial and administrative satellite of the English National Opera, but it is now fully autonomous, presenting up to ten productions a season under the musical directorship of David Lloyd-Jones. It has built up a large and committed following not only in Leeds, but in the other north-eastern cities to which it regularly tours. The standards of musical preparation and production have been consistently high, although the management have so far eschewed the more radical staging experiments associated with Welsh National Opera.

Wilfred Josephs' opera *Rebecca*, based on the novel by Daphne du Maurier, had some popular success when it was given its world première in Leeds in 1983. Other notable productions include an *Aida* by Philip Prowse, a *Bohème* by David Freeman, and part one of *Les Troyens* by Tim Albery. In 1987 the Company ambitiously presented the first-ever British production of Strauss's *Daphne*.

The company is based in the Grand Theatre, Leeds, an elaborate late Victorian edifice with an attractive auditorium and Moorish decoration.

The 1984 Opera North production of 'Orpheus and Eurydice'

65

English National Opera

London Coliseum, St Martin's Lane, London

Director: Peter Jonas
Musical Director: Mark Elder
Season: September–July
Productions: 18, 7 new
Performances: 10 – 18 of each
Capacity: 2,358
Ballet: July–August for visiting companies

Box Office(01) 836 3161
Telex: 264867 ENOG
Box open: Mon–Sat 10.00a.m.–8.00p.m.
Postal: As above
Cards: (01) 240 5258; all major cards accepted
Recorded Information: (01) 836 7666
Prices: £4.50–£21.50
Concessions: 90 seats on day of performance from 10.00a.m. at £2.00. Standing from 3.00p.m. only if performance sold out

Recordings: Mary Stuart (EMI), Julius Caesar (EMI), La Traviata (EMI), Otello (EMI), Rigoletto (EMI), The Ring (EMI), Mikado, Orpheus in the Underworld (all SLS)

The opera company and the theatre, inextricably linked for more than fifteen years in the minds of London's operagoers, have historically independent origins, yet with hindsight they seem to have been made for each other. The English National Opera has only been known as such since 1974 and there were many at the time of the change who thought they would never get used to no longer calling the company Sadler's Wells Opera, though by 1974 the company had been gone from its theatre namesake for six years. So the story of the ENO, as it is affectionately abbreviated, is a tale of two theatres and a succession of companies, whose descendents form the backbone of British cultural life: the National Theatre, the Royal Ballet (and its adjunct Sadler's Wells Royal Ballet) and the English National Opera.

All three derive from the pioneering work of the redoubtable theatre manager, Lilian Baylis, first at the Old Vic, south of the Thames beyond Waterloo Station and subsequently at Sadlers' Wells Theatre in the north London borough of Islington. Baylis had been mounting productions of Shakespeare and opera, often in the most rudimentary circumstances until the beginning of the 1930s. The move to Sadler's Wells resulted from Baylis's conviction that London needed a permanent company performing five nights a week in one theatre, or rather in two theatres since the Shakespeare outfit and the opera ensemble commuted between the Vic and Wells for a number of years until the problems of transportation between either side of the river necessitated the stabilisation of the two companies. During one such journey, the sets for *La Traviata* blew off the top of a lorry travelling over Blackfriars Bridge and into the Thames. So the Vic became the home of Shakespeare (and subsequently the provisional residence of the National Theatre) and Sadler's Wells that of opera.

From the start of her theatrical activities, Baylis had determined on a policy of performing serious entertainment at price which 'labourers and artisans' could afford. The Sadler's Wells Theatre, designed with spartan restraint and functionality by the architect F. M. Chancellor, opened on 6th January, 1931 with Shakespeare's *Twelfth Night*, an apt choice which was followed two weeks later by the first performance by the

The interior of the London Coliseum

Vic-Wells Opera, a production of *Carmen* from the Old Vic stock, conducted by Lawrence Collingwood, produced by Sidney Russell and choreographed by Ninette de Valois who was later to cultivate the Royal Ballet from the seeds planted at the Vic and Wells by Baylis.

With an ever-watchful eye on the box-office, Baylis mustered a surprisingly adventurous repertoire, inaugurating a Russian series with Rimsky Korsakov's *The Snow Maiden* in 1933 and following it up with the same composer's *Tsar Saltan*, Mussorgsky's *Boris Godunov* and Tchaikovsky's *Eugene Onegin* and specialising in contemporary, or recent British operas such as Holst's *Savitri*, Vaughan Williams's *Hugh the Drover* and the music dramas of Baylis's friend, the eccentric Wagnerian, Dame Ethel Smyth whose *Boatswain's Mate* and *The Wreckers* were both performed before the outbreak of the 1939–45 war. It was on the first nights of such operas that Baylis gave her famous first night exhortations to her loyal audiences warning them that if they didn't come to the less familiar pieces there wouldn't be enough money to afford to stage the ones they knew and loved.

Two years after Lilian Baylis's sudden death in 1937, Tyrone Guthrie was appointed Director of Sadler's Wells Opera and his productions set a lasting precedent for British theatre directors in the then notoriously untheatrical world of opera. It was unfortunate, perhaps, that his directorship coincided with the belt-tightening experience of the war, but the acuity with which the company adapted to straitened circumstances proved a measure of its will to survive. Not for the first time productions thrived on ingenuity in place of spectacle. Once the air-raids over London had begun, in 1940, the company, now directed by the soprano Joan Cross, hit the road and spent the rest of the war years touring the British regions.

After the war, the Sadler's Wells Opera reopened with the first performance of *Peter Grimes* by the then little-known Benjamin Britten. A new period of innovation, particularly in terms of repertoire, was ushered in by the appointment of Norman Tucker in the late forties. Twentieth-century operas, Stravinsky's *Rake's Progress*, Bartók's *Bluebeard's Castle*, Pizzetti's *Murder in the Cathedral*, above all the hitherto unknown works of Janáček were pioneered after the hugely successful first British performance of *Katya Kabanova* in 1951. By some curious arrangement or unwritten rule, Sadler's Wells and its successor, English National Opera, have given all of Janáček's operas, including *Osud*, except the most popular, *Jenůfa* which in London is 'owned' by the Royal Opera.

By 1968, when the company moved from Sadler's Wells to the Coliseum the direction of the Opera was in the hands of a man whose vision and determination saw the transformation of a still fairly humble, predominantly touring operation, into a metropolitan and national asset. Stephen Arlen conceived the notion of combining the two companies which now comprised Sadler's Wells Opera – a legacy from the demise of the Carl Rosa Touring Opera – and throwing the entire physical resources of both into the venture.

Alberto Remedio's Walther, Norman Bailey's Sachs, Derek Hammond-Stroud's Beckmesser and Clifford Grant's Pogner, launched each singer into the Wagner repertoire and all, along with Rita Hunter's Brünnhilde, featured in the famous production of the *Ring*, which established Reginald Goodall as the country's foremost Wagner conductor.

Under Arlen's successor, George, Lord Harewood, the company not only changed its name, to English National Opera in August 1974, but embarked on a most adventurous repertoire policy. Harewood's own personal tastes, and the emergence of Valerie Masterson as a star soloist, revived almost forgotten French repertoire in London. To the obvious *Carmen*, a great hit in 1970, were added Berlioz's *Damnation of Faust*, Massenet's *Manon* and *Werther*, Gounod's *Romeo and Juliette* and *Mireille* and Charpentier's *Louise*. The Janáček series was extended to include *The Adventures of Mr. Brouček* (*Osud* came later) and under Charles Mackerras's musical direction, a host of unusual works were programmed to leaven London's staple operatic diet: he himself conducted the British première of Martinů's *Julietta* (1978) in association with the New Opera Company, but that collaboration bore diverse fruits: Szymanowski's ecstatic *King Roger* (1976), Ginastera's strange story of perversity in the Italian renaissance, *Bomarzo* (1976), in which Graham Clark made his ENO debut, Shostakovich's Gogol setting, *The Nose* (1979). Other new works championed during this period included Henze's *The Bassarids* (1979) (British stage première) conducted and produced by the composer, Penderecki's *The Devils of Loudon* (1973) and Ligeti's *Le Grand Macabre* (1982), were all given their British stage première at the Coliseum. The company has commissioned and performed première productions of native works, including David Blake's *Toussaint* (1977), Harrison Birtwistle's *The Mask of Orpheus* (1986), and Iain Hamilton's *The Royal Hunt of the Sun* (1977) and *Anna Karenina* (1981).

Towards the end of Lord Harewood's reign at the Coliseum – he retired in 1984 – he welcomed the new wave of young British producers and designers. Controversy initially shattered the former peace of the auditorium when radical stagings of Tchaikovsky's *Queen of Spades* (1983), Dvořák's *Rusalka* (1983), both by David Pountney, of Wagner's *Rienzi* (1983) and Tchaikovsky's *Mazeppa* (1984), in startling modern dress productions by Nicholas Hytner and David Alden respectively. The Coliseum audience has gradually accepted the changes brought by the new team at the top, conductor Mark Elder and director of production, David Pountney, but Lord Harewood enabled them to carry forward their often stimulating programme. The ENO's reputation for one of the world's most comprehensive repertoires – acknowledged in a 1978 Society of West End Theatres' award has been maintained and even enhanced and the standards of productions have risen to our all-time peak. A night at the Coliseum, even without stars, can provide the most rivetting dramatic experience and the musical standards remain high.

The exterior of the London Coliseum

Covent Garden

The Royal Opera House, Covent Garden, London WC1

Director: Sir John Tooley
Musical Director: Bernard Haitink
Season: September–July
Productions: 23, 5 new
Performances: 5–10 of each
Capacity: 2,000
Ballet: 20 per season
Recorded Information: (01) 836 6903

Box Office: (01) 240 1911/1066
Telex: 29788 COVGAR G
Box open: Mon–Sat 10.00a.m.–7.30p.m.
Postal: PO Box 6, London WC2 7QA
Prices: £2.00 – £42.00, Occasional standby discounts for students, senior citizens, unwaged, unemployed and Friends of Covent Garden. 65 Amphitheatre tickets available from 10.00 a.m. on day of performance.

Recordings: The Trojans, Midsummer Marriage, Il Trovatore, Tosca.
Video: *Un Ballo in Maschera*

Opera has been performed on the site occupied by the present Royal Opera House for over two hundred and fifty years. In 1732, John Rich opened the first of three buildings devoted to the entertainment of the public, the Theatre Royal, with the profits he had accrued from the runaway success of *The Beggars' Opera*, the musical satire which 'made Gay rich and Rich gay' – it made him very rich too. Initially this auditorium served as a playhouse, opera house and ballet theatre, occasionally as an arena for lowlier sports, bawdy farces and pantomimes. Almost immediately, though, the Covent Garden theatre became the focus for opera and oratorio at its most sophisticated. Handel, who had made and lost fortunes with his Royal Academies at King's Theatre in the Haymarket, created two of his most important works for the stage there: the magic opera, *Alcina* and its more intimate companion piece, *Ariodante*, crowned his operatic career. Both made use of the Theatre Royal's capacity for spectacle – for the first time Handel could make use of a resident ballet troupe – but eventually the composer, straitened by the cost of lavish 'cloathes and scenes' and growing public resistance to the Italian *opera seria*, devised large-scale works for concert performance of *Messiah* and premières of *Samson, Joseph* and *Belshazzar, Hercules* and *Semele*. These last, musical dramas on mythological and controversially erotic subjects, were given in the manner of an oratorio – in other words with stage directions printed in the libretto and action left to the listener's imagination – but they are English operas in all but name. The Royal Opera celebrated the two hundred and fiftieth anniversary of theatrical activity at Covent Garden with a new production of *Semele* on 1982.

In 1808 Rich's Theatre Royal succumbed to the fate of so many eighteenth century candle-lit buildings. It was thought that a spark from a gun during a performance of Sheridan's *Pizarro* smouldered overnight and caused the blaze which reduced the theatre to ashes. The following year the manager Thomas Harris opened a second Theatre Royal to designs by Sir Robert Smirke. Under the direction of the actor John Philip Kemble the stage was given over predominantly to the spoken theatre. It was during this period of the theatre's history that Covent Garden's most famous commission was created. To a text which indulged the British taste for elaborate changes of scenery and a sub-Shakespearean amalgam of high-flown tragedy and low-life comedy,

70

INTERIOR OF THE ITALIAN OPERA HOUSE, COVENT GARDEN.

A mid-nineteenth-century view of Covent Garden

Carl Maria von Weber produced his English opera, *Oberon*, a pantomime elevated by the richest music of his early Romantic imagination. The effort of mounting so vast a work so far from home, coupled with the inclement weather, apparently overwhelmed him; less than four months later, after having presided over twelve performances, he died and was buried at St Mary's Moorfields.

In 1847, the auditorium underwent renovation and reconstruction to accommodate the Royal Italian Opera, the first stable company to give opera regularly on the site since the days of Handel. Then, the operatic world was dominated by Italian, or Italian-trained, singers so the repertoire was predetermined. The new-look opera house reopened with Rossini's *Semiramide*, sung by the prima donna Giulia Grisi who was to reign as 'queen' of Covent Garden until the arrival of Adelina Patti. Although the operas performed by the Royal Italian company reflected the prevailing Italian taste at first, with Rossini, Bellini and Donizetti, and subsequently Verdi, German and French operas were also sung but in Italian. London audiences heard *Il Flauto Magico* rather than *Die Zauberflöte*, *Il Franco Cacciatore* rather than *Die Freischutz*. The practice persisted right until the end of the century so that the first performance of Wagner's early operas, late arrivals on London's operatic scene, were given in Italian at the present theatre.

The fire which destroyed Smirke's theatre erupted during a benefit gala, a masked ball, in March 1856. Not until the following year did Edward Middleton Barry's plan for the new opera house emerge, and this reflected the growing prosperity of British society during the mid-Victorian era, even though it cost substantially less than had

Smirke's building. Barry used the site in a practical manner using height to accommodate as many spectators – up to two thousand – as had its broader and deeper predecessor. Auditorium and stage were now at right angles to, rather than parallel to, Bow Street. By European standards the exterior of the building seems restrained, almost austere in its monochrome classicism. This can in part be explained by the unpropitious location of the theatre, surrounded by other buildings at close proximity which prevent an unhindered view of it, but the interior conforms to the prevailing magnificence of 'Empire' opera houses. The traditional horseshoe shape, now upholstered in royal crimson and gold, and the clean square lines of the proscenium give the Royal Opera House an unfussy elegance rarely encountered in houses of similar vintage. In marked contrast to so many of its European and Latin American counterparts, however, and in common with British theatres in general, its restricted foyer space gives the impression of clutter. Although the Victorians clearly went to the theatre as much for social as artistic reasons – the horseshoe gallery and box structure is the manifestation of this dual purpose – they clearly did not believe in the leisurely foyer-fraternising of their European contemporaries.

The full-time company which currently resides in the Royal Opera House, The Royal Opera, is an international ensemble comparable with those of the premier European theatres, the State Operas in Vienna, Munich and Hamburg, the Opéra in Paris, or La Scala, Milan, giving performances for most of the year in Britain. After the Second World War, the Covent Garden Opera, as it was then called, was founded as a permanent ensemble of mostly British singers (though the young Schwarzkopf was an early member) performing the standard operatic repertoire in English. Under the German conductor, Karl Rankl, a standard of performance was established and consolidated so that by the end of the forties and early fifties distinguished foreign guests began to appear. The administrator, David Webster, invited Hotter and Flagstad to sing Wagner (in English), Welitsch as Salomé and eventually Callas as Norma and Aida (both in Italian). But these were special occasions: English-language ensemble was the norm. Webster introduced some experiments in the staging of opera by exposing singers to the unconventional theatrical ideas of Peter Brook but these foundered after the scandalous reception of his *Salomé*, designed by Salvador Dali, in 1949. In recent years, Covent Garden has flirted with audacious, challenging producers – the East German Götz Friedrich was a short-lived 'principal producer' here – but its directors have repeatedly shown a marked preference for conventional stagings, traditional design and conservative intellectual concepts.

After Rankl's withdrawal in 1951, the Czech conductor Rafael Kubelik built up the repertoire, introducing, famously, a complete version of Berlioz's *Les Troyens* and Janáček's *Jenůfa* until then unknown in Britain, and nurtured a company of excellent British singers. Though he was much criticised at the time – it was a highly personal attack in the press by Sir Thomas Beecham which precipitated his resignation – he laid the groundwork for the emergence of a number of British and Commonwealth stars towards the end of the decade. Both Joan Sutherland and Jon Vickers grew out of this period and they were backed up by other outstanding artists who subsequently made international reputations: Geraint Evans, Amy Shuard, Josephine Veasey, Michael Langdon and Donald McIntyre.

The 1902 Covent Garden production of 'Lohengrin' (photo: Mary Evans Picture Library)

The revolution arrived with Georg Solti at the beginning of the sixties. By this time Sadler's Wells Opera, based at the famous theatre of that name in Islington, had developed into a national company, also performing opera in English, with a strong identity of its own. So, between them, Solti and Webster set about moving the Covent Garden Opera into the international league. The Solti era probably brought the Royal Opera House to its artistic peak: the repertoire was expanded and diversified; the major Strauss operas were seen in new productions and *Ring* cycles became annual events. Leading conductors, notably the Italian Carlo Maria Giulini, were invited in to complement the special tastes of the Musical Director. New productions, cast from company strength alongside the greatest international singers, invariably attracted world attention. Solti's legacy can certainly be detected today in the Royal Opera's artistic make-up. The notion of the resident ensemble had been abandoned in favour of original language casts drawn from all over the world. Inevitably, the Royal Opera competes for the most prominent artists with the other international houses, but most of the great contemporary singers appear regularly, especially in the Italian repertoire: Domingo, Carreras, Vickers, Ricciarelli, Cortrubas, Bruson and Milnes appear almost every season and Pavarotti, Sutherland, Caballé, Cappucilli and Ghiaurov are frequent visitors. The finest German repertoire is primarily cast with British guest singers: Jones, McIntyre, Minton, Lloyd are all international artists who appear regularly at Covent Garden. Recent seasons have seen a sharp decline in the number of new productions offered at Covent Garden, the result of comparatively low-funding for a house of international standing, and a consequent decline in standards. Although the Royal Opera at its best can match the musical level of any great house in Europe or America,

Covent Garden as it looks today

many of its productions are old and tired. Some of the great successes of the Solti regime, Visconti's *Don Carlos*, Zeffirelli's *Tosca* and *Rigoletto*, have been required to outlive their artistic usefulness.

There are, however, indications that the thinking is changing among the management. Fewer of the old sets are being resuscitated and many productions are being replaced with new stagings, but at the cost of a contracted repertoire. Since the publication of a report into the financing of the Royal Opera House in 1983, there have been very few novelties or experimental works. Although the company has commissioned some contemporary pieces – only three operas, by Henze, Tippett and John Taverner in the last decade – it remains the custodian of the stage-works of Benjamin Britten and Michael Tippett. At least one opera by either composer can be seen each season. At the opposite end of the spectrum – baroque opera – the picture is bleak, though the auditorium is scarcely ideal for the operas of Monteverdi and Handel. Nor has it the desirable intimacy for Mozart, although the Musical Director between 1971 and 1986 , Sir Colin Davis, overcame this with some sparkling, magical performances of six out of the seven major operas. In 1986 Bernard Haitink took over as musical director promising to maintain the highest artistic standards

You can get priority booking by joining the *Friends of Covent Garden*, which also entitles you to various privileges including the opportunity to go to dress rehearsals attend regular lectures and receive the Opera House magazine *About the House*. Applicants who are under twenty-six will receive free ticket vouchers up to the value of £54 per season.

Wexford Festival

Theatre Royal, High Street, Wexford

Director: Elaine Padmore
Season: 12 days Oct–Nov
Productions: 3, all new
Performances: 4 of each
Capacity: 550

Box Office: (353) 532240
Postal: Booking forms can be obtained from above address
Box open: 9.30a.m.–10p.m.
Prices: IR £22–27
Cards: Access, Visa
Concessions: Half-price for students and senior citizens
Agencies: Tickets can also be booked through McCullongh Piggort Ltd, 11–13 Suffolk Street, Dublin 2

Opera for connoisseurs can take many forms – from the luxury casting at Salzburg, to the intensive monomania of Bayreuth or the intimate perfection of Glyndebourne – but one of the rarest operatic pleasures the world has to offer is to be found in the south-west corner of Ireland in an unremarkable little town with no great tradition of professional musical performance. Why Wexford should have become the host of an opera festival at all and the destination of those opera-lovers who crave the rich diet of specialities long since forgotten by the repertory houses of metropoli, is one of the delightful accidents of musical history. Each year at the end of October and November (when most other festivals are wrapped up for the winter) the tiny Theatre Royal presents twelve performances of three operas, invariably well-known to collectors of old records of opera arias, but rarely seen on stage.

The pattern of performances has remained unchanged since the sixties, when Brian Dickie, a young administrator 'on loan' from Glyndebourne arrived in Wexford to apply the expertise and discrimination he exercised at the Sussex opera festival to the local enthusiasms which had hitherto been the Wexford festival's principal motor and which, even today, contributes enormously to maintain it in business. For, though Wexford is expensive in Irish terms and regarded as elitist in some quarters, one can truly speak of it as a festival which came from the townspeople. In no sense does one feel in this friendly little town that the festival has been imported from outside.

Wexford's attraction is its repertoire policy. Operas which at Covent Garden or La Scala, though not necessarily the Met, would be regarded as box-office poison are meat and drink to Wexford's artistic directors and patrons: in early years, it was the Italian *bel canto* repertoire, principally Donizetti and the once-rare Rossini comedies, that came to be regarded as 'Wexford' operas, though, interestingly, the festival began in 1951 with a former resident of the town, J. M. Balfe, the Irish composer who enthralled the Victorians with his English version of the *bel canto* prototype: *The Rose of Castille*, *The Siege of La Rochelle* (performed at the 1963 festival) and *La Bohème* (not yet given at Wexford but famously advocated by Sir Thomas Beecham in the past).

In recent years, the byways of the French and German repertoires (with side glances at Slavonic works) have been successfully explored, with productions of Gounod

The Wexford Festival production of 'Königskinder'

(Mireille and *Roméo et Juliette)*; Bizet *(La Jolie Fille de Perth* and *The Pearl Fishers)*; and, above all, Massenet *(Don Quichotte, Thaïs, Hérodiade, Grisélidis* and *Le Jongleur de Notre Dame* rather than *Manon* or *Werther)*. That section of the repertoire much beloved by the subscriber at the smaller German house, the *Spieloper*, has been given an airing at Wexford. Otto Nicolai's *The Merry Wives of Windsor*, a work almost unbelievably ignored by British companies, Eugen d'Albert's *Tiefland*, Peter Cornelius's *Der Barbier von Baghdad* (which like *The Merry Wives* should have been sung in English), Weber's *Oberon* and Lortzing's *Der Wildschütz* and, more recently, Engelbert Humperdinck's *Königskinder;* the cinderellas of familiar composers' outputs, get priority at the Theatre Royal.

The programme is arranged so that patrons can take in the complete repertory in any three consecutive days: Wexford might have been made for the musical weekend break.

WESTERN EUROPE

The 1986 Bregenz Festival production of 'The Magic Flute'

Bregenz Festival

Postfach 119, A–6901 Bregenz, Austria

Director: Franz Salzmann
Artistic Director: Alfred Wopmann
Season: July–August
Productions: 2 new
Performances: Varies
Capacity: Floating stage 4,388, Festival House 1,751

Box Office: 0 5574/22811–0
Telex: 57 539
Box open: Daily 9.00a.m.–5.00p.m.
Postal: As above
Prices: 90–1,150 SCH

Bregenz has an annual summer festival, whose chief attraction is the famous floating stage on Lake Constance installed in 1979. The auditorium on the facing shore seats four thousand and four hundred people.

The event actually started in 1946 on the initiative of the town's citizens and in the first week registered an audience of seventeen thousand. From the onset the Vienna Symphony Orchestra provided whatever orchestral roles were necessary although there were no productions of opera until the 1950s when the stage director Adolf Rott, conductor Anton Paulik and the designer Walter Hoesslin were invited to collaborate on one major operatic work a year; a contribution that lasted for almost twenty years. Since then the important events have included a *Flying Dutchman* given as a single act in 1973, a Haydn opera, *Il Finta Stanislas* given the following year in the courtyard of the local castle Hohenems (where a separate festival is devoted exclusively to the music of Schubert) an *Otello* with Domingo and Tomowa-Sintow and Gruberova's Elvira in Bellini's *I Puritani*.

The festival was given new impetus in 1985 by the stage director Jérôme Savary and the designer Michel Lebois, whose production of *The Magic Flute* in 1985 was so successful it was repeated the following year. Constituting another team in the history of the Bregenz festival, Savary and Lebois went on to recreate Offenbach's *The Tales of Hoffmann* in 1987; a production that made use of reflecting plates to effect the various transformations required to show Hoffmann's surrealistic dream-world. Operetta is also an essential part of the festival as well as symphony concerts, plays, ballet and recitals. There are usually two productions each year taking place on the floating stage and in the Grand Festival Hall with a capacity of one thousand seven hundred and fifty. Some of the well-known singers who have appeared recently include Luis Lima, Renato Bruson, Katia Ricciarelli, Francisco Araiza, Yevgeni Nesterenko, Aprile Millo and Paata Burchaladze.

Salzburg Festival

Grosses Festspielhaus, Hofstallgasse 1, Salzburg

Director: Dr Willnauer
Artistic Director: Otto Sertl
Season: mid-July to end-August
Productions: 6, 1 new
Performances: 5 of each
Capacity: 2177, no standing
Ballet: 5 per season

Box Office: (662) 842541
Telex: 633880
Box open: Feb to July, Mon–Fri mornings.
From July, Mon–Fri 9.00a.m.–5.00 p.m.
From end-July, also Sunday
Postal: Postfach 140, A5010 Salzburg
Prices: 150–3000 SCH
Cards: None

*Recordings: Carmen (CBS), Don Giovanni (DG), Falstaff (HMV),
Don Carlos (HMV), The Ring (DG), Così fan Tutte (DG),
Salome (HMV), Tristan (HMV)*

This beautiful Baroque town, the birthplace of Mozart, has held numerous festivals to commemorate its famous son. Yet the operatic tradition there predates the composer's lifetime: the first opera ever to be performed north of the Alps, Caneggi's *Andromeda*, was given in 1618 in the garden of Schloss Hellbrunn. Later in the seventeenth century, Antonio Caldara presented nineteen of his operas to the local court, probably in the Heckentheater of the Mirabellgarten. It was here, too, that the young Mozart's intermezzo *Apollo et Hyacinthus* (1767) and his *Il Sogno di Scipione* (1772) were performed.

An international Mozart Society was set up here in 1870, and began to publish the first systematic and scholarly edition of Mozart's works. Under the Society's auspices, the Viennese Hofoper were invited to give performances of *Figaro*, *Don Giovanni*, and *Così fan Tutte*. Further special performances followed, conducted by Mottl, Richter, Muck and Strauss. Highlights included two performances of *Don Giovanni* in 1901, rigorously rehearsed by the soprano Lilli Lehmann, who sang the role of Donna Anna; and Mahler's performance of the same opera in 1906, with sets by the great designer Alfred Roller.

The success of such events inspired Schalk and Strauss, along with the poet and playwright Hugo von Hofmannsthal and producer Max Reinhardt, to institute a regular Festival. Since 1922, when the Festspielhaus was opened, the event has maintained very high standards, and won a unique aura of prestige and glamour. Indeed, this has actually led to a barrage of complaints about the expense of the tickets and the elitism of the organisation. Apart from opera, lieder recitals, orchestral concerts and serenades have taken place in several attractive and atmospheric venues, including the Felsenreitschule (the riding school with a seating capacity of five hundred and sixty), the Mozarteum, and the courtyard of the Residenz, the seat of the Archbishop.

The 1930s were particularly exciting years for Salzburg: the opera performances enlisted top-quality singers and the orchestra of the Vienna Staatsoper, as well as a train of great conductors including Bruno Walter, Clemens Krauss, Wilhelm Fürtwängler, Hans Knappertsbusch, Karl Böhm, Tullio Serafin, and Felix Weingartner. Toscanini conducted memorable performances of *Falstaff*, *Meistersinger*, *The Magic Flute*, and an outstanding production of *Fidelio*, with Lotte Lehmann in the title role. The Anschluss in 1938, and the onset of war a year later, meant that the Festival's activities were severely curtailed. A particularly dramatic incident occurred in 1944 when the première of Strauss's *Liebe der Danae* was cancelled at the last minute owing to Hitler's declaration of the supreme war effort to the German people: Strauss is said to have conducted the public dress rehearsal with tears in his eyes. By the time the opera received its next Salzburg performance in 1952, the composer was dead.

With the co-operation and financial help of the US Army, the Festival was able to resume its programme as early as 1946, showing an impressive commitment to new works while continuing to produce the more traditional Mozartian fare. Premières have included Einem's *Dantons Tod* (1947) and *Der Prozess* (1953), and Henze's *The Bassarids* (1966) and Berio's *Il Re in Ascolto* (1984). The Festival has also made some remarkable resuscitations of early operas, such as Cavalieri's *Rappresentazione di Anima e di Corpo* in 1968 and Henze's magnificent version of Monteverdi's *Il Ritorno d'Ulisse in Patria* in 1986.

Herbert von Karajan has dominated the Festival, both as conductor and director, since the mid 1950s. In 1960 he conducted the performance of *Der Rosenkavalier* which inaugurated the new Festspielhaus. Designed by Holzmeister to incorporate the original façade of the former court stables, dating back to 1603, the opera house has one of the largest stages in the world – over one hundred and thirty five feet wide and seventy feet deep.

In 1967 Karajan instituted an annual Easter Festival, which presents one operatic production each season under his musical control. *Carmen, Otello, Rosenkavalier, Meistersinger* and the *Ring* have featured, as well as operas by Mozart. Famous productions at the Summer Festival have recently included Giorgio Strehler's *Die Entführung aus dem Serail* and Ponnelle's *Le Nozze di Figaro*. The conductors Karl Bohm and James Levine have been frequent visitors, as have an astonishing array of major singers: Lucia Popp, Agnes Baltsa, Anna Tomowa-Sintow, Paata Burchaladze, Kathleen Battle, Jon Vickers, and Dietrich Fischer-Dieskau have been particular favourites in recent years.

It is almost impossible to hear major operatic performances at the Festival without booking in advance. The summer programme should be subscribed to in early January, and the Easter Festival six months in advance. It is not necessary to send money, but order forms, available through Austrian National Tourist offices, should be sent to the Festival Box Office, who will reply not later than April. Some tickets are available at extra cost from the agency Theaterkartenburo, Polzer, Residenzplatz 4; tel: (662) 846500. Returns are sometimes available three quarters of an hour before the performances begin.

Vienna Staatsoper
Opernring 2, 1010 Wien

Director: Dr Egon Seefehlner
Musical Director: Claudio Abbado
Season: Sept–June
Productions: 45, 7 new
Performances: Approx 5 of each
Capacity: 1642 and 567 standing
Ballet: 26 per season.

Box Office: (51444) 53 24 26 55
Telex: 113775
Box open: Mon–Sat 9.00a.m.–5.00p.m., Sun and hols 9.00a.m.–12.00p.m.
Postal: Kassenleitung Vienna I Staatsoper, Hanuschgasse, 3 Goethegasse 1 A 1010 Wien. Advance postal bookings fron onside Vienna are accepted up to 12 days before performance
Prices: 150–1800 SCH, standing room available one hour before performances
Special order form: to be used for postal bookings. Written orders can only be received up to 42 days before performance

Recordings: Turandot, Frau Ohne Schatten, Wiener Staatsoper 1933 and 1934 (EMI), Die Fledermaus (Decca), Rosenkavalier (CBS). Video: Turandot.

The Royal and Imperial Court Opera (Königliche und Kaiserliche Hofoper) in the capital of the former Austro-Hungarian Empire remains, despite occasional challenges from the houses in Berlin, Munich, Dresden and Hamburg, the principal musical theatre of the German-speaking world. Yet its traditions are predominantly interpretative rather than creative: the great Viennese opera classics started life before the great opera house 'am Ring' was built. Mozart's *Die Entführung aus dem Serail, The Marriage of Figaro* and *The Magic Flute* opened at either the Burgtheater – now Vienna's premier theatre company – or at the suburban Theater aud der Wieden, Schikander's disreputable popular establishment. While *Fidelio* had its first performance at the Theater an der Wien, still used to this day for operetta and small-scale opera productions at the annual Vienna Festival.

The present building dates from the golden age of Imperial Vienna, though, of course, the institution it houses dates back to the infancy of opera as a public entertainment. Cesti's famous spectacle, *Il Pomo d'Oro* (The Golden Apple, not the tomato!) celebrated the wedding of Emperor Leopold I to the Infanta, Margareta of Spain in 1666. Almost a hundred years later, during the long reign of Maria Theresa, Gluck's reform opera, *Orfeo ed Euridice* was unveiled at the Burgtheater. During the early years of the nineteenth century the official court opera performances took place in the Theater am Kärntnertor (close to the Carinthian Gate). Among the musical highlights of this period were the first performances of Beethoven's Choral Symphony – with the famous German bel-canto soprano, Caroline Unger singing the top solo line), of Schubert's all-but-forgotten singspiel, *Die Zwillingsbrüder* (The Twin Brothers) of Weber's *Euryanthe* and Donizetti's *Linda di Chamonix* in 1842.

By the mid 1850s, as the city of Vienna began to expand, it became necessary to demolish the city walls and with them, the Kärtnertor Theatre. In keeping with the Imperial pretensions of the city, a magnificent new opera house was planned to occupy a dominating site on the Ring, the new boulevard which circled the city centre. The architects of the Court Opera House, August Siccard von Siccardsburg and Eduard van der Nüll, were the first victims of the Viennese opera-mania which, even today, seems to preoccupy inhabitants of the city more than any political issue. Van der Nüll, driven to distraction by press and public hostility, committed suicide before his building had opened its doors and von Siccardsburg, shocked and demoralised, died of a heart attack within months of his colleague. Their achievement of providing Vienna with one of the world's most beautiful opera houses – not, it has to be said, quite the same building as the one to be found on the Ringstrasse today – was recognized only after their demise.

The building work took seven and a half years from the end of 1861 until the 25th May 1869 when the house opened with a production of *Don Giovanni*. Of Siccardsburg's original ground plan and van der Nüll's elaborate interior decoration only the external façade, the great staircase, the foyers, the tea-salon and the loggia containing Moritz von Schwind's celebrated frescoes of scenes from *The Magic Flute* remain today, the auditorium having been redesigned in a modern classical style by Erich Boltenstern for the post-war reconstruction from 1949 until 1955. The works of art that adorn the interiors of the old parts of the theatre are of an Imperial splendour surpassed only – in the German-speaking domain – by that of the newly restored Semper Opera in Dresden. Among the artists who adorned the walls and galleries of the old building were Carl Rahl – responsible for the auditorium ceiling and the stage curtain – Josef Gasser, Josef Preleuthner, Michael Rieser, Eduard van Engerth and Friedrich Sturm. The old foyer is still one of the most striking rooms in the opera house, notable above all for the series of paintings – after von Schwind – depicting scenes from contemporary operas, some of them popular at the time but now rarely revived: Cherubini's *Les Deux Journées*, Boieldieu's *La Dame Blanche*, Marschner's *Hans Heiling*, Spohr's *Jessonda* and Schubert's *Der Häusliche Krieg* among a handful of survivors.

The first golden age of the Vienna Court Opera's grand musical tradition coincided with the directorate of Wilhelm Jahn, who presided as Intendant and stage director from 1881 to 1897. Although the Wagner operas had been introduced to the Viennese under the auspices of his two immediate predecessors, *Die Meistersinger* during Johann Herbeck's time and the complete *Ring* during Franz Jauner's period as Intendant, Jahn could draw on the talents of Hans Richter for this important area of the repertory. Richter conducted the Vienna première of *Tristan und Isolde* and Jahn himself introduced other subsequently popular works to the theatre: *Pagliacci*, *The Bartered Bride* and *Hänsel und Gretel*. The most notable world première of the Jahn era was of Massenet's *Werther* given in German on February 16th 1892 with the Belgian Wagner tenor, Ernest van Dyck in the title role and Marie Renard as Charlotte.

With his clarion call against slovenly routine – in the oft-cited part-quotation *Tradition ist Schlamperei* (Tradition is sloppiness) – Gustav Mahler swept through the corridors of the Court Opera like a new broom. He established the Vienna Opera's reputation as the most outstanding ensemble company in the world. Singers of the finest quality were lured to the Austrian capital – Mahler's sometime mistress, the dramatic soprano Anna Bahr-Mildenburg, Selma Kurz, Leo Slezak (a famous Lohengrin and humourist who invented the joke about the departure time of the next swan, having missed the first one at his entrance during the opera) and Richard Mayr, the bass Richard Strauss wanted – but failed to get – for Ochs in the Dresden première of *Der*

Rosenkavalier. Mahler laid the foundations of the Vienna Opera's pre-eminence as an international house of the highest quality. Not only were musical performances meticulously cast and prepared, but stagings, often with superb designs by Alfred Roller, acquired a more dominant artistic profile. Like so many of his successors during the twentieth century, Mahler was eventually drummed out of his job in 1907, the butt of hostile press and public criticism. From 1911, Hans Gregor steered the opera through the last years of the Habsburg monarchy, building on Mahler's groundwork and gathering a nucleus of outstanding soloists including the rival sopranos, Lotte Lehmann and Maria Jeritza and the English-born tenor Alfred Piccaver.

It fell to Franz Schalk, Intendant from the end of the First World War, to restore the lustre of the house, now the Vienna State Opera, after the upheavel of the monarchy's demise. With Richard Strauss as his co-director from 1919, he saw the première of Strauss and Hofmansthal's most ambitious collaboration, *Die Frau ohne Schatten*, first given on October 10th 1919 with Jeritza and Lehmann as Empress and Barak's Wife, Lucie Weidt as the Nurse, Karl Oestvig as the Emperor and Mayr as the Dyer Barak. Schalk conducted this most glittering occasion and Roller designed the sets and costumes, though neither, apparently, were to the composer's and librettist's liking.

The Vienna Staatsoper (photo: BBC Hulton Picture Library)

The other notable première of the Schalk-Strauss partnership was Hans Pfitzner's *Palestrina* which Schalk also conducted in 1917. Now rarely performed outside the German-speaking lands, it still retains a special place in the repertoire of the Vienna State Opera. Strauss withdrew from the administration of the Opera after his sixtieth year, but returned frequently to conduct Mozart and the local first performances of *Intermezzo* with Lehmann repeating her brilliant portrait of the composer's wife after the Dresden première, and *Die Aegyptische Helena* with the beautiful Jeritza as the face who launched a thousand ships.

After Schalk, a succession of directors, including the great conductors Clemens Krauss, Felix von Weingartner (Mahler's successor in 1908) and Karl Böhm, maintained the high standard of the ensemble until the end of the war. By this time the Vienna State Opera had attracted many of the young singers who were to form the unrivalled Mozart and Strauss interpreters of the post-war period: Elizabeth Schwarzkopf, Lisa Della Casa, Hilde Gueden, Irmgard Seefried, Sena Jurinac, Leonie Rysanek and Ljuba Welitsch among the sopranos, Christa Ludwig, Anton Dermota, Paul Schoeffler, Walter Berry, Erick Kunz and Ludwig Weber. Most of these permanent members of the Vienna ensemble appeared as international stars at the Salzburg Festival.

After the destruction of Siccardsburg and Van der Nüll's house in March 1945, the opera company's activities transferred to the Theater an der Wien until the opening of the reconstructed and re-designed building on November 5th 1955 with a new production of *Fidelio* conducted by Böhm, director for the second time, after a brief period of *Arbeitsverbot* (prohibition). His reign endured all too briefly as his international career, particularly in North and South America, blossomed. After frequent absences, he conducted a new production of Alban Berg's *Wozzeck* (one of his special operas) to storms of audience disapproval and he promptly resigned. The same fate eventually befell his successor Herbert von Karajan, though not before almost a decade of near-permanent festival standards with great singers under his direction.

By the mid-sixties when Karajan left no less peremptorily than had Böhm, the international opera scene underwent radical changes. Although the State Opera retained the services of some of its greatest artists, among them Rysanek, Jurinac, Ludwig and Berry and still had, in the Vienna Philharmonic, the world's finest opera orchestra in its pit, the tightly-knit ensemble began to loosen in favour of international star casts. The need to provide a quickly changing programme of operas – as many as twenty in any given month – necessitated a dilution of the ensemble spirit. Even today, the State Opera can give evenings of unrivalled operatic splendous, with starrily cast first nights and charmed revivals. During the seventies many of these occurred under Böhm in his favourite Mozart and Strauss operas with a new generation of singers including the creamy voiced soprano Gundula Janowitz, but demands on the world's greatest singers meant routine repertoire on some nights.

Lorin Maazel, on his appointment as Director in 1982, attempted to raise everyday standards by introducing a limited stagione system, playing series of performances of an opera with the same hand-picked cast, but the plan succumbed to audience resistance and he withdrew after less than two years in office. During his short administration he did preside over some important new productions; a thrilling *Turandot* with Eva

Marton, Katia Ricciarelli and José Carreras; a very distinguished *Aida* with Maria Chiara and Luciano Pavarotti and the Vienna première of the three act version of Berg's *Lulu* completed by Friedrich Cerha.

Today, Vienna can call on the services of the world's best singers and has developed a handful of its own stars, including the Czech coloratura, Edita Gruberova, and it looks poised to enter a new period of glory under the administration of Claus Helmut Drese and musical direction of Claudio Abbado, who have already announced five extremely exciting seasons from 1987. It would appear that Abbado is doing unusually well for a new director to the Staatsoper and he has already achieved a great success with a new production of *Un Ballo in Maschera* starring Pavarotti which was given extensive TV coverage.

Vienna Volksoper
Behringstrasse 78, Wien 9

Director: Eberhardt Waechter
Season: Sept – end June
Productions: 30, 4 new
Performances: 25 of new productions,
10 of old
Capacity: 1473, 102 standing
Ballet: 6–10 per season

Box office: (51444) 3318
Telex: 113775
Box open: Mon–Sat 9.00–5.00p.m.,
Sun 9.00–12.00a.m.
Postal: Goethegasse 1, Wien 9
Prices: 15–500 SCH; student concessions 50
SCH, 1hr before performance
Cards: Visa, Mastercharge, American Express

Recordings: Die Fledermaus, Wienerblut.

The second opera house in Vienna, the Volksoper, was founded in 1898 by the playwright Adam Müller-Gütenbrünn in the unfashionable Währinger Strasse for the purpose of giving plays in the Viennese dialect. The theatre rapidly lost money and was forced to close. But in 1903, following the appointment of Rainer Simons as director, it reopened with the intention of becoming a credible alternative to the Hofoper. In 1904 Alexander von Zemlinsky, then the most celebrated conductor in Vienna after Mahler, gave the opening performance – of Weber's *Der Freischütz* – and during the next decade he produced some important Austrian premières, including *Tosca* (conducted by Puccini himself and starring the then little-known Maria Jeritza) in 1906 and *Salomé* in 1907.

In 1917 the theatre was taken over by the municipality, and Felix Weingartner, another superb conductor, took charge. There followed a difficult period of massive inflation and fuel shortages, causing the theatre to close for long periods, but it remained an enterprising institution, giving the world premiere of Schönberg's *Die Glückliche Hand* (1924), Schubert's *Der Hausliche Krieg*, and the first Viennese performance of *Boris Gudunov*. Another composer favoured by the Volksoper was the English Wagnerian Joseph Holbrooke, whose *The Children of the Don* (1912) and *Dylan, Son of the Wave* (1914), satisfied the Viennese demand for Wagnerian kitsch. Important singers making their debuts here at this time included Emanuel List and Ludwig Weber.

The house was closed in 1928, reopening the following year as the Neues Wiene Schauspielhaus. It now expanded its repertoire to embrace operetta and assumed a position relative to the Hofoper similar to that of the Opéra-Comique to the Opéra in Paris, hosting a body of works that were light and small-scale. The famous Max Reinhardt production of Offenbach's *La Belle Hélène*, in Korngold's arrangement, appeared here in 1932, as well as many other operettas in the Viennese tradition.

In May 1945, six weeks after the bombing of the opera house on the Ringstrasse, the Staatsoper company moved to the Volksoper, making it one of their two temporary homes, the other being the Theater an der Wien. The Staatsoper itself reopened in 1955, with Franz Salmhofer as director and Marcel Prawy as producer.

During the 1950s the Volksoper introduced the American musical to Vienna with Cole Porter's *Kiss Me Kate*, and this was followed in the 1960s by productions of

The Vienna Volksoper production of 'Die Csardasfurstin'

Bernstein's *West Side Story* and Lerner and Loewe's *My Fair Lady*. Karl Dönch was appointed director in 1973, and oversaw extensive modernisation of the sombre and undecorated auditorium; a centre box, closely associated with Hitler's presence during the Anschluss, was tactfully removed.

A recent star of the house has been the American soprano Julia Migenes-Johnson, who sang here for eight years before becoming world-famous through her portrayal of *Carmen* in the film by Francesco Rossi.

Opéra Nationale de Belgique
Théâtre de la Monnaie, rue Leopold 4, 1000 Bruxelles

Director: Gérard Mortier
Musical Director: Sylvain Cambriling
Season: Sept–July
Productions: Approx 14–16, 6 new
Performances: Approx 9 of each
Capacity: 1140, no standing
Ballet: Approx 4 per season

Box Office: 02 218 1266
Telex: 24575
Box open: Mon–Sat 11a.m.–6p.m. Mon–Sat
Postal: As above, one month in advance.
Tickets unsold 5 minutes before performance
are sold at 120 FB to those under 25
Prices: 150–1600 FB
Cards: American Express, Diners

*Recordings: La Clemenza di Tito (SEPA), Lucio Silla (PAVANE),
Kiri Te Kanawa recital (EMI)*

If opera ever made money, it ought to do so in the Belgian capital, where the Muntschouwberg, which houses the National Opera and Ballet, is built on the site of an old mint. When in 1675 the Maréchal de Villeroi began to re-draw the map of central Brussels, its ruler, Maximilian Emanuel of Bavaria, decreed that a 'grand théâtre' should be built on the square once occupied by the Hotel d'Ostrevant where coins were minted up to the fifteenth century.

In 1700 under the direction of the governor's treasurer, the Italian Giovanni Paolo Bombarda, a playhouse was erected to rival the great theatres of Europe. In this first 'théâtre sur la Monnoie' French dramatic entertainments were regularly given (among the notables who visited it were the Duke of Marlborough, Napoleon and both his wives) until 1817, when the second 'theatre on the mint' was built – Bombarda's house having attained almost unprecedented longevity for the candle-lit theatres of the day.

Outwardly, the second theatre, designed by Damesne and erected between 1817 and 1819, differs little in appearance from 'La Monnaie' of today. The auditorium followed the prevailing Italian mode, enriched with fashionable Empire style decoration. Damesne conceived his theatre as a neo-classical temple to the lyric and dramatic arts, and soon after its inauguration it became an important focus for predominantly new French plays and operas, performed here almost immediately after their Paris premières. During a performance of Auber's opera, *La Muette de Portici* (The Mute Maiden of Portici) on the 25 August, 1830, shortly after the duet 'Amour sacré de la patrie' a riot started in the auditorium when the tenor singing the role of Masaniello, one Lafeuillade, cried 'Aux armes, aux armes!'. The angry crowd flooded onto the streets of Brussels, sparking off the Belgian rising against their Dutch masters.

This period also witnessed the supremacy of the great Franco-Jewish tragedienne, Rachel, who breathed new life into Racine's *Phèdre*, *Andromaque* and *Iphigénie*. Plays continued to be performed at La Monnaie until 1853, when under the administration of Theodor Letellier the stage was devoted exclusively to opera and dance. In 1845 the Opera gave its first performance abroad, at Covent Garden, to considerable acclaim. By this time the repertory included not only the latest French works of Auber and Boïeldieu, but also the *bel canto* operas of Rossini, Bellini and Donizetti, often in French translations sung by French artists. The great tragic tenor Adolphe Nourrit quickly transferred the operas in which he had created the principal tenor in Paris to Brussels: Rossini's *Le Comte Ory* and *Guillaume Tell*, Adam's *Le Postillion de Longjumeau*, Halévy's *La Juive* and early works by Meyerbeer, the German-born composer who had moulded the taste of the French for extravagant spectacle, lengthy balletic *divertissments* and undemanding tunes.

It was during preparations for a performance of Meyerbeer's *Le Prophète* on the 21st January 1855, that fire broke out on stage, spreading rapidly to the auditorium and gutting the interior, but leaving Damesne's shell intact. Only a year before the plain pediment above the portico had been furnished with a relief depicting the Harmony of Human Endeavour. Within the existing walls the architect Poleart conceived an entirely new auditorium, modelled to a great extent on the Grand Opéra in Paris, though without Garnier's Imperial excesses. La Monnaie is the perfect medium-scale opera house, intimate enough for Mozart's comedies and yet large enough to accommodate the spectacle of the Romantic operas.

However, it was in the latter half of the nineteenth century that the house reached its zenith of its artistic fortunes, to the extent that it could rival the glittering éclat of 'La Grande Boutique' (Verdi's name for the Paris Opéra) itself. In March 1860 Richard Wagner came to conduct two concerts of his works on his way to Paris, but it was not until the following decade that any of his operas were staged at La Monnaie: *Lohengrin* in 1870 and *The Flying Dutchman* in 1872. Under the direction of Letellier, and later of Stoumon and Calabresi, the house consolidated its position as one of the finest and most progressive in Europe. As early as 1883 they contrived, with the help of the German impresario Angelo Neumann, to bring the original 1876 Bayreuth production of Wagner's *Ring*, lock, stock and barrel to Brussels. On the 19th December 1881, La Monnaie had given Massenet's *Hérodiade* its world première, a success so spectacular – fifty-five performances in four and a half months – that it seems to have prejudiced the Paris Opéra against the work (it was not performed there until 1921). In succeeding seasons Meyer's *Sigurd* (1884) and Chabrier's *Gwendoline* (1885), both highly regarded in their day, had their first performances here. In the twentieth century Ernest Chausson's *Le Roi Arthus* (1903) Milhaud's *Les Malheurs d'Orphee* (1925) and Honegger's *Antigone* (1927) were 'creations mondiales' by the La Monnaie company. Most recently Knussen and Sendak's *Where the Wild Things Are* (then called Max and Maximonsters) was staged here, unfinished, in 1981, the European Year of the Child.

The directorship of Maurice Kufferath from 1900 to 1914 ushered in a new period of artistic innovation. These years saw the growth of a fully fledged company of singers, dancers and musicians, who performed for eight months of the year. Felix Mottl, the great Bayreuth conductor came to supervise productions of Tristan und Isolde and Die Walkure; Richard Strauss conducted his own operas, Salome and Elektra; and Vincent d'Indy and Gabriel Faure also appeared in the pit. The repertoire ranged from Gluck to contemporary works, operas and ballets from Russia were included, and the Expressionist artist, Ferdinand Khnopff numbered among the set and costume designers.

After the Great War, La Monnaire re-opened its doors on the 21st December, 1918, under a new administration led by Jean van Glabbeke and Paul Spaak. During the inter-war period the house was quick to produce the most significant contemporary operas; Puccini's Turandot in 1926, only months after the La Scala premiere, Max von

Schilling's Mona Lisa and Prokofiev's The Gambler in 1929, given simultaneous world premieres in Paris and Brussels – La Monnaie was not to be outdone. This was the golden age of singers in the Belgian capital, with artists such as Ernest van Dijk, Anton van Rooy, Fanny Heldy and Fernand Ansseau appearing beside the great international stars of the day – Chalipapin, Caruso, and Destinn.

Although basically a repertory company, the Belgian National Opera has always used 'star' singers: Maria Malibran in 1829; the 18-year-old Adelina Patti in 1861 before beginning her reign as 'Queen' of Covent Garden, and returning to sing her celebrated Lucia, Violetta, Gilda, Juliette, Marguerite and Valentine in Meyerbeer's *Les Huguenots;* Maria Sasse, the *créatrice* of Sélika in the same composer's *L'Africaine;* Marietta Alboni; Emma Albani; the noble French baritone Jean-Baptiste Fauré, who repeated the role of Hamlet he had created in Paris; Gali-Marié, the first Carmen and Mignon; Emma Calvé; the great Wagnerian Félia Litvinne; even Nelly Melba sang Gilda here.

La Monnaie remained open during the Second World War, though in straitened circumstances. After the war, some of the most notable performances were those given in conjunction with Bayreuth. As with Neumann earlier, Wieland Wagner took his productions to Brussels. Clutgens, Sawallish and Keilberth conducted such fine Wagnerians as Martha Modl, Gré Brouwensteijn and Wolfgang Windgassen.

After a blaze of glory under Maurice Haussman's directorship, a period crowned by Elizabeth Schwarzkopf's farewell to the stage in Strauss's *Rosenkavalier* in 1971, La Monnaie's reputation declined. Schwarzkopf returned in 1979 to direct the same opera with Elisabeth Söderström in her old role, but the experience was enjoyed by neither. The appointment of Gérard Mortier in 1978 has transformed the artistic profile of the house in the eighties. With two musical directors, or rather principal conductors, Mortier reorganized the Company and planned the repertoire around a policy of concentrated work on one opera at a time, with promising young singers and international stars prepared to dedicate themselves to thorough rehearsal schedules and radical productions. This, together with generous government funding, has made La Monnaie one of the most enterprising and envied houses in Europe. Its series of Mozart productions directed by Karl-Ernst Herrmann, Luc Bondy and Gilbert Deflo (the resident producer) has encouraged audiences to look afresh at these timeless masterpieces. Mortier has also revived the French repertoire, most notably the magical production of Massenet's *Cendrillon* with Frederica von Stade in 1982, Charpentier's *Louise* in 1983 and *Les Contes de Hoffmann* in 1986. By restricting the number of productions given each year and mounting them to the highest possible quality, Mortier has taken La Monnaie to the top of the European league. It is a theatre with a proud tradition, but one not hamstrung by the glories of its past.

The Théâtre Royal de la Monnaie, Brussels

Royal Theatre, Copenhagen

Kongens Nytov, Copenhagen K, DK 1050

Director: Paul Jorgensen
Season: September–June
Productions: 7
Performances: 7 to 10 of each
Capacity: 1,100
Ballet: 15–20 per season

Box Office: (1) 141765
Telex: 15524 DKT
Box open: Mon–Sat 12.00–7.00p.m.
Postal: As above
Prices: 30–150K
Concessions: For students and senior citizens

Opera in Denmark can be traced back to the mid-seventeenth century; the first performance was probably Caspar Forster's *Il Cadmo* in 1663. There are records of an opera by Schindler *Der Vereinighte Götterstreit*, given in 1689 at the ill-fated Amalienborg Theatre which burned down shortly after the première, killing a hundred and eighty people. Foreign companies provided the bulk of entertainment; indeed Italian, French and German companies were performing at the Court Theatre until well into the nineteenth century. The German composer Reinhard Keiser was master of the King's music between 1721 and 1723 and in 1722 his opera *Ulysses* was given to celebrate Frederick IV's birthday. Another important state event was the commissioning of Gluck's *La Contessa dei Numi* in 1749, although the composer's prestige had by then hardly been established.

From the end of the eighteenth century a series of important musical directors kept the medium very much alive for the city's inhabitants. These included Schulz (1787–1795), Kunzen (1795–1817) and finally Johan Svendsen (1883–1908) who oversaw the building of the new Royal Theatre which opened in 1874. His successor from 1908 was Denmark's greatest composer Carl Nielsen, who had recently been honoured with two premières at the Royal Theatre, *Saul og David* in 1902 and *Maskarade* in 1906. Nielsen was instrumental in bringing Wagner to Denmark, some productions having been given in close collaboration with the Stockholm Opera. He was unable to give the complete *Ring* and the task was undertaken by his successor Georg Heberg (1944–30) in 1910.

Before the Second World War there were attempts by the musical directors Johan Hye-Knudsen and Egisto Tango to update the repertoire and include works like *Wozzeck* and *Elektra*. During the occupation they courageously continued to produce works that had been banned by the Nazis, including the first performance outside the United States of *Porgy and Bess* in 1943.

It must be added that one of the greatest of all heldentenors, Lauritz Melchior (1890–1973) began as a baritone in Copenhagen, making his debut in *Tannhäuser* in 1918. He went on to sing Tristan over two hundred times and kept close links with the Royal Opera. There have been a number of Danish operas, one of the most popular being F. L. A. Kunza's *Holger Danske* (1789) which is based on the *Oberon* theme.

In 1931 a new stage was built alongside the original stage, allowing for the performance of both ballet and drama. After two years of restoration during which the backstage facilities were altered considerably, the Royal Theatre reopened in 1986 with *Elverhøg* by Kuhlau, one hundred and thirty eight years after its first performance.

Finnish National Opera
Boulavardi 23–27, Helsinki 18

Director: Iika Kuusisto
Artistic Director: Jorma Hynninen
Season: August–June
Productions: 4, 2 new
Capacity: 600
Ballet: 4 per season

Box Office: (358) 90 12921
Telex: 13401
Box open: Mon–Fri 9.00a.m.–5.00p.m., Sat 10.00a.m.–1.00p.m.
Postal: As above
Prices: 40–120 Mks
Concessions: Discounts for senior citizens and students

The first operatic voices to ring through Helsinki were those of touring German and Italian companies in the early nineteenth century. In 1873 the first resident company was founded, but it wasn't until 1911 that regular opera could be heard and in 1914 the Suomalainen Opera company was set up. The Finnish National Opera was formed in 1918, staging its first production, *Aida*, a year later. It has since been at the same small, beautiful, classically designed but utterly impractical venue, though there are now plans for it to move to a new base in Toolo Bay, and Aulis Sallinen has been commissioned to compose an opera for its opening night, hopefully some time in 1990.

The company prides itself on its high standard of singing, and performs most works in Finnish though some classics are sung in the original language. The fine tradition in Finnish language opera actually began with Oskar Mericanto's *Pohjan Neiti* in 1908, and continued with works by Madetoja and more recently Aulis Sallinen. The Finnish bass Martti Talvela has contributed much to opera in Finland and was the artistic director of the Savonlinna Festival until 1980. The Finnish National Opera holds an annual May festival, and also tours abroad, its major venture of 1987 being a visit to the Edinburgh festival.

The Finnish National Opera House, Helsinki

Savonlinna Opera Festival

Olavinkatu 35, SF 57130 Savonlinna, Finland

Director: Pentti Savolainen
Season: July
Productions: 5, 2 new
Performances: Varies
Capacity: 2,157

Box Office: (358) 57 22684
Telex: 81057007 OPERA SF
Box open: Mon–Sat 10.00a.m.–6.00p.m.,
Sun 10.00a.m.–3.00p.m. during festival
Postal: As above
Prices: 180–280 Mks

In addition to offering exquisite lakeside scenery, the Savonlinna summer festival holds its annual July opera in an atmospheric medieval castle. It began in 1912 with a performance of Melartin's *Aino* in the castle courtyard featuring Aïno Acte, the first singer from Finland to win international acclaim, with her portrayal of *Salome* in Strauss's highly controversial opera. The following year Merikanto conducted his own work, *The Killing of Elina*.

War prevented the 1914 opening, and from 1916 to 1930 politics again halted the festival. Over the years there were further problems, so that it wasn't until 1967 that the festival became an annual summer event. In spite of a well received *Fidelio*, the Finnish Broadcasting Corporation decided not to provide the enterprise with much needed financial backing, and in 1972 there were strong fears that it was about to end. Fortunately the festival survived and an artistic board was specially created to sort out its financial and artistic policies. Notable operatic successes from then on include the 1972 production of *The Magic Flute* produced by August Everding, revived every year, and *Boris Godunov*. Martti Talvella was artistic director from 1972 to 1980. He was succeeded by former tenor and businessman Timo Mustakallio, then by pianist Ralf Gothoni, and the present director is Pentti Savolainen.

Ulf Söderblöm conducted the famous *Fidelio*, first in 1961, and has conducted at every festival since. Besides Talvella, other important singers are Matti Salminen and the sopranos Ritva Auvinen and Tam Valjakka. Talvella succeeded in bringing big names to Savonlinna including Jessye Norman, Nicholai Gedda, Birgit Nilsson, Elli Ameling and Ileana Cotrubas for either opera or recitals.

Finnish operas are also staged, with Finland's most famous composer, Aulis Sallinen's *Horseman and Red Line*, and Joonas Kokkonen's the *Last Temptation*. The 1987 season featured the revival of *The Magic Flute, Aida, Carmen, Khovanschina, The King Goes Forth to France*, and *Orpheus in the Underworld*. There is also a wide programme of classical concerts, recitals and choral works.

Aix-en-Provence Festival
Palais de l'Ancien Archêveché, 13100 Aix-en-Provence

Director: Louis Erlo
Season: July
Productions: 5
Performances: Approx 4 of each
Prices: Opera 200–620 F; concerts 140–220 F
Concerts: Approx 9 per season

Box Office: (42) 23 11 20
Box open: May 4–30 box office is on the ground floor of the Palais de l'Ancien Archevêché, Mon–Sat 9.00–12.00a.m., 4.30–6.00p.m.; June 1–July 31 it is at the cloisters of Saint Sauveur, Place de l'Archêveché, 10.00a.m.–1.00p.m., 3.00–7.00p.m.
Postal: Festival d'Aix, Palais de l'Ancien Archevêché, 13100 Aix-en-Provence

An annual summer festival (the Festival International d'Art Lyrique et de Musique) takes place in Aix, this beautiful Provençal city that has inspired artists and musicians for centuries. Opera takes place in the courtyard of the Archbishop's Palace, originally designed by Cassandre, and concerts are held in the nave and cloisters of the nearby Cathedral of Saint Sauveur. Founded by Gabriel Dussurget and Roger Bigonnet in 1948, the festival's emphasis was initially on Baroque and Classical opera, especially Mozart and Rossini, supplemented by Cimarosa, Rameau, Grétry, Gluck, Monteverdi, Haydn and Purcell. High standards were achieved largely through the efforts of Hans Rosbaud, the director until 1959, who assembled local talent and introduced many important singers such as Graziella Sciutti and the American soprano Teresa Stich-Randall, who became a regular. Other singers launched by the festival include Berganza in Purcell's *Dido and Aneas* and Troyanos as the composer in Strauss's *Ariadne auf Naxos*.

After Rosbaud's retirement, the festival rapidly fell into decline, although public interest was maintained by an expansion of the repertoire to include bigger works such as *Falstaff*, *Pelléas et Mélisande* and *Der Rosenkavalier*. The Festival recovered its high standards when Bernard Lefort took over in 1973 and a policy was established of getting one or two big names for each production and giving lesser mortals a chance in supporting parts. For a while Caballe was brought in every year, and a famous production of *Semiramide* by Pierre Luigi Pizzi in which she sang the title role renewed interest in an otherwise neglected opera. Other favourites have included Katia Ricciarelli and Marilyn Horne and in 1976 an important production of *La Traviata* by the ex-theatre director Lavalli introduced Sylvia Sass to West European audiences. English singers such as Valerie Masterson, Philip Langridge and Robert Lloyd have also become regular guests. Recent triumphs of the festival, now under the directorship of Louis Erlo, include an *Ariadne* with Jessye Norman and José Van Dam in *Falstaff*. The tricentary of Lully's death was celebrated in 1987 with Claude Penchenat's production of *Psyché*, originally written for the re-opening of the Salle des Tuilleries in 1678.

Grand Théâtre de Bordeaux

Place de la Comédie, 33074 Bordeaux

Director: M. Lespinasse
Artistic Director: Gerard Boireau
Season: October–May
Productions: 12, 1 new
Performances: 6 of each
Capacity: 1,100

Box Office: 56 909160
Telex: OPERMAI 560994 F
Box open: Mon–Fri 9.00a.m.–5.30p.m.
Postal: As above
Prices: 80–200 F

Opera in Bordeaux dates back to 1688, but the opera house built in the Municipal Gardens and the academy were not founded until the middle of the next century. The most significant development of the century was the building of the Grand Théâtre which opened in 1780. Designed by Victor Louis, it was one of the finest opera houses in France, with a capacity of one thousand, one hundred and fifty eight. Although damaged during the Revolution, the theatre was fully restored in 1799.

During the nineteenth century, its importance considerably increased. It hosted performances by leading Parisian companies and periodically had its share of the usual kind of operatic controversy. *La Traviata* was not considered to be up to the standard of Meyerbeer; *Manon* was an incoherent muddle; and Rheingold's currency, it was suggested, would have been better dumped in the Garonne! In 1938 the theatre was modernised, and from 1948–51 it benefited from the leadership of Vanni Marcoux (singer turned director). In 1950 the Bordeaux Arts Festival was launched, with operatic works taking a prominent part. The last thirty years have also seen several important premières, the most notable including Bizet's *Ivan IV* and *Mathis der Maler*.

Bordeaux produces about twelve operas a year, but rarely attracts big names. Despite this it is a reasonably innovative repertoire. In addition to the main works of Wagner, Bizet, Verdi, Mozart, there have been performances of Massenet's *Le Jongleur de Notre Dame*, Yumi Narci's *Trois Contes de l'Honorable Fleur* in 1984, Landowski's *Montségur* in 1985, Rossini's *La Pietra del Paragone* in 1986 and Salieri's *Falstaff* in 1987. Each year there is at least one new production.

The Grand Théâtre de Bordeaux (photo: Roger-Viollet)

Opéra de Lyon
Place de la Comédie, 69001 Lyon

Director: Louis Erlo
Musical Director: John Eliot Gardener
Artistic Director: Jean-Pierre Brossmann
Season: October–June
Productions: 8, 4 new
Performances: Varies
Capacity: 3,000

Box Office: (78) 28 09 05
Telex: OPERALY 305286F
Box open: Mon–Sat 11.00a.m.–6.00p.m.
Postal: As above
Prices: 80F–160F

Recordings: Etoile (EMI)

Opera in Lyons began with the opening of the Académie Royale de Musique in 1676. This was renowned for its performances of Lully's *Phäeton, Bellérophon, Armide* and *Atys* which were staged four times a week until the building was destroyed by fire in 1688. For a while opera could then be heard at the governor's residence before it was put under the control of Nicolas Levasseur, who initially staged concerts in the local stables before a suitable building was constructed. In the early eighteenth century the opera moved to the rue St. Jean, but further fires and economic problems hampered its future. In 1756, a new theatre was erected, which presented *opera buffa* and *opera comique*, featuring the works of Grétry, Piccinni and Gluck. The theatre was rebuilt in 1831 and was enlarged in 1842, increasing its capacity from one thousand eight hundred to three thousand. The company staged a number of worthy productions of Wagner during the late nineteenth and early twentieth centuries, including the first production of *Die Meistersinger* in France. The sentimental strain in French opera exploited by Massenet and Gounod, as well as the popular Italian works of Verdi, Bellini and Donizetti were also adequately represented at Lyon.

In recent years, with Louis Erlo as director since 1969, and Theodor Guschlbauer as musical director, there have been on average six to eight operas a year. Erlo has injected new life into the Opéra with a number of bizarre productions that have generated interest. A good many have been first-rate productions of rarely performed operas, with the highlights including Dallapiccola's *Vol di Notte* (1969), Weill's *Mahoganny* (1970), Martinŭ's *The Three Greetings* (1972), Schönberg's *Pierrot Lunaire* , Honegger's *Jeanne au Bûcher* (both 1973), and Rameau's *Zoroastre* (1974). In 1986 the appointment of John Eliot Gardener, an ex-pupil of Nadia Boulanger, as musical director, marked the first time an Englishman had been given a position of prominence in a French opera house. Under him, the emphasis shifted from contemporary works to less-known Baroque and classical operas such as Charpentier's *David and Jonaphas* and revivals of Rameau and Cavalli. The 1987 season included more curiosities such as Rossini's *Le Comte Ory*, Offenbach's *Les Brigands* and Messager's *Fortunio*.

Opéra de Marseilles
2 rue Molière, 13000 Marseilles

Director: Jacques Carpo
Season: October–May
Productions: 10, 6 new
Performances: Approx. 3 or 4 of each
Capacity: 1,786
Ballets: 2 or 3
Concerts: 7 or 8

Box Office: (9) 155 2110
Box open: Daily 2.00–5.00p.m.
Postal: As above
Prices: 50–135 F
Concessions: 30% discount for students

Marseilles is one of France's minor musical strongholds. From the second century BC, when a Roman theatre was built for plays and concerts, it has exerted a notable influence on French musical life. In the fifth century it was renowned for its religious music, and in the sixteenth century it boasted one of the earliest printed musical texts. Opera in Marseilles flourished particularly during the sixteenth and seventeenth centuries.

The Marseilles Music Academy was built in 1685, and was France's first provincial opera house. Opening with Gautier's *Triomphe de la Paix* it had a turbulent beginning, having to move home more than once. Experiencing some financial difficulties, it even had to suspend several productions, but its artistic purpose was never undermined by these practical setbacks. It specialised in rescue opera, comedy, and operas by Gluck, Lully and Rameau, soon becoming the first stop for many works which had recently opened in Paris.

Marseilles' lively musical public and first-rate company gained a new opera house almost a hundred years after the first one had opened. Enlightened managerial policy led to the introduction of Grand Opera, in particular the works of Halévy, Meyerbeer and Spontini. The theatre burned down in 1919 and was reopened in 1924. This is the theatre used today, based in the centre of Marseilles' red light area. Leonie Rysanek, the Austrian soprano known for her parts in Verdi and Strauss operas, has appeared there regularly. A recent offshoot is the Marseilles Operetta, which is rather sober and unexperimental, although it has staged some modern works including Berg and Penderecki.

Marseilles is now considered to be an 'Italian' house with lesser-known Italian singers bought in, and it tends to have a limited repertoire.

Orange Festival

Choregies d'Orange, Place des frères Mounet, 84105 Orange

Director: Raymond Duffaut
Season: July
Productions: 2
Performances: approx 3 of each
Capacity: 13,000
Concerts: 5 per season

Box Office: (90) 34 2424/(90) 34 1552
Box open: Daily June–Aug 8.00a.m.–6.00p.m.
Postal: BP 180 Orange 84105 (enclose cheque plus 25F for postage)
Prices: 120–600 F

Often referred to as the French Verona, this open-air Roman amphitheatre in Provence plays host to a highly enjoyable summer music festival every July. During the latter part of the last century, occasional plays were mounted there by the Paris-based Comédie Française but it wasn't until 1899 that anyone had the idea of using the arena for opera. However, within twenty years a repertoire had been built up, usually of French Grand Operas such as *Le Prophète*, *Faust* and *Samson and Delilah*. The people responsible for creating a yearly event and maintaining a standard of excellence were Jacques Bourgeois and Jean Darnel who from 1971 set out a policy of two or three big operas per festival supplemented by a symphony or orchestral concert, an orotorio and several recitals, the latter given in the cloisters of a local church. Top stars were called in to grace the stage for these elaborate productions and often visiting choruses have been accompanied by local orchestral talent and production staff. Over the past twenty years there have been several notable productions; a 1973 *Tristan und Isolde* under Karl Böhm with Jon Vickers and Birgit Nilsson. Tristan und Isolde brought international attention to Orange and the following year's production of *Norma* with Montserrat Caballe established the festival as the most important of its type in France, surpassing even that of nearby Aix-en-Provence. Since 1982 Raymond Duffaut, ex-director of the Avignon Festival, has directed proceedings and recent successes have included a *Macbeth* with Maria Zampieri and Renato Bruson (1986) and a *Flying Dutchman* (1987) with the Belgrade Opera Chorus.

While the acoustics can often disappoint largely due to the wind or 'mistral', there is something majestic about seeing opera at Orange. Obviously some voices are more suited to the setting than others and really only the biggest voices can be heard adequately.

Paris Opéra
Place Garnier, 75009 Paris

Director: Jean Louis Martinoty
Season: End September–mid July
Productions: 10, 6 new
Performances: Average 10 of each
Capacity: 1,991
Ballet: 10 per season

Information: (1) 47 42 53 80
Box Office: (1) 47 42 53 71
Box open: Daily by telephone 12.00p.m.–6.00p.m.; in person 11.00a.m.–8.00p.m. (not Sun)
Postal: Location par correspondance, 8 Rue Scribe, 75009 Paris.
Prices: 40F–550F
Concessions: Tickets at 100F available to students 10 mins before performance

The first significant event in the genesis of opera in Paris was the Royal Privilege of 1669 granted to Robert Cambert and Abbé Pierre Perin for the performance of *'representations en musique et en langue francoise sur le pied de celles d'Italie'*. This meant that at last opera could be staged, albeit heavily under the control of Louis XIV. The producer, the Marquis de Sordeac, who joined forces with the ballet-master Beauchamp, succeeded in launching what was officially known as the Académie de Musique at the Salle de Jeu de Paume on March 16th, 1671, with a pastoral by Cambert called *Pomone* which is now regarded as the first French opera. Having to cope without any state subsidy, the enterprise went bankrupt within a year but was revived by one of the most talented men of the King's Court, the composer and conductor extraordinaire Jean-Baptiste Lully. In a famous collaboration with the librettist Philippe Quinault, Lully managed to produce seventeen operas at the Palais Royale by the time of his death in 1687. Lully's influence was far reaching: he dominated the first significant period in the history of the Opéra and with a succession of masterpieces such as *Alceste* (1675), *Isis* (1677) and *Armide et Renaud* (1686), created a formal if sometimes pompous style that came to be known as *tragedie lyrique*.

The second great period of the Académie was marked by the presence of France's next important composer Jean-Philippe Rameau who wrote his first *tragedie lyrique*, *Samson* in 1733, which was followed shortly by his debut at the Opéra with *Hippolyte et Aricie* in 1733. He went on to write another forty works, some of which were highly controversial in their attempt to break new ground. His great contribution was the relaxation and sophistication of Lully's rather rigid style of recitative coupled with a much more heightened sense of dramatic unity. *Les Indes Galantes* (1735), *Dardanus* (1737), *Castor et Pollux* (1737) and *Zoroastre* (1749) are all masterworks, the penultimate having been written to inaugurate a new theatre at the Tuileries after the destruction by fire of the theatre at the Palais Royale.

The Académie was by this time a flourishing and heavily subscribed affair. Events took on an exciting turn towards the later part of the eighteenth century with the arrival of two non-native composers to Paris, whose intense rivalry both delighted the Parisian public and established the French capital as the most important city for opera in Europe. These were the German Christoph Willibald von Gluck and the Italian Niccolo Piccinni; composers of extraordinarily differing styles. The former attempted to rid opera of superfluous decoration in favour of dramatic unity, the latter preferred to flatter the vanity of singers rather than make any concessions to the demands of form. The rivalry continued for several years during the 1770s and 1780s with operas by both composers running almost concurrently: *Iphigénie en Aulide*, *Armide*, *Iphigénie en Tauride* and *Echo et Narcisse* by Gluck, *Roland*, *Iphigénie en Tauride* (written in competition with Gluck) and *Didon* by Piccinni. Meanwhile, the venue for opera transferred to the Salle des Menu-Plaisirs in 1781, and then again to the Salle Montasiers in the rue de Richelieu.

The staircase at the Paris Opéra

The period immediately after the French Revolution was an interesting one for the Académie as the new regime immediately banned works considered to be 'Ancien Régime' and thus many *tragédies lyriques* were replaced by new forms, such as *rescue opera* and *opéra comique*, with many new composers such as Méhul, Gossec and Philidor arriving on the scene. But the old Grand Operas were to make something of a comeback – Napoleon rehabilitated some of them in an attempt to make the institution the privileged showcase it had always been. He also encouraged composers to use historical subjects in a way that reflected the splendour of his burgeoning empire. The ensuing period was dominated by a style now known as Grand Opera with two composers leading the field, both personally approved by Napoleon – the Italians Spontini and Cherubini. The premières of the former's *La Vestale* (1806) and *Fernand Cortez* (1809) as well as Cherubini's *Faniska* (1807) were considered state events. Fortunately, Mozart's works enjoyed great popularity in Paris and Gluck's earlier works such as *Orfeo et Euridice* were revived regularly.

The company continued to move from one venue to another: in 1820 it went to the Salle Favart and the Théâtre Louvois, and the following year to new permanent premises in the rue Lepeletier (the Salle Lepeletier). It was here that gaslight was first used, in the 1822 production of Isouard's *Aladin, ou la Lampe Merveilleuse*. The audience at the Opéra at this time was wittily described by Stendhal: 'Most of the seats at the Grand Opéra, are taken, either by members of the lower classes, or else by gaping provincials freshly disembarked from the stage-coaches – the two classes of mortals who are by instinct admirers of anything expensive. Add a sprinkling of newly-arrived English landed gentry (in the boxes) and a score or so of licentious rakes who have paid to stare at the *corps de ballet* (in the balcony)' Stendhal, like many Parisians, preferred to go to the Théâtre Italien which arose at this time as a result of Napoleon's preference for Italian music and competed successfully with the Académie. Its directors included Spontini and Rossini, who gave many of his own operas as well as Meyerbeer's *Il Crociato in Egitto* (1825), the composer's first work for Paris.

Both Bellini and Donizetti were commissioned to write operas for the Théâtre Italien: The première of *I Puritani* and the first Paris production of *Norma* were both given in 1835 with a cast that included the famous quartet of Giulia Grisi, Lablache, Rubini and Tamburini. These four appeared regularly at the theatre as a kind of cabal: they would all insist on appearing together or not at all. Donizetti's commissioned opera, *Marino Faliero* (1835) was less successful and prompted the following comments from Bellini: '*Marino Faliero* had a mediocre effect . . . the newspapers, influenced by his [Donizetti's] behaviour, as he goes and acts the clown in all the houses of Paris and especially with the journalists, have tried to praise him'. Donizetti's time was still to come: *L'elisir d'amore* (1839), *Lucia di Lammermoor* (1837) and finally *Don Pasquale* (1843) were unequivocally successful.

As the Théâtre Italien and Opéra Comique habitually put on lighter French and Italian works, the Académie dominated as the centre of 'Grand' opera, attracting important composers from foreign countries. Rossini was commissioned to write his two last pieces for the Opéra (*Le Comte Ory* 1827 and *Guillaume Tell*, 1828). Meyerbeer came in 1826 and with the librettist Scribe successfully exploited the then current demand for extravagant, sometimes bloodcurdling spectacles with intricate and essentially historical plots, second act ballets, absolutely no dialogue and plenty of complex stage machinery for maximum visual effect. His mammoth and successful *Robert le Diable* (1831) epitomized this style, as did the French contributions of Auber (*Gustav III*, 1833), Halévy's *La Juive* (1835), and Berlioz's *Benvenuto Cellini* (1838), which was an unfortunate failure. Established operas were altered to suit this fashionable style – Mozart's *Don Giovanni* was extended to five acts and a ballet (by Auber) thrown in. The staggering receptions given to Meyerbeer's epic *Les Huguenots* (1836) and his master-piece *Le Prophète* (1849) confirmed his standing as the Cecil B. de Mille of opera composers.

In 1858 Napoleon III and the Empress Eugénie were the victims of an attempted assassination, as their carriage was passing down the rue Lepeletier after an evening at the Opéra. This incident appears to have moved the Emperor to announce a competition for a design of a new house 'more splendid that anything that has been put up before'. It was won by Charles Garnier in 1860 and the following year work commended. The façade was finished after six years but there were long interruptions: during the Franco-Prussian War it became necessary to store arms in what existed of the new building and later a deep swamp linked to a river was discovered under the foundations. After many years of toil, the 'Salle Garnier' finally opened on January 5 1875. It is one of the largest and grandest theatres in the world, situated at the top of a long avenue created specially for an uninterrupted view. Both interior and exterior are saturated with embellishments of every kind, creating a profusion of detail that for some is more offensive than pleasing to the eye. There are a myriad of halls and antechambers adorned with a variety of materials and colours and a staircase of outrageous proportions, after which the auditorium appears, small, dark and a bit gloomy. 'To the uninformed passer by', wrote Debussy, 'the Opéra looks like a railway station . . . inside one might be forgiven for thinking it was the central lounge of a turkish bath'. At its opening it was variously described as a 'brothel', 'an evil haunt' or a 'paradise', but the overwhelming emotion created was pride: the Parisiens could now proclaim that they had the largest, most glamorous and modern opera house in the world.

To avoid offending living composers, the opening night programme mostly consisted of music by the dead (overtures by Rossini and Auber, two acts of Halévy's *La Juive* and a scene from *Les Huguenots*). Since that time the new Opéra has been notorious for the various ways select groups from the audience have tried to influence the policies of the house. The case of Wagner is the most infamous: having re-written his opera *Tannhäuser* in French and with the obligatory ballet, Wagner's insistence of having the ballet at the beginning of the opera rather than during the second act, resulted in a fiasco. The opera was howled off the stage by two *claques*: the reactionary Jockey Club, who, in Berlioz opinion were paid for their services, and the 'abonnées' – subscribers who objected to all foreign works with the exception of Verdi, who was tolerated for political reasons, and Rossini who had become a resident of the city. When the director Pedro Gailhard was brave enough to present Wagner's *Lohengrin* in 1891, stinkbombs were thrown and demonstrations mounted. It was the influence of the abonnées that caused France to become the first major country to reject Wagner (the *Ring* was not given until 1911) and Strauss, whose *Elektra*, written in 1908/9 had to wait until 1933 for a Paris performance. Verdi, who called the Opéra 'La Grande Boutique' was successful there with two major works – *Les Vêpres Siciliennes* (for the Grand Exhibition in 1855) and *Don Carlos* (1867), but his wife's comments to a friend hinted at the frustration he suffered: 'What a punishment for the sins of a composer is the staging of an opera in that theatre, with its machinery of marble and lead! Just think! I am burning with impatience to go to Genoa and put in order and enjoy the apartment, and at the Opéra they argue for twenty-four hours before deciding whether Fauré or Lasasse is to raise a finger or the whole hand.'

There was predictably great enthusiasm for the French composers Massenet and Gounod, whose *Faust*, though first given with dialogue at the Opéra Comique, was more successfully revived in the Salle Garnier in 1869. In 1888 there was a famous revival of Gounod's *Romeo and Juliet*, with Adelina Patti and Jean de Reszke which established him as one of the leading French composers of the day.

When André Méssager became director in 1908, the *claques* largely disappeared and the Opéra was able to develop along standard lines, incorporating a broader repertoire. His successor Jacques Rouche occupied the post for thirty years and introduced some seriously neglected operas *(Boris Godunov, Der Rosenkavalier, Falstaff, Fidelio, Les Troyens* and *Turandot)*. With a few notable exceptions (Lily Pons, Régine Crespin) the Opéra during this period and later, suffered a great shortage of native singers of any quality. It also continued to be slow in responding to new trends and had a lot of catching up to do; *Wozzeck*, for instance, was not given until 1965.

During the War the Opéra was closed for a time, the last work to be presented before the occupation being Milhaud's *Medée* (1940). On Hitler's specific orders it was reopened under the direction of Germaine Lubin, a Wagnerian soprano who had been admired by Hitler in 1939 at Bayreuth. Her efficiency in collaborating with the Nazis was undisputed: she brought in German producers, directors and conductors giving them strict instructions on rehearsal techniques, and certain German operas (Pfitzner's *Palestrina* and Werner Egk's *Die Zaubergeige)* were commendably staged. Not surprisingly Lubin's career came to an abrupt halt on the liberation of Paris.

In 1959 A. M. Julien was asked by the De Gaulle government to administer both the Opéra and the Opéra Comique under an amorphous body calling itself the Réunion des Théâtres Lyriques Nationaux. The institution is today heavily bureaucratized and directly under the control of the Ministry of Culture. In 1971 Rolf Liebermann was appointed administrator with Solti as musical director in an attempt to enliven the opera, and the new regime was inaugurated with a performance of the *Marriage of Figaro* at Versailles in 1973.

Liebermann's great achievement was to reorganize the Opéra as an international rather than an ensemble house, along the lines of Covent Garden and Vienna. He also established a policy of hiring interesting producers such as the ex-theatre director Jorge Lavallie, whose *Faust* was considered extremely shocking, Jean-Pierre Ponnelle, Giorgio Strehler and Patrice Chéreau, and within a few years standards were considerably raised. Bernard Lefort's short tenure from 1980 was fairly unremarkable except for an essentially unsuccessful attempt to create a school of singing at the Opéra similar to those of Buenos Aires or Moscow. Finding the whole institution too cumbersome to handle both Lefort and his successor the Italian Massimo Bogianckino left the Paris Opéra somewhat frustrated men. Bogianckino was relieved to have been offered the

The grand foyer at the Paris Opéra

post of Mayor of Florence, taking up his position in 1986 paving the way for the new director, Jean Louis Martinoty.

Although it has mysteriously retained its glamour, the Paris Opéra is still considered an élitist and stuffy institution with a massive workforce of one thousand one hundred people, over twice that of Covent Garden. Despite receiving 28% of the national music budget, it has recently raised its ticket prices by 25% and has in the last few years created a deficit. As a producer of singers, it has always failed miserably in comparison with its counterparts in other capital cities and despite some successful productions, including the première of Messiaen's *St Francis of Assisi* (1983), there has been no consistently good house style for many years.

The Chagall ceiling in the auditorium, executed during the late sixties was controversial at the time, being considered out of keeping with the Opéra's Second Empire style but as with most civic-inspired modernist conceptions in Paris the time span between general disgust and adulation is fairly short.

The new opera house at the Bastille, presently under construction, which was the brainchild of François Mitterand has run into various problems due to petty political rivalries. The original idea – to mount cheap, updated opera productions for more people to see – has met with opposition from Chirac, the present French leader who recently forced the resignation of the original team of administrators. The present plan is for the Bastille opera house – which will have a capacity of two thousand seven hundred – to open in the autumn of 1989; the bicentenary of the Revolution. It will have a separate team to the Salle Garnier, with Daniel Barenboim as musical director, Pierre Vozlinsky as general director, and Eva Wagner as director of programming. The man in charge of the whole organization is the civil servant Raymond Soubie.

Opéra Comique
Salle Favart, 5 rue Favart 75002 Paris

Director: Jean-Louis Martinety
Season: End Sept–mid July
Productions: 7, 6 new
Performances: Variable
Capacity: 1331
Ballet: 4

Box Office: (1) 47 42 53 71:
Box open: Mon–Sat 11.00a.m.–6.30p.m.
Postal: 8 rue Scribe 75009 Paris
Prices: 25 F–350 F
Concessions: Tickets available 10 mins before
performance at 100 F

Recordings: La Fille du Régiment, Barber of Seville

The institution of the Opéra Comique was the result of an agreement between two groups – the *Comédiens*, a company of entertainers who combined speech and song, and the *Academie Royale de Musique*, which held the monopoly on the performance of French opera in Paris. In 1715 the latter organization was forced to sell some of its privileges, and so the *Comédiens* bought the right to present operas containing a certain amount of dialogue known as *opéras comiques*. The great success of this repertory forced the Académie to close in 1745; seventeen years later the *Opéra Comique* was amalgamated with an Italian company, the *Comédie Italienne*, under the direction of Charles-Simon Favart, at the theatre known as the Salle Favart. In 1789, a rival company attempted to perform a similar repertory in the neighbouring Théâtre de Monsieur – an enterprise which resulted in the ruin of both houses.

In 1801 the two companies were united by an act of government and formally entitled the Théâtre National de l'Opéra Comique. For twenty years the new company occupied the Salle Feydeau, seriously attempting to provide an alternative to Grand Opera. Spontini's earliest French operas were given here, along with celebrated *opéra-comiques* such as Boieldieu's *La Dame Blanche* (1852). After further peregrinations, the company moved to the second Salle Favart, where it has remained ever since, almost without a break.

The Opéra Comique soon became the most popular venue for middle-class and middle-brow musical entertainment: the premières of Auber's *Fra Diavolo* (1830), Hérold's *Zampa* (1831), Adam's *Le Chalet* (1833), and Donizetti's *La Fille du Régiment* (1840) were all given here. During the 1840s the management branched out to allow Berlioz to perform his highly original hybrid oratorio *La Damnation de Faust* there.

In 1855 the advent of a new house for operetta, the Bouffes Parisiens, which championed the work of Offenbach, caused the Comique some alarm. Any threat to its supremacy in the field was averted when the director Emile Perrin secured a comic opera from Meyerbeer, *L'Etoile du Nord* (1854), which broke all box-office records. Thomas's *Mignon* (1866), a more sombre piece based on Goethe's *Wilhelm Meister*, was another moneyspinner; and in 1875, there emerged Bizet's *Carmen* which, despite its notorious opening-night failure, soon established itself as the greatest and most enduring of all *opéras-comiques*.

By the end of the century, the company had expanded their repertoire to include works duplicated at the Opéra; but this was also the period of the house's greatest artistic enterprise and daring. Under the inspired direction of Léon Carvalho and Albert

Carré, a series of works was commissioned from France's finest composers – Offenbach's *Les Contes d'Hoffmann* (1881), Delibes' *Lakmé*, (1883), Massenet's *Manon* (1884), Chabrier's *Le Roi malgré lui* (1887), Lalo's *Le Roi d'Ys* (1888), Charpentier's *Louise* (1900), Debussy's *Pelléas et Mélisande* (1902), Dukas' *Ariane et Barbe-Bleu* (1907), Ravel's *L'Heure Espagnole* (1910), Fauré's *Pénélope* (1919) and Ravel's *L'Enfant et les Sortilèges* (1926; first performed in Monte Carlo, 1925). In sharp contrast to the petrification which had invaded the Opéra, it is evident from this list how the Opéra Comique was continually being infused with new blood.

Since 1920 the Opéra Comique has had several directors, but has produced nothing new of comparable importance. In 1959 it was merged with the Opéra. There are now various peculiarities in the way the two houses divide their repertoires – peculiarities baffling to the outsider. The old rule, for instance, that there should be no spoken dialogue on the stage of the *Opéra* (Salle Garnier) has been broken on several occasions, as the original version of Gounod's *Faust* and Mozart's *The Magic Flute* and *Die Entführung aus dem Serail* are frequently given here. However, *The Marriage of Figaro*, which has only accompanied recitative, is rarely performed at the Opéra; and some very un-comique works such as *Tristan und Isolde* have graced the Salle Favart. Strauss' operetta *Die Fledermaus* customarily plays at the Opéra.

The interior of the house is plain and dominated by dull stone colours. The exterior was aptly described by Debussy as 'French railway station Baroque'.

The Opéra Comique in 1910 (photo: BBC Hulton Picture Library)

Opéra du Rhin, Strasbourg
19 Place Broglie 67008 Strasbourg

Director: René Terrason
Musical Director: Theodore Guschlbauer
Season: September–July
Productions: 7, 3 new
Performances: Approx. 8 of each
Capacity: 1,000
Ballet: 2 per season

Box Office: (8) 8364566
Telex: 890261F
Box open: Mon–Sat 9.00a.m.–12.00p.m.; 2.00p.m.–6.00p.m.
Postal: As above, one month in advance
Prices: 20–180 F
Concessions: Discounts for students groups

Recordings: Carmen (ERATO)

In 1972 the operas of Colmar, Mulhouse and Strasbourg joined forces under the artistic director Alan Lombard to form the Opéra du Rhin. It has clearly been a successful venture, particularly for Colmar which had never been an operatic stronghold. Its theatre had opened in 1849, but without a resident opera company until the 1940s, it had been forced to rely on touring companies. Mulhouse, on the other hand, had been a major operatic centre since the mid-1940s, staging the French première of Britten's *Rape of Lucretia*, and Buser's *Roxane*. Under the directorship of Pierre Deloger, more premières followed, notably the French premières of *Boris*, *The Consul*, and Tomasi's *l'Atlantide*.

Strasbourg has always been one of the focal points of French musical life, gaining its first opera house in 1701 at the Place Broglie, which eventually disintegrated in fire in 1799. The new theatre lasted from 1821 (opening to the sounds of Grétry's *Fausse Pie*) until 1870, when it burnt down again during the Franco-Prussian War. The current theatre opened in 1873, and has numbered among its conductors Pfitzner, Klemperer and Szell. The opening of the house was made possible by a grant from the magistrate Jean Guillaume Apfel, who insisted on the highest standards. The repertoire was exclusively in German, as Alsace was under Prussian occupation at the time. After the First World War, Paul Bastide (who was musical director until 1938) reclaimed the French repertoire for Strasbourg, and delighted the city's inhabitants with *verismo* works, particularly those of Puccini. During the Second World Hans Rosbaud took over, and maintained standards until 1945, when Bastide returned to completely reorganize the establishment.

Since 1972, the new Opéra du Rhin has mounted several French premières of important French operas, such as *Peter Grimes*, *Bluebeard's Castle*, *Wozzeck*, *Lulu*, *Jenůfa*, *Mathis der Maler*, and *The Love of Three Oranges*. It also involves itself in co-productions with Lyon, Toulouse, and Aix-en-Provence. Its policy is to increase the number of French works performed, and not just to stage works by better-known composers such as Verdi, Puccini, Mozart and Wagner.

Théâtre du Capitole de Toulouse
Place du Capitole, 3100 Toulouse

Director: Robert Gouaze
Musical Director: Jacques Doucet
Season: October–June
Productions: 6 or 7
Capacity: 1,500

Box Office: 61 22 80 22
Telex: 530891
Box open: Mon–Sat 9.00a.m.–12.30p.m.,
2.30a.m.–6.00p.m.
Postal: As above
Prices: 30–220 F

Recordings: La Belle Hélène (EMI), La Grande Duchesse de Gerolstein (CBS), La Périchole (EMI), Mireille (EMI)

Toulouse has a long, celebrated musical tradition. It is famous for its troubadours, based here for four hundred years up to the mid-seventeenth century; and church music, practised here from the fifth to the seventeenth centuries. In the mid-eighteenth century the rapidly growing interest in church music was capped by the creation of the Théâtre du Capitole de Toulouse, erected in 1737.

Fire destroyed the first opera house, which was later rebuilt in the early 1750s, soon to gain a considerable following under its directors Prin, Devaux, Granier and Delainville. They saw it successfully through its first fifty years to the end of the century, developing a specialisation in *opera buffa*. Toulouse then gradually became notorious for its extraordinary relationship between artists and audience. On one occasion the badly out-of-form Cavandoit explained to the displeased audience at curtain call 'I know I was awful, but I've just had a terrible row with Modeste (the stage manager). It has ruined my voice!' In the 1820s the theatre often sounded like a music hall, with the outraged audience whistling down anything they didn't like. The local paper noticed that 'the whistling craze has reached a frightening degree.' In 1829 Mme. Saint Clair fainted on stage at a climax of booing, and in the same year Mlle Pouilly protested against the protesters by promptly walking off stage.

The theatre was twice redesigned, in 1835 and 1880, but a fire in 1917 led to a hiatus before the grand re-opening in 1923. From 1948–68 the tenor Louis Izar was the musical director: during his reign Toulouse staged the Bayreuth production of the *Ring* in 1958, with Birgit Nillson making her French debut. From 1966 onwards the company has pursued a policy of singing all its productions in the original language. Toulouse's distinguishing trademark is that it performs nineteenth-century revivals from the Paris Opéra. In 1962 *William Tell, La Juive, Il Trovatore* and *Fra Diavolo* were performed; in 1963 *Les Huguenots*, in 1966 *I Puritani;* in 1967 *La Reine de Saba*, and in 1970 the Glyndebourne production of *La Pietra del Paragone*. There has also been an annual international singing competition, with the greatest discovery to date being Teresa Berganza.

The present status achieved by the opera in Toulouse has much to do with the personal popularity and prestige of Michel Plasson, who has made numerous recordings from the Théâtre du Capitole and has masterminded various co-productions with other companies.

Théâtre Gabriel, Versailles

Théâtre Gabriel, Versailles

Productions: Occasional performances an average of 1 or 2 per year – usually given by Paris Opéra
Capacity: 600

Booking: Contact Versailles Tourist Board or Paris Opéra

Louis XIV's palace, south-west of Paris, was originally built without an opera house, although several plans were made for a permanent theatre during his reign (1643–1715). Instead, temporary stages were erected in various state rooms, the courtyard, or in one of the numerous gardens. As Lully was writing both operas and ballets, and Molière and Racine were providing plays, there was no shortage of theatrical entertainment for the Sun King.

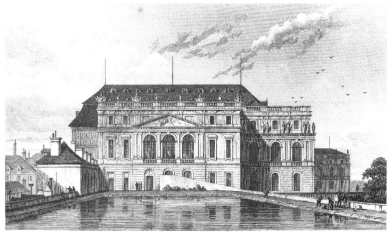

The Théâtre Gabriel at Versailles (photo: BBC Hulton Picture Library)

In 1748 a permanent opera house, the Théâtre Gabriel, designed by Ange-Jacques Gabriel was commissioned by Louis XV; and after many delays due to lack of money, it was finally opened for the occasion of the marriage of the then Dauphin (later the ill-fated Louis XVI) and his Austrian bride Marie-Antoinette. The performance was of Lully's *Persée* and starred the great French soprano Sophie Arnould. There is no doubt that the prevailing theoretical treatises on the building of the opera houses, such as Chaumont's *La Véritable Construction d'un théâtre d'opéra a l'usage de France*, influenced Gabriel a great deal. At the same time M. de Marigny, the brother of Madame de Pompadour and *Directeur des Bâtiments du Roy* had recently returned from an official visit to Italy, where he had scrutinized the new theatres. For his assistants he recruited the finest craftsman: Pajou for sculpture, Rousseau for trophies, Dropsy for marble-work, Vernet for the garlands, Durameau for the ceiling. The result is perhaps the most beautiful small theatre in the world with high fluted columns, chandeliers reflected in mirrors, golden trophies hanging on either side of the proscenium, and a deep blue curtain and seats. For the poet Paul Valéry 'it calls all that the most sensitive company could wish for, when it gathers together for entertainment. The architecture has – to perfection – succeeded in making each viewer enjoy the view of his fellows set in an admirably balanced structure of interior spacing.'

During the Revolution of 1789, the Jacobins used the theatre as a meeting-place for political debates; and it continued to be neglected or simply abandoned – until the reign of Louis-Philippe, who restored it in 1837. The re-opening performance included the overture to Gluck's *Iphigénie en Aulide*, several scenes from Meyerbeer's *Robert le Diable*, with Falcon and Duprez, and a ballet by Auber. In 1848 Berlioz was asked to conduct a concert involving four hundred and fifty-six performers.

But these were rare occasions – little else happened at the theatre beyond state visits or other ceremonial functions: Queen Victoria and Prince Albert were entertained there in 1855, the King of Spain in 1864 (with a rendering of Lully's *Psyché*) and more recently it saw the first state visit of Queen Elizabeth and Prince Philip in 1957, when the programme included the 'Acte des fleurs' from Rameau's *Les Indes Galantes*. Since then there has been a little more activity at the theatre, and restoration work has continued slowly and meticulously. The whole complex of seventeeth-century stage machinery is now in working-order, alongside the new possibilities provided by electrical equipment. These developments have facilitated certain notable revivals, including operas by Monteverdi and Gluck. In 1973 Rolf Liebermann inaugurated his directorship of the Paris Opéra with a performance here of Mozart's *The Marriage of Figaro* conducted by Sir Georg Solti.

Works that have had their premières at Versailles include Rameau's *Platée* (1745), Grétry's *Aucassin et Nicolette* (1774) and Sacchini's *Oedipe Colonne* (1785). Operas given at Versailles are occasionally open to the public but generally speaking the theatre is most frequently visited by those who wish to admire its architecture.

Bayreuth Festival

9 Luitpoldplatz, Bayreuth

Director: Wolfgang Wagner
Season: August
Productions: 7, including a further 4 if the Ring is performed
Performances: 3–6 of each (3 complete performances of the Ring)
Capacity: 1,800

Box Office: 8921 5722
Box open: Beginning–end festival, daily 10.00–12.00a.m. and 1½ hours before beginning of performance
Postal: Postfach 2320 D-8580
Prices: 16–200 D.M.
Recorded Information: (0921) 202221 Mon–Fri 11.00a.m.–12.00a.m.

Recordings: All major Wagner operas have been recorded on Philips and D.G.

Bayreuth is where Wagner built his ideal opera house, and it is justly associated with some of the greatest productions of his works. Wagner had originally hoped to build his own theatre in Munich, but his plans were rebuffed several times by the city authorities. However, while travelling through Germany in 1871 in search of a suitable stage for the *Ring* cycle, the composer discovered Bayreuth. Attracted by the town's setting and inhabitants, he decided to build his opera house, and a home for his family, there.

Wagner commissioned the Leipzig architect Otto Bruckwald to draw up the plans, and he then conducted a series of fund-raising concerts to finance the building. Since these failed to raise as much money as hoped, the building had to be constructed in the cheapest materials, namely wood and brick. The theatre was always planned as a temporary structure, a sketch of the ideal to be realised once the newly-united Germany attained her full imperial power. The auditorium, modelled on a classical amphitheatre, is on a single raked level, with a stage thirty-three metres wide. The acoustics are exceptionally good, largely due to Wagner's innovative concept of a covered orchestra pit. The sound from the pit travels upwards to mingle with the voices before being projected into the auditorium, to produce what Wagner described as 'a mystic chasm'.

In August 1876 Wagner staged his *Ring* for the first time. Because of his meagre budget, he travelled widely in search of performers and helpers prepared to work more for love than money. Pilgrims to the first *Ring* festival included celebrities such as Liszt, Mahler, Nietzsche, Bruckner and Grieg, but tourist facilities were scanty. A contemporary related how 'food forms the chief interest of the public: cutlets, baked potatoes and omelettes are discussed more eagerly than Wagner's music . . .' Despite this minor irritation, the first *Ring* was an artistic triumph for Wagner and an impressive debut. Although the festival made losses financially, the king cleared the debts, and donated sufficient funds to ensure the future. The second festival, in 1882, was devoted exclusively to the first performances of *Parsifal*, the only one of Wagner's operas to be conceived directly for the Bayreuth stage.

On Wagner's death the task of running the festival fell to his tyrannical widow Cosima. Her most significant achievement was the recreation of all the major Wagner operas including *Die Meistersinger* in 1888, *Tannhäuser* in 1891, *Lohengrin* in 1894, a new *Ring* in 1896, and *The Flying Dutchman* in 1901, and the establishment of the festival as an institution rather than just an experiment. However Cosima's conservatism prevented any innovation in production.

The Opera House at Bayreuth

When both Cosima and her son Siegfried died in 1930, Heinz Tietjen, of the Berlin Staatsoper was appointed Director. Under him, a number of grandiose and lavish productions were staged, and the festival was frequently graced with the presence of Hitler, a personal friend of Siegfried's widow Winifred. Due to the Führer's influence the festival became an annual event lasting until the end of the Second World War. Despite Winifred's Hitlerian connections, she was successful in securing a free and safe passage for Jewish singers at Bayreuth, but in 1947 she was declared a Nazi collaborator and dismissed from running the festival.

In 1951 her two sons Wieland and Wolfgang were permitted to assume control of the festival, and Bayreuth was relaunched with a traditional *Die Meistersinger* and new productions of the *Ring* and *Parsifal*. Wieland set a new style during the fifties that repudiated naturalism, introducing the concept of the stage as an 'illuminated space' containing symbolic representations of inner conflicts rather than outward events. Although the sparseness of these productions was partly determined by lack of money, they were successful in preserving a single, simple idea, emphasising the uniformity of the opera as a whole. When Wieland died in 1966 Wolfgang took over as chief producer, effecting a return to naturalism in some of his interpretations.

In May 1973 exclusive family ownership of the festival ended with the creation of the Richard Wagner Foundation, whose members include local politicians as well as artists. Recent productions have continued the impressive and talented tradition of Bayreuth. Most notable, the 1976 *Ring*, directed by Patrice Chereau with Boulez conducting, created great controversy by setting the operas in their historical nineteenth-century context, leading to accusations of Marxism which stirred the passions of many Germans for whom the festival remains a symbol of national pride.

In contrast to the Chereau *Ring* cycle which was both recorded and filmed, Sir Peter Hall's 1983 production of Wagner's masterpiece looked extremely conservative and even reactionary in its deferential adherence to what Hall considered to be Wagner's original stage directions. The singing continued to be of the highest quality. Peter Hoffmann, Jeanine Altmeyer, Rene Kollo, Sigmund Nimsgern, Waltrud Meier, Peter Seiffert, Gabrielle Schnaut have all appeared recently but the real revelation was Hildegard Behrens' first Brünhilde in the Hall production.

There is currently a production of *Lohengrin* by the film-maker Werner Herzog, and the forthcoming *Ring* cycle of 1988 will be produced by Harry Kupfer and conducted by Daniel Barenboim.

Tickets for Bayreuth can be hard to obtain. The box office on receiving your application will put you on the bottom of what may be a very long list – some people have to wait two or three years for their turn. There is, however, a chance of picking up seats at the last minute for performances on the day when the box office opens at 10.00a.m.

Berlin Deutsche Oper
Bismarkstrasse 34–37, Charlottenburg, Berlin

Director: Prof. Götz Freidrich
Musical Director: Jesus Lopez Cobos
Season: September–beginning March
Productions: 55, 3 or 4 new
Performances: 4 or 5 of each
Capacity: 1,900
Ballet: 57 different works per season

Box Office: (030) 341 4449
Box open: Mon–Fri 2.00p.m.–8.00p.m.; Sat–Sun 10.00a.m.–2.00p.m.
Postal: 10 Richard Wagnerstrasse 1, Berlin 10
Prices: 15–92 DM

Recordings: Olympie (Orfeo), Martha (EMI), Marriage of Figaro (CBS)

West Berlin's principal opera house on the Bismarckstrasse opened on November 12th 1912 with Beethoven's *Fidelio*. The first Intendant was Georg Hartmann; a champion of Wagner (he organized the first performance of *Parsifal* outside Bayreuth in 1914, the year after the copyright had expired) and the later works of Verdi, and he assembled an impressive production team to create a plausible rival to the city's Staatsoper, now in East Berlin. But it was during the period after the company was taken over by the state in 1925 that it reached its artistic peak, with a string of great conductors (Bruno Walter, Leo Blech and Fritz Stiedry) under the leadership of its new director Heinz Tietjen (1925–1930). The rise in standards continued during Carl Ebert's regime, and notable contributions were made by the conductor Fritz Busch and the set designers Wilhelm Reinking and Caspar Neher. Productions of such operas as *Pelléas et Mélisande*, *Euryanthe* and Wolf's *Der Corregidor* were singled out for praise while premières were mounted simultaneously, the most important being Schreker's *Der Schmied von Ghent* and Weill's *Die Burgschaft*, both given in 1932.

During the Nazi period, the renamed Deutsches Opernhaus was reorganized by Goebbels, who installed a puppet manager in the form of the baritone Wilhelm Rode. Although standards of singing were largely maintained under the musical directorship of Hans Schmidt-Isserstedt and Leopold Ludwig, the excellent expressionist staging, which had become a hallmark of the institution, was surplanted by a naïve naturalism.

The house was destroyed during the Second World War and company, once again called the Stadtisches Oper, was rehoused in the Theater des Westerns – the former home of Volksoper – under the direction of the bass-baritone Michael Bohnen. In 1948 as musical life in the city recovered rapidly, Tietjens returned to take over from Bohnen and the following year he invited back Leo Blech, who served as music director until the third great name associated with the company, Carl Ebert, resumed his post there. In 1961 the company was renamed yet again and returned as the Deutsche Oper, to its former location. The old theatre had been completely rebuilt in a somewhat austere manner, with spacious functional foyers and a large auditorium. An abstract metal sculpture by Hans Uhlmann is displayed in front of the house. The inaugural production was *Don Giovanni*, which was followed the next night by the première of Gisèle Glebe's *Alkmere*.

The following period was marked by the opera's attempt to win back its reputation as an innovative establishment dedicated not only to the classics but to modern repertory.

Many works that had been neglected during the Nazi period were duly mounted, including *Wozzeck*, *Peter Grimes*, *The Rake's Progress*, and *Cardillac*, and premières of Henze's *König Hirsch* (1956) and Egk's *Circe* (1948).

Lorin Maazel became musical director in 1965 and was responsible for performances of Henze's *Der Junge Lord* (1965), Dallapicola's *Ulisse* (1968), Blacher's *Two Hundred Thousand Thalers* (1969) and Fortner's *Elizabeth Tudor* (1972). The Deutsche Oper also gave the first stage performance of Schönberg's *Moses und Aron* in Germany. In 1976 Seigfried Palm was appointed Intendant and the company has continued to build an adventurous repertoire which, at seventy-five different operas including works by least-known composers such as Lortzing, Von Grien, Sutermeister and Zillig, is now one of the largest and most interesting of any opera house. Presently the proceedings are dominated by Palm's successor Götz Friedrich and the musical director is Dr Jesus Lopez Cobos. Many great singers associated with the house include Ludwig Suthaus, Ernst Häfliger, Julia Varady, Dietrich Fischer-Dieskau, Rene Kollo, Brigitte Fassbaender and most recently Karin Armstrong.

The Oper der Stadt Köln production of 'Agrippina'

Oper der Stadt Köln

Buhnen der Stadt Köln, Offenbachplatz, 5000 Köln 1

Director: Michael Hampe
Music Director: Sir John Pritchard
Artistic Director: Claus H. Henneberg
Season: September–June
Productions: 21, 5 new
Performances: Varies
Capacity: 1,346, 16 standing
Ballet: 13

Box Office: (0221) 21 25 81
Box open: Mon–Fri 11.00a.m.–6.00p.m.; Sat 11.00a.m.–2.00p.m.
Postal: As above
Prices: 16–66 Mks
Concessions: 12Mks ½ hour before performance.

Recordings: Die Soldaten (Wergo); La Sonnambula (Laudis)

Cologne's operatic history stretches back to 1882 when the first permanent theatre was built. The first director was Sobald Ringelhardt, who staged works by Beethoven and Rossini, amongst others. The company's second director was F. Hiller who from 1850 to 1954 gave Cologne its first taste of Wagner with performances of *Tannhäuser* in 1853 and *Lohengrin* in 1855. Neither was particularly well received.

In 1872 the Glockengasse was opened with one theatre, the Habsburger, used specifically for opera. The theatre's best years were undoubtedly between 1917 and 1924, when Klemperer conducted the première of Korngold's *Die Tote Stadt* in 1920 and the first German performance of *Katya Kabanova*. In 1943 the theatre was hit in an air raid, leaving Cologne without an opera venue for fourteen years.

The Grosses Haus, designed by Wilhelm Riphahn, opened to *Oberon* in 1957. Later that year Fortner's *Bluthochzeit* was premièred, followed by the first German performance of *The Fiery Angel* in 1960, Nono's *Intolleranza* in 1962, the première of Zimmerman's *Die Soldaten* in 1965, and Britten's revised *Billy Budd* in 1966. István Kertesz, a Mozart specialist, was musical director from 1964 to 1973, and it was he who brought widespread attention to the company. Since 1975, when Michael Hampe took over, the repertoire has grown to fifty-five operas, ranging from Monteverdi and Handel to Wagner and Richard Strauss, with special emphasis given to Mozart and adventurous productions such as those by Gilbert Deflo and Hans Neugehauer.

The success of the company is reflected in the number of invitations to tour to venues in Paris, London, Washington, Stockholm, Tel Aviv, Venice, and the Edinburgh and Holland festivals. The chief conductor is currently Sir John Pritchard who will be replaced in 1989 or 1990 by James Conlon. Workshops and rehearsal rooms are also contained within the complex that contains the Opera House. A covered passage connects the theatre to a restaurant, another to a car park and another to a large shopping centre. Riphahn also designed a smaller theatre beyond the Opera House, with a capacity of nine hundred and twenty.

Deutsche Oper am Rhein

Heinrich-Heine-Allee 16a 4000 Dusseldorf 1
&
Neckarstrasse 1, 4100 Duisburg

Director: Dr Kurt Horres
Season: Mid September–mid July
Productions: 37, 9 new
Performances: Varies
Capacity: Dusseldorf 1,344; Duisburg 1,200
Ballet: 6 per season

Recorded Information: (211) 283417
Box Office: (211) 133940/133949
(Dusseldorf); (203) 39041 (Duisburg)
Box open: Mon–Fri 10.00a.m.–1.00p.m.;
5.00p.m.–6.300p.m.; Sat–Sun 11.00a.m.–
1.00p.m.
Postal: As above
Prices: 10–60 DM Dusseldorf; 8–45 DM
Duisburg
Concessions: 50% reduction for
schoolchildren, students and senior citizens

In 1956 the industrial towns of Duisburg and Düsseldorf combined resources to create one of West Germany's leading opera companies, the Deutsche Oper am Rhein. Alberto Erede was the first musical director and his collaboration with the Intendant Hermann Juch was notable for a number of important premières of German works like Klebe's *Die Räuber* in 1957, and a revised version of Krenek's highly successful *Karl V* in 1958. An innovative production style had already been established, aided by Heinrich Wendel's superb set designs, and this continued until well into the 1970's under the new Intendant Grischa Barfuss. During this period the company specialized in twentieth-century opera, revivals of Monteverdi, under the musical directorship of Gunter Wich, who produced an excellent *Poppea* in 1965, and most recently complete cycles of works by Mozart, Strauss, Puccini, Janáček and Rossini. The twenty-fifth anniversary, in 1981, was marked with Alexander Goehr's *Behold The Sun*, a commissioned piece. They have also pioneered the work of Benjamin Britten and spectacularly revived some neglected modernist works, such as Honegger's *Judith* in 1965, Dallapiccola's *Ulisse* in 1969 and Othmar Schoeck's *Penthesilea* in 1986.

The opera house in Düsseldorf was built in 1875 and renovated after partial wartime destruction in 1956. It has a larger auditorium and better backstage facilities than the Duisburg house, which is more modern, originally dating from 1912 but reconstructed in 1950.

The Deutsche Oper am Rhein is now directed by Dr Kurt Horres and now has a broad repertoire of around a hundred operas. Productions have continued under more interesting European directors such as Jean-Pierre Ponnelle, Otto Schenk, Georg Reinhardt and Bohemul Herlischka. Since it begun, the company has always attracted major singers, from Martha Mödl, Astrid Várnay and Helga Pilarczyk during the early period, to contemporary artists like Kollo, Baltsa, Behrens, Randova and Zylis-Gara. Karl Ridderbusch has sung there often since 1965. The company tours regularly to neighbouring countries and came to the Edinburgh Festival in 1972.

Frankfurt Oper
Theaterplatz 3, D-6000 Frankfurt 1

Director: Gary Bertini
Season: October–June
Productions: 26, 5 new
Performances: Average 6 of each
Capacity: 1,430

Box Office: (49 69) 23 60 61
Box open: Mon–Fri 10.00a.m.–6.00p.m.; Sat 10.00a.m.–2.00p.m.
Postal: Unter Mainanlage 11, 6000 Frankfurt 1
Prices: 10–60 DM
Concessions: 50% discount for disabled; discount for students 1 hour before performance

The first known staging of an opera in Frankfurt was a performance of Theile's *Adam und Eva* at the Haus zum Krachbein in 1698. Frankfurt had no court opera and therefore no tradition of *opera seria*. Travelling companies made *opera buffa* and German *singspiel* popular, the latter becoming increasingly important in the second half of the following century when troupes such as those of Abel Seyler and Ferdinand Grossman all had resident composers. Even Goethe was moved to write a *singspiel*, *Erwin und Elmire*, which was set to music by André and given in Frankfurt in 1777.

In 1782 the Stadtisches Comödienhaus opened with a repertoire centred on lesser known Germans such as Winter and Weigl, gradually absorbing Mozart and, at the beginning of the nineteenth century, French *opéra comique*. During this period Frankfurt acquired a reputation for sumptuous set design, which in the hands of Giorgio Fuentes, at the opera between 1796 and 1805, centred on the use of perspective and anticipated the sets of Pierre-Luc-Charles and Ciceri at the Paris Opéra. His sets for Mozart's *La Clemenza di Tito* and Salieri's *Palmira* considerably expanded the expressive range of stage designs.

The year of 1810 saw the première of Weber's *Silvana*, given here rather than at Stuttgart where the composer had a court position. In 1818 Louis Spohr was briefly associated with Frankfurt when he directed his own *Zemire und Azor*. Grand Opera dominated the next important period with great demand being sustained for spectacular productions of Halévy, Auber and Meyerbeer, culminating in Wagner's arrival in 1862 to conduct *Lohengrin* with Johanna Wagner as Elsa. Other singers from this period to have appeared at Frankfurt include Jenny Lind, Wilhelmine Schröder-Devrient and Henriette Sontag.

A new theatre, solely for opera, with good facilities opened in 1880 with Otto Dessoff as artistic director. Under his successor Ludwig Rottenburg, who stayed with the company until 1923 there was a great period of German premières including those of *Pelléas*, *Louise*, and the world première of Schreker's *Der Ferne Klang*. In contrast to the conservatism of musical life in Frankfurt during the nineteenth century, there was a burgeoning interest in contemporary music of this century, initiated by Rottenberg but climaxing during the early twenties when Furtwängler, Clemens Krauss and Hans Rosbaud all worked there as conductors. Hindemith, too, was for seven years Konzertmeister at Frankfurt and wrote *Cardillac* while living there, although the première took place in Dresden. Under Krauss his wife, the Rumanian soprano Viorica

121

Ursuleac, established her authority in Strauss and other singers in the company included Adele Kern and Siegler. In 1930 Frankfurt staged the première of Schönberg's *Von Heute auf Morgan* under the new musical director William Steinberg and production of Herbert Graf. Important premières continued under the Nazis under Bertil Welzelberger including Egk's *Der Zaubergeige* in 1935, Orff's *Carmina Burana* in 1937, and his *Die Kluge* in 1943.

The opera house was wrecked during the 1943 bombing and moved first to the Stock Exchange and then to the rebuilt Schauspielhaus. Productions improved under the direction of Georg Solti (1952–1961), Lovro von Matačič (1961–1965) and Christoph von Dohnányi (1968 to 1977). Under the direction of Michael Gielen (1978 to 1987), the company was considered to be one of the finest in Europe, with a strong emphasis on ensemble, new and original productions and design. With producers such as Ruth Berghaus with *The Ring* in 1986 and *The Makropoulos Case* in 1986, Hans Neuenfels with *Doktor Faust* in 1986, the film director Volker Schlöndorff with *Katya Kabanova* in 1984 and Christopher Nel with *Falstaff* in 1985, the vast stages and excellent technical resources of the Frankfurt opera have been used to great imagination. It has also been the policy until very recently to employ only a limited number of international stars, a factor that for a while caused low attendance, although one can now hear Catarina Ligendza, Rosalind Plowright, Manfred Schenk, Anja Silja and Giorgio Zancanaro in leading roles. Gary Bertini has recently taken over as general director.

The old opera house at Frankfurt

Staatsoper, Hamburg

Grossetheaterstrasse 34, 2000 Hamburg 36

Director: Hans Joachim Zirkel
Artistic Director: Renate Kupser
Season: August–June
Productions: 22, 5 new
Performances: Varies
Capacity: 1,675
Ballet: 13 per season

Box Office: (40) 302448
Telex: 215020
Box open: Mon–Fri 11.00a.m.–6.30p.m., Sun 11.00a.m.–1.00p.m.
Postal: As above
Prices: 4–180 Mks

Hamburg can boast the first independent opera house in Germany, the Goosemarket Theatre, founded in 1678 by Johann Fortsch. The church put up fierce opposition from the start, and the first productions such as Theile's *Adam und Eva* which opened the theatre, reflected the sort of subjects imposed from above. The opera house needed a strong personality to free it from these constraints and to inject it with new life, and it was significantly helped from 1695 by the powerful leadership of Reinhard Keiser.

Keiser not only wrote around one hundred and sixteen operas for Hamburg, including the popular *Störtebecker und Goedje Michel* in 1701, but was also its director from 1703. Working closely with Johann Matheson, the performances of whose *Boris* in 1710 and *Heinrich IV* in 1711 were important events, Keiser created an atmosphere that attracted young musicians to Hamburg to learn the operatic trade. Among his violinists (later harpsichordists), was George Frederick Handel, whose first opera *Almira*, written directly under Keiser's influence, was premièred at the Goosemarket in 1705. The initial period reached its peak with Telemann's operas, *Sokrates* in 1721 and *Pimpinone* in 1725, after which the city fell under the influence of visiting companies from Italy, temporarily eclipsing German opera.

From the 1780s, the most important events were, naturally enough, the introduction of Mozart's operas followed by a period of intense interest in Gluck. Between 1771 and 1779 Freidrich Schröder gave *Die Entführung, Don Giovanni, Figaro* and in 1793 *The Magic Flute*. Lesser-known directors who were to follow later mounted spectacular productions of Gluck's *Iphigénie in Tauride* in 1811 and *Alceste* in 1818.

In 1809 the building became the Stadttheater but a new opera house was still required and the architect Schinkel was commissioned to design it. The Theater am Damtör was inaugurated in 1827 with Spohr's *Jessonda* and within it a strong company grew up with what soon became the largest repertoire of any house in Germany.

New for the public was the establishment of the big virtuosi concerts such as those of Clara Wieck in 1835 and Franz Liszt in 1840, and it was not long before Richard Wagner was rehearsing his *Rienzi* (1844). The first Verdi opera to reach the international stage, *Nabucco*, came to Hamburg in 1845 starring the Swedish soprano Jenny Lind. From then on both composers were well represented with the former's *Tannhäuser* appearing in 1853, *Lohengrin* in 1855, and *Die Meistersinger* in 1871.

The director Hofrat Pollini oversaw in an exciting era at the Hamburg Opera from 1873, giving the company's first *Ring* cycle in 1887 and capturing the thirty-one-year-old Gustav Mahler for six years. There were the usual disagreements between the management, musical director and the critics who did not see eye to eye with Mahler's interpretations. The conductor's uncompromising nature earned him few friends, but between them Mahler and Pollini together turned the establishment into one of the greatest international strongholds of opera with a fine group of singers, including Katharina Klafsky, Albert Niemann and Ernestine Schumann-Heinck, and with at least sixty operas in the repertoire.

Under the musical direction of Klemperer, (1911 to 1912), Pollack (1917 to 1932), Jochum (1933 to 1944) during whose tenure the stage was enlarged, and Böhm (1931 to 1934), the company continued to thrive, with Hans Hotter and Lauritz Melchior making substantial contributions. The building was bombed in 1943 and the auditorium was destroyed. Plans were immediately made to create a new structure around the existing stage, and the company moved into the Thalia Theatre until the end of the war. In 1949 the auditorium was enlarged and a new exterior, based on a design by Gerhard Weber, was inaugurated in 1955 with a new production of *The Magic Flute*, by Gunther Rennert.

Since then the opera has staged more than forty contemporary works and was for a number of years considered the most important house in West Germany, largely due to the inspirational directorship of Rennert, who ran the theatre between 1955 and 1965. He extended the repertoire from Handel and Purcell to Berg, Britten and Dallapiccola, and was responsible for a number of great productions. Following in his footsteps Heinz Tietjen (1956 to 1959) and Rolf Liebermann (1959–1972) continued to offer commissioned works of contemporary opera, some of the best including *Der Prinz von Homburg* by Hans Werner Henze in 1960, *The Devils of Loudun* by Penderecki, where Tatiana Troyanos created the role of Jeanne in 1969, Gunther Schuller's *The Visitation* and Humphrey Searle's *Hamlet* in 1968. A fire in 1975, during August Everding's period of directorship, was a disaster in terms of lost repertoire and cost the company twenty-five million marks. A rather unstable period followed during which Liebermann briefly returned on the instructions of a private industrialist willing to financially help the company, and Horst Stein and Christoph von Dohnanyi both took up the baton. During the 1980s Hamburg has maintained a high standard with the usual international élite of singers appearing with the company. Since 1983 it has revived a number of operas by the composer and teacher of Scönberg, Alexander von Zemlinsky, with *Der Kriederkreis*, *Das Zwerg* and *Eine Florentische Tragödie*.

Ludwigsburg Festival
Ludwigsburg Schloss, D-7140 Ludwigsburg

Director: Dr Rüdiger Krüger
Artistic Director: Prof. Wolfgang Gönnenwein
Season: May–September; early October
Productions: Varies, 1 new every two years
Performances: Varies
Capacity: 150–1000 depending on room

Box Office: 07141/28000
Telex: 7264 451
Box open: Mon–Fri 9.00a.m.–4.00p.m.
Postal: Ludwigsburge Festspiele, Postfach 1022, D-7140 Ludwigsburg
Prices: 10–50 DM

Recordings: Così fan Tutte, Don Giovanni, Gli Amori di Teolinda

This intimate festival contains a variety of musical events including one opera production a year and takes place at Ludwigsburg, Germany's largest Baroque castle, within easy reach of Stuttgart. The former home of the rulers of Württemburg, the estate has a choice of settings, including a magnificently decorated opera house, a chapel, an order hall, a courtyard and the palace gardens.

At the heart of the programme are Mozart operas, including a recent *Marriage of Figaro* which was presided over by the musical director of the festival and, since 1985, Intendant at Stuttgart Opera, Wolfgang Gönnenwein. It featured a young cast and was an enormous success. This came soon after a *Così fan Tutte*, produced by the same team, and a *Don Giovanni*, both of which were recorded on disc. Other events include oratorio and recitals of various kinds. The Ludwigsburg Festival Ensemble was set up to maintain a high artistic level, and tours all over Europe and the Far East, often accompanied by South German Madrigal Choir. Some of the singers who have been associated with the festival include Peter Schreier, Doris Soffel, Teresa Zylis-Gara, Edith Mathis and Siegfried Jerusalem. Handel's *Semele* and Monteverdi's *Orfeo* are also included in the repertoire.

The programme for the festival is published in late February, and ticket sales from written orders start in early March. Orders by phone can be made from mid-April, but most performances are already sold out by then: because of this it is advisable to be put on the mailing list.

Bayerische Staatsoper, Munich

Max Joseph Platz, Postfach 745, 8000 München

Director: Wolfgang Sawallisch
Artistic Director: Otto Herbst
Season: September–July
Productions: 50, 7–10 new
Performances: Varies
Capacity: 2,100, standing 320

Box Office: (89) 22 13 16
Box open: Mon–Fri 10a.m.–1.00p.m., 3.00–6.00p.m.; Sat 10.00a.m.–1.00p.m.
Postal: Eintrittskartenkasse der Bayerischen Staatsoper, Maximilianstrasse 11, D–8000 München 22
Prices: 12–250 DM during opera festival, otherwise 6.50–102.50 DM
Other Booking Procedures: ABR Theatrekass; München am Stachus; Max Heiber authorized ticket agencies.

Recordings: Die Meistersinger; Arabella; La Traviata; Die Frau ohne Schatten; Die Fledermaus (all DG)

Munich was the very first German city to have a theatre specifically devoted to opera, the Opernhaus am Salvatorplatz. The one-time granary was opened in 1656 with Kerll's *Oronte* and survived until 1922. Initially performances were almost entirely of Italian Baroque opera, with German works performed at another venue, and it was not until the nineteenth century that both were accommodated under the same roof. To begin with opera was a court affair, with works by Torri and Albinoni being used to celebrate the marriage of the heir apparent, Karl Albrecht, with lavish sets by Galli-Bibiena. Munich was very fortunate in having opera lovers in charge of the city: when Albrecht was sent into exile for two years, his replacement Maximilian III continued funding the art, promoting more Neapolitan opera.

In the early 1850s a new theatre was built in the Court Palace or Residenz by the architect Cuvilliés and it remains one of Europe's most beautiful Baroque theatres. Premières of Mozart's *La Finta Giardiniera* in 1775, and *Idomeneo* in 1781, were both performed here, starting a long and distinguished association with the composer that reached a high point in the 1890s, when Munich's performances were unrivalled anywhere in the world. Bruno Walter's period as musical director from 1913 to 1922 continued the Mozart tradition. In 1787, however, Carl Theodor was so worried by the Italian influence that he banned Italian operas, though some were performed in German translations. In 1805 the Italian ban was removed, with Mozart and his contemporaries soon becoming predominant in Munich. The other great event around this time was the opening in 1818 of the Nationaltheater. It was designed by Karl von Fischer but soon had to be rebuilt after a fire in 1821 with money raised by adding an extra pfennig to the beer tax. The building was later damaged by bombs in 1943, and was again rebuilt and given a classical facade modelled on the Paris Odéon. Many works were given their first performance here, the most significant being Weber's *Abu Hassan* and Meyerbeer's *Jephtas Gelübde* in 1812.

In 1836 Munich's operatic life entered its period of greatest fame with the arrival of the conductor and composer Franz Lachner and not too long afterwards Richard

The interior of the Nationaltheater, Munich

The exterior of the Nationaltheater

Wagner. Lachner began by giving some fine performances of Italianate works, with which he had a special affinity, but by the time of his appointment as musical director in 1852 he had considerably reshaped the repertoire to include the early works of Verdi, Marschner and Lortzing and had plans to introduce operas by the French composers Gounod and Saint-Säens, as well as his own, somewhat derivative Italian efforts such as *Caterina Cornaro*. The grand entrance of Wagner in 1864 proved to be a headache as the younger composer had certain ideas for Munich that it seems were incompatible with prevailing tastes. Lachner had already succumbed to pressure from Ludwig II to give *Tannhäuser* in 1855 and *Lohengrin* three years later, which were two operas he greatly disliked; the prospect of Wagner's taking over the cultural life of the capital was one he was determined to resist. Fortunately for him the King's decision to roll out the red carpet for Wagner turned out to be a political and financial embarrassment. Not only were the composer's arrogant demands of the city badly received but his obvious exploitation of the King's infatuation with himself and his music caused nothing less than a constitutional crisis.

With thirty thousand thalers to finish the *Ring*, all his debts paid and a yearly allowance of eight thousand florins, Wagner was allowed, in the King's words, to 'have nothing to do with the common things of the world' and this he did – in lace, satin and silk matching dressing gowns at expensive pianos, under velvet curtains, in rent free apartments. Various other scandals contributed to Wagner's eventual banishment; the most notorious centred around his love affair with Liszt's daughter Cosima who was at the time married to the conductor Hans von Bülow. But Wagner had his supporters, and amazingly enough Von Bülow was top of the list. Eventually to replace Lachner as musical director, he conducted the premières of both *Tristan und Isolde* in 1865 and *Die Meistersinger* in 1868, the latter in Wagner's absence. Wagner hoped to give *Tristan* in the smaller Cuvilliés Theatre and directed several rehearsals there but Ludwig objected strongly, feeling that this event, more important to him than the current war being waged by his people, should be a grand state occasion. Writing to Wagner at the time of preparation, he proclaimed: 'My loved one . . . I shall never forsake you. Oh Tristan, Tristan will come to me and my boyhood and youth will be realized.'

Despite a healthy degree of opposition during the first performance, *Tristan* was a success, partly due to extensive rehearsals – but by that time Wagner was destined to leave Munich.

In 1869 and 1870 *Das Rheingold* and *Die Walküre* were given at the Hofoper and the following year Wagner returned to settle in nearby Bayreuth where he hoped to realize his long-standing ambition of building his own opera house. Wasting no time, he directly approached the King and secured an advance of one hundred thousand thalers for the project, much to the wrath of the Bavarian government who were enraged that Wagner should dare to reappear on the scene. Support for Wagner's music was growing despite this, and Munich's reputation as a Wagner centre was further consolidated by the appointment of Hermann Levi to the post of Kapellmeister in 1872. Levi was later to be the conductor of the first *Parsifal* and was considered by Wagner, despite his being Jewish, the finest conductor of his music.

A line of great Munich Wagner conductors continued into this century with Herman Zumpe (1900–3), who conducted parts in the newly opened Prinzregententheater and

Felix Mottl (1903–11), one time assistant to Wagner during the first Bayreuth festival, who was so carried away by the intensity of the music he collapsed of a heart attack and died whilst conducting *Tristan*.

At the end of the century the pulse of Munich's operatic life was maintained by the opening of the summer festival in 1875, which concentrated on the works of Mozart and Wagner. From 1913 to 1922 Bruno Walter began a period of prodigious activity as musical director, conducting premières of Schreker's *Das Spielwerk und die Prinzessin*, 1913, Korngold's *Violanta* and *Der Ring des Polykrates*, both in 1916, culminating in Pfitzner's epic *Palestrina* in 1917. In 1922 Hans Knappertsbusch became the musical director but had to relinquish the post in 1935 when he made no secret of his dislike of the Nazis. He was soon replaced by Clemens Krauss, who conducted premières of *Friedenstag* in 1938, and *Capriccio* in 1942 in collaboration with Richard Strauss. Strauss had an enormous effect on Munich. His work was performed between the years 1889 and 1899 and later when the Nationaltheater was bombed in 1943 he composed the *Requiem Metamorphosen* in its honour. While the main theatre was out of action, operas were staged in the Prinzregententheater, built by Possart on the Bayreuth model and originally intended for Wagner. The Nationaltheater was reopened in 1963 to Strauss's *Die Frau ohne Schatten*. Since the war there have been an outstanding series of musical directors, including Ferdinand Leitner (1944–1946), Georg Solti (1946–1952), Rudolf Kempe (1952–1954), Ferenc Fricsay (1955–1959) and Joseph Keilberth (1959–1968). Under Wolfgang Sawallisch's directorship, Munich is expanding its repertoire, though maintaining the rich, well-established ties with the past.

The Nationaltheater is the second most important German language opera house after Vienna and has such important singers as Lucia Popp, Margaret Price, Edita Gruberova, Hildegard Behrens and, Rene Kollo and Brigitte Fassbaender singing there regularly. Its audience has a reputation of being one of the friendliest in Europe. As well as the Nationaltheater, special productions are mounted at the Altes Residenztheater of smaller scale works such as Strauss's *Capriccio*, *Ariadne auf Naxos*, and Mozart's *La Clemenza di Tito*. Since its partial destruction during the Second World War it has been rebuilt to the exact specifications of the original architect, much of the detailed decorative work having been removed before the bombardments and stored in the mountains. It now boasts a magnificent Rococo horseshoe-shaped auditorium in which each of the four tiers are decorated differently and where the acoustics are superb. The theatre is also used for concerts given by the Bavarian Radio Symphony Orchestra.

The Munich Opera Festival has been going now for more than a hundred years, and draws the greatest companies in the world, including Bayreuth, La Scala, and the Paris Opéra. Artists who have given either operatic performances or recitals there include Hermann Prey, Thomas Allen and Peter Schreier. It runs from the second week in July to the first week in August and takes place not only in the Nationaltheater but also in the Altes Residenztheater and the Prinzregententheater. It was first organized by Intendant Carl von Perfall for Mozart and Wagner in 1875.

Wurttembergisches Staatstheater, Stuttgart.

Oberer Schlossgarter 6, 7000 Stuttgart 1

Director: Wolfgang Gönnenwein
Musical Director: Garcia Navarro
Season: Mid September–end June
Productions: 49, 12 new
Performances: Varies
Capacity: 1,400 (Small House 850)
Ballet: 44 per season

Box Office: (711) 20 32 206
Box open: Tues–Fri 10.30a.m.–1.00p.m.,
3.00p.m.–5.00p.m.
Postal: P.O. Box 982, 7000, Stuttgart 1
Prices: 10–80 DM
Cards: All major cards
Concessions: 8 DM for students on day of
performance

Although known today primarily as a commercial centre, Stuttgart has a fine operatic tradition which goes back to the end of the seventeenth century. The first permanent company was established in 1696, and the first opera performed was *Amalthea*, written by the director of the company, Theodor Schwartzkopf. No German-language opera existed at the time, and visiting Italian companies were in constant demand. There are records of Cuzzoni and Riccardo Boschi, the brother of Farinelli, singing at the new Hoftheater from 1751, and the composer Niccolo Jommeli was invited to fill the post of Kappelmeister at the Duke of Württemberg's court between 1753 and 1771. Much of this was instigated by the director of the theatre, Ignaz Holzbaur, who gave both *opera seria* – such as Hasses's *Demofoonte* – and *opera buffa* – including Galuppi's *Le Virtuose Ridicule* as well as some of the finest examples of German *singspiel* such as *Der Liebe auf dem Lande* in 1768.

During the early part of the following century both Conradin Kreutzer and Johann Hummel were employed as Kappelmeister at the Stuttgart court, and introduced French Grand Opera and Opera Comique to the Hoftheater, including the works of Méhul, Boieldieu (*La Dame Blanche*) and Spontini (*La Vestale*), as well as Beethoven's *Fidelio* as early as 1817.

From 1819 to 1856, Lindpainter, a conductor highly esteemed by Mendelssohn and Berlioz, brought further glory to the opera house by hiring outstanding singers, instigating longer hours of rehearsal and directing regular subscription concerts for virtuosi such as Paganini and Liszt. He was also responsible for Meyerbeer successfully directing his own *l'Etoile du Nord* at Stuttgart in 1854, which led to a further invitation to conduct *Dinorah* five years later.

The present theatre opened in 1912, and was almost immediately honoured with the world première of Strauss's *Ariadne auf Naxos*, conducted by the composer and produced by Max Reinhardt. Since then, there have been a number of important directors working at the Hoftheater (as it is now called). Max von Schillings was ennobled by the King of Württemberg during his seven year tenure, during which he made Stuttgart one of the major centres for opera in Germany, and successfully premiered his own *Mona Lisa* in 1915. After his departure in 1918 for Berlin, the post was taken by Fritz Busch who managed in less than three years to introduce Stuttgart to the major works of Pfitzner, Schreker (*Der Schatzgräber*) and Stravinsky (*Mavra*), as well as première Hindemith's one-act opera *Das Nusch-Nuschi* in 1921. Carl Leonardt's tenure lasted fifteen years, during which time he performed complete cycles of Wagner and Weber, although his activities tended to reflect the more conservative preferences of the Nazis. Productions during the war under Herbert Albert and Philip Wüst were positively uninspired, although there were some fine singers in the company including Karl Erb, Fritz Windgassen and Ludwig Suthaus.

After the Second World War, the theatre re-opened in 1946 with the première of Hindemith's *Mathis der Maler*, previously banned by the Nazis. The following year, another great period was inaugurated when Ferdinand Leitner took over as artistic director. A notable interpreter of Strauss, he broadened the repertoire considerably, organising the first production of Orff's *Die Bernauerin* in 1947, Stravinsky's *The Rake's Progress* in 1951, and introducing works from the second Viennese School. His singers included Martha Mödl, Wolfgang Windgassen, Astrid Varnay, Leonie Rysanek, George London and Fritz Wunderlich. Both Wieland Wagner and Gunther Rennert directed for him, in collaboration with Vaclav Neumann (1969 to 1972) and Silvia Varviso (1972 to 1980) as musical directors. He continued to give premières, notably of Orff's works, including *Oedipus der Tyrann* in 1959 and *Prometheus* in 1968. On Varviso's appointment as musical director of the Paris Opera, his position was taken by Dennis Russell Davies, and from 1985 the Intendant has been Wolfgang Gönnenwein.

The present Stuttgart company has a large, broad-based repertoire that includes the majority of operatic masterpieces as well as the occasional new work. Singers who have worked there recently include Karin Armstrong, Vladimir Atlantov, Eva Marton, Gabrielle Benackova, Janine Altmeyer, and Hanna Schwarz. The ballet company, which achieved fame during the sixties under John Cranko, performs in the Kleines Haus, which is part of the same complex.

Schwetzingen, which lies some thirty miles away from Stuttgart, holds an annual festival during May and June in a Rococo theatre in one of Germany's most perfect eighteenth-century castles. There is no permanent ensemble, but visiting companies of great worth help make this a unique event, as do the kind of operas performed here. These are usually revivals of early Italian or French opera in keeping with the setting. In 1987 Michael Hampe's production of *Italiana in Algeri* for Zurich Opera was a great success. Wernicke's production of Gluck's *Le Cinesi* coupled with *Echo et Narcisse*, with the Hamburg State Ensemble accompanied by the Concerto Köln playing old instruments was intended as a tribute to the composer on his anniversary.

The Greek National Opera

59 Akadimias Street, Athens 10679

Director: Nick Pertroupoulos
Season: November–May
Productions: 12, 6 new
Performances: 5–8 of each
Capacity: 1,000
Ballet: 10 per season

Box Office: (1) 361261
Box open: Daily 9.00a.m.–1.00p.m.,
5.00p.m.–7.00p.m.
Postal: No postal booking
Prices: 250–100 Dr.
Athens Festival: Information can be obtained from 1 Voucourestion St, Athens 10564, tel: 32 35172

The first professional Greek company was formed in 1888 and after a successful performance of Donizetti's *Betly* toured round Egypt, France and Rumania with a repertoire that included French Grand opera and some works by the Greek composers Karrer and Xyndas. Suffering from inadequate planning and insufficient public interest in this part of the Mediterranean, the company closed within two years giving less ambitious amateur companies a chance to resuscitate operatic life in the capital.

A degree of permanence was only established in 1939 when the *Ethniki Lyriki Skini* (The Greek National Opera) was founded as part of the National Theatre, which was to encompass all the performing arts. Fortunately unhampered by wartime events, it opened at the Ethnikon Theatre with *Die Fledermaus*, then moved to the Olympia Theatre and was finally given its own home at the National Lyric Theatre in 1946. Unfortunately none of these houses have really adequate facilities for opera and for this reason as well as a reluctance to subsidize the art form by a series of governments, there has rarely been a permanent company giving a permanent season. This situation still exists today although the new democratic state has promised to help the present company purchase the burnt out wreck of the Kotopouli Theatre. By 1990 this will have been turned into a new cultural centre with a permanent opera base. For the time being, opera is given at the Olympia Theatre which seats one thousand.

There is a summer festival in Athens during which opera is usually put on at the Herodatticus Theatre in the Acropolis (which has a capacity of five thousand) by visiting companies. The Royal Opera, for instance, recently put on its production of *King Priam*. The present company also perform there after touring to Patras and Salonika. At the last count it had around thirty soloists and fifty chorus, an orchestra of fifty and a *corps de ballet* of thirty, although when it is happily installed in the new building it hopes to expand its activities considerably. At present the season continues intermittently between November and May, an average of twelve productions being staggered over this period.

Although Athens may never have been a prestigious venue, a few distinguished singers have begun their careers there, notably Maria Callas who later sang *Norma* and *Medea* in the antique Epidaverus Theatre. Other Greek-born expatriots such as Teresa Stratas and Tatiana Troyanus have also been persuaded to sing for the company. During the 1987 season, the National Opera gave the world première of the Greek opera *Fotea* by Lefen.

Tel Aviv Opera
101 Dizenkoff Street, Tel Aviv

Musical Director: Yoav Talmi
Season: April–May, then tours
Productions: 1 or 2 new
Performances: 3 of each
Capacity: 900

Box Office: (972 3) 24521
Box open: Daily 10.00a.m.–1.30p.m., 5.00–8.00p.m.
Postal: New Israeli Opera, 69 Iben Gabirol Street, Tel Aviv 64162
Prices: 25–50 Shekels
Concessions: Reductions for students and subscriptions

The Israel National Opera Company came into existence on November 29th, 1947, the same day that the United Nations voted to partition Palestine. In 1958, thanks to the dedication and hard work of its founder the soprano Edis de Philippe, it moved into a permanent home, the former Parliament building, or Knesset, with a capacity of nine hundred. The opening gala performance was a pot-porri of operatic excerpts, and the first production was of Massenet's *Thaïs* with de Philippe in the title role.

The identity of the National Opera Company is inextricably linked to the foundation of the Jewish state and a varied repertoire of operas and musicals includes many works specially associated with the history of its people, such as *Samson and Delilah*, Verdi's *Nabucco*, Goldmark's *Die Königin von Saba* and Bock and Harnick's *Fiddler on the Roof*. At the same time it has been the policy of the country to ban the works of Wagner and Richard Strauss, both considered anti-semitic, and a recent attempt by the conductor Zubin Mehta to include the Prelude and Liebestod from *Tristan und Isolde* in an orchestral programme failed at the outset. Mehta began performing Wagner but was interrupted by violent protesters. It has not been official government policy to ban Strauss or Wagner; more a sort of consensus of opinion. Most operatic performances are given in Hebrew.

The National Company had its heyday during the sixties, during which Israeli composers such as Menachim Avidon and Ami Maayani helped create an indigenous style with works like *Alexandra* in 1959 and *The War of the Sons of Light*, both based on Jewish history. The young Placido Domingo made a sterling contribution between 1962 and 1965, singing more than three hundred performances of twelve different operas.

The company's fortunes declined in 1978 when Edis de Philippe died, and productions have since become rather haphazard affairs. In recent years, however, there have been attempts to overcome organizational and financial problems, and to some extent the company has undergone a revival.

The Knesset building closed its door to opera in 1982 and the company disbanded until 1985 when the *New Israeli Opera* was formed thanks to £200,000 grant from Ministry of Education. The debut performance was *Dido and Aneas* in June 1985. Using the Israel symphony orchestra and the Rinat national choir the company mounts an average of two productions a year in the Cameri Theatre in Tel Aviv. Out of six productions, *The Marriage of Figaro*, *La Traviata* and Kurt Weill's *The Rise and Fall of the City of Mahagonny* have been successful. The company also tours to Haifa and Jerusalem.

Teatro Communale di Bologna

Piazza del Teatro, via Zamboni 28–30, Bologna

Director: Dr Carlo Fontana
Musical Director: M Riccardo Chailly
Season: Sept–June
Productions: 9
Performances: 6 of each
Capacity: 1,500

Box Office: 051–529 999
Telex: 226386 ENLIBO
Box open: Daily except Monday 10.00a.m.–1.00p.m.; 4.00p.m.–6.30p.m. A large number of tickets are sold in advance. Telephone booking recommended.
Postal: Large Respigni 1, 40126 Bologna
Prices: 5000–60000 Lire

Recordings: Favorita; Oberto Conte di S Bonifacio

Opera was first produced in Bologna at the Teatro da Casa with a private performance of Cavalieri's *La Disperazione di Fileno* in 1600. Performances were organized and subsidized by prominent intellectuals: Zoppio, Malvezzi, Fantuzzi and Malvasia, who sought out Venetian companies, and sometimes singers from nearby Modena. The first public performance was at the Teatro del Publico in the Palazzo del Podestà with Giacobbi's *L'Andromeda* (1610). In 1623 it burned down but was replaced by a wooden structure which by virtue of its arrangement of superimposed rows of boxes rather than graded seats made it accessible not only to the aristocratic classes but to the bourgeois paying public. Other theatres in the city in use until the eighteenth century included the Teatro Formagliari, the Teatro Malvezzi (for Bolognese operas) and the Teatro Marsigli-Rossi (for *opera buffa*).

The Teatro Communale came into existence as a result of an initiative by a group of noblemen, and was constructed between 1754–7 with financial backing from the Papal government and the Bolognese Senate. It was designed and built by Antonio Galli Bibiena and given a magnificent auditorium capable of seating one thousand five hundred people, as well as a hall dominated by a bronze relief of Wagner opposite one of Verdi. The theatre opened its doors in 1763 with a performance of Gluck's *Il Trionfo di Clelia*, given under the composers' supervision. It rapidly became the most important musical institution in the city, giving between 1820 and 60 three seasons annually of the most important Italian works of the time by composers such as Mercadante, Rossini, Donizetti, and, from 1843 Verdi.

The theatre was thoroughly renovated in 1859 and the following year appointed Angelo Mariani as its chief conductor. Under his regime, which lasted until 1872, production standards notably improved and repertoire became more adventurous. The theatre staged operas by Meyerbeer, as well as the Italian première of Verdi's *Don Carlos* (1867) and the first performances of Wagner's works in Italy with *Tannhauser* (1872) and *Lohengrin* (1897). Mariani's successors, the brothers Mancinelli and Franco Faccio, continued first Italian performances of Wagner operas with *Tristan und Isolde* (1888) and *Parsifal* (1914) and introduced Slavic and Spanish operas. The Teatro Communale does not have a permanent company, but brings in different singers, producers, set designers and conductors for each production. Because of this, it does not have a repertoire policy, although under the musical directorship of Riccardo Chailly and administrator Carlo Fontana the usual quote of Italian Romantic opera has been supplemented by contemporary works by composers such as Henze (*La Gatta Inglese*, 1985) and operetta (Lehar's *Merry Widow*, 1984. In 1984 the house gave *Tristan und Isolde* under the exiled Russian producer Yuri Liubimov. In fact, there has been a marked emphasis recently on German repertoire as well as on the comic operas of Rossini.

The Teatro Communale di Bologna in the twenties

Teatro Massimo Bellini, Catania

Via Perrotta 12, Catania, Sicily

Director: Ubaldo Mirabella
Artistic Director: Gerolamo Arrigo
Season: December–June
Productions: 6, 2 new
Performances: 6–9 of each
Capacity: 1,470
Ballet: 1

Box Office: (095) 327376
Box open: Daily 10.00a.m.–1.00p.m.,
5.00p.m.–7.00p.m.
Postal: Botteghino Teatro Bellini at above
address
Prices: 10,000–50,000 Lire

The Teatro Massimo Bellini in the Sicilian town of Catania, where Vincenzo Bellini was born in 1801, was built to replace the old and inadequate Arena Pacini. Work on the new house begun as early as 1812, but was halted by the invasion of Algerian pirates and only resumed in 1874. Carlo Sada completed the work in 1890, using the original designs of Andrea Scala, and the house opened in the same year with Bellini's *Norma*. The Teatro Massimo has since produced all Bellini's operas, alongside many by his most distinguished contemporaries Rossini and Donizetti.

During the Second World War it was closed until the Allied forces entered Catania in 1943: here the troops were entertained and some operas were given in conjunction with the Teatro Massimo in Palermo. Between 1948 and 1952, the theatre was modernized. In 1951 on the one hundred and fiftieth anniversary of Bellini's birth, 'the Swan of Catania' was celebrated with productions of *Norma*, *La Sonnambula*, *I Puritani* and *Il Pirata*.

Since the foundation of the Liceo Musicale Bellini in the same year, musical life has intensified in Catania. The Massimo has contributed to this significantly by creating a forum for performances of otherwise forgotten works by native nineteenth-century composers, such as Coppola, Plantania, and Pappalardo. Although there is no resident maestro, the season – which runs from December to June – has attracted a number of important singers. Antoinetta Stella, Maria Caniglia, and Paolo Silveri have all been there.

The exterior of the theatre has a Baroque façade; inside the style is nineteenth-century imitation Rococo, following a red, white and gold colour scheme. An oval centrepiece inside the auditorium contains the painting 'The Apotheosis of Bellini' by Ernesto Berlandi, and depicts scenes from *Norma*, *La Sonnambula*, *I Puritani*, and *Beatrice di Tenda*.

Teatro Communale, Florence

Corso Italia 12, Firenze

Director: Francesco Romana (Teatro Communale); Massimo Bogianckino (Festival);
Season: December–February (Teatro Communale); May–June (Festival)
Productions: 6 (Winter season); 4 (Festival)
Performances: Varies
Capacity: Teatro Communale 1,806; Teatro della Pergola 1,000

Box Office: (055) 2779236
Box open: Daily (except Mon) 9.00a.m.–1.00p.m., and ½ hour before performance
Postal: Via Solferino 15, Florence 50100
Prices: 13,000–100,000 Lire. Standing room places sold 1 hour before performance
Agencies in Florence: Universal Tourismo; Globus; Newtours; Arno

Recordings: La Bohème (DG), Lucia di Lammermoor (EMI) (both from Festival)

Opera was born in Florence when the Camerata, a group of intellectuals and musicians, met in the house of a leading nobleman, Count Bardi, to discuss ways of setting dramatic texts convincingly to music. In reaction to the predominant style of the day – counterpoint – they conceived a form, monody, which consisted of endless recitatives which reflected the meaning of the text. The first true opera is generally thought to be *Daphne* (1594–8) with music by Peri – but along with many works of the period this has not survived.

Operas, or Pastorales as they were sometimes called if based on a pastoral subject, were first presented to the select public of the Florentine court in a number of venues, including the Boboli gardens, the theatre in the Pitti Palace (where Peri's *Euridice*, 1600, the earliest extant opera, was first performed), and the larger theatre in the Uffizi. Opera at this time was generously supported by the ruling Medici family and continued to be presented at court, usually allied to some social or political function: Caccini's *Euridice* (1602) for visiting members of the clergy; Monteverdi's *Orfeo* (1607) for a visit by Cardinal Gonzaga; Salvadori's *La Flora* (1628) for the celebration of the Medici-Farnese wedding.

Towards the latter part of the century opera was being organized by twelve or more academies: one of the largest, the *Immobili*, a group of noblemen, commissioned the architect Ferdinando Tacco to build the Teatro della Pergola in 1652. Originally built of wood, it was eventually reconstructed in masonry in 1755 and had a capacity of one thousand. The death of Gian-Carlo di Medici in 1663 precipitated its closure, it was reopened in 1718 with Vivaldi's *Scanderbergh* and continued to perform works by Neopolitan or Venetian composers such as Porpora, Galuppi and Vinci. Among composers who wrote operas specially for the Pergola are Wagenseil, Piccinni and Sachini. In 1830 it appointed the impresario Alessandro Lanari as manager and several important premières were given there, including Donizetti's *Parisina* (1833) and later Mascagni's *Rantzan* (1892), the first Italian performances of Weber's *Die Freischütz* (1843) and Meyerbeer's *Dinorah* (1867) and, in 1847, Verdi's *Macbeth*.

The Teatro Communale, originally the Teatro Politeama Fiorentino Vittorio Emmanuele was built as an open air theatre in 1864 and covered in 1883. It was radically transformed between 1935 and 1937 and finally completed in 1961 by Alessandro

Giuntoli and Corinna Bertolini in an ugly municipal style. Since 1932 it has been controlled by Florentine authorities and a year later it was established as the principal residence of the Maggio Musicale, the annual May–June festival, initiated by the conductor Vittorio Gui.

The festival grew quickly in stature giving Italian premières of Stravinsky's *Oedipus Rex*, (1937), Dallapiccola's *Vol di Notte* (1940) and Prokofiev's *War and Peace* (1953). Opera is still performed in the Boboli gardens and in both the Communale and the Pergola Theatres. Under the direction of Mario Labrocca (1936–44) and Francesco Siciliana (1950–56), the festival gave many Italian first performances of foreign works, including Bartók's *Bluebeard's Castle* (1938), Ravel's *L'Enfant et les Sortilèges* (1939), Busoni's *Doktor Faust* (1942), Janáček's *Jenůfa* (1960) and Schönberg's *Die Glückliche Hand* (1964).

One notable event of the first festival was the only appearance outside the United States and Covent Garden of Rosa Ponselle in Spontini's *La Vestale*, conducted by Tullio Serafin. When the audiences demanded an encore after the aria, the conductor is reputed to have said: 'let them have their encore – God knows when we will hear singing like that again'. The revival of seventeenth-century operas during the 1950s set a fashion for the works of Cavalli (*Didone*, 1952) and Peri (*Euridice*, 1960). Since then there has been a series of radical and sometimes scandalous productions of standard operas by theatre and film directors: Jancso's *Otello* (1981) and Jonathan Miller's *Tosca* (1986) were generally admired unlike Yuri Liubimov's *Rigoletto* (1985) and Ken Russell's *The Rake's Progress* (1982).

Various important composers and conductors have been called upon to direct the festival's proceedings. In 1986 it was Zubin Mehta and in 1984 Luciano Berio. Berio directed an *Orfeo* workshop in which Monteverdi's score was transcribed for modern instruments and pop techniques. Its first performance was given by Luca Ronconi. The musical director for 1987 is Bruno Bartoletti who is conducting Henze's version of Monteverdi's *Il Ritorno d'Ulisse in Patria* with Julia Hamari and James King.

A sixteenth-century view of the Pitti Palace and the Boboli Gardens where opera was first performed in Florence

Teatro Communale dell'Opera, Genoa

Via xxv Aprile 1, Genoa

Director: Franco Ragazzi
Season: Jan–July
Productions: 7, 2 new
Performances: Approx 5 of each
Capacity: 1500
Concert: Several concerts given Oct–Dec

Box Office: (10) 589 329/591 697
Box open: Daily 10.00a.m.–12.30p.m., 3.30–7.00p.m., Sun 10.00a.m.–12.30p.m.
Postal: Biglietteria del Teatro Margherita
Prices: 6000–15000 Lire

Genoa was without a proper opera house until 1821 when King Carlo Felice of Sardinia ordered the demolition of the Church of San Domenico and replaced it with the Teatro Carlo Felice. Designed by the architect Carlo Barabino, the theatre actually opened in 1828 with Bellini's *Bianca e Fernando*. It held two thousand five hundred people, with the rights to over one hundred and fifty boxes being sold to wealthy families to cover the costs of the project. In addition, there were several gaming rooms and a large salon which also served as a billiard room. The repertoire included several works by Rossini and Donizetti. For nearly forty years Verdi spent the winter in Genoa (where his *Simon Boccanegra* is set), maintaining strong professional ties with the Carlo Felice – his friend Angelo Mariani was musical director there between 1852 and 1873: later both *Aida* and *Falstaff* were given there with Verdi's active co-operation. 1874 saw the première of *Salvator Rosa*, an opera by the Portuguese-Brazilian composer Antonio Carlos Gomes, whose operas (notably *Il Guarany*) enjoyed a brief vogue in Italy.

In 1892 Genoa commemorated the four-hundredth anniversary of the discovery of America by its most famous son, Christopher Columbus. The theatre was redecorated and an opera called *Cristoforo Colombo* was specially commissioned from Alberto Franchetti. The third performance of this work was conducted by the young Arturo Toscanini, whose work at the Carlo Felice continued until 1894 and included celebrated productions of *Simon Boccanegra*, Mascagni's *L'Amico Fritz*, Catalani's *Loreley* and the previously mentioned *Falstaff*. The operas of both Wagner and Richard Strauss have always enjoyed enormous popularity here: Strauss visited Genoa in 1934 to conduct the Italian première of his *Arabella* in 1934. The all but total neglect of Mozart until the 1970s seems strange in comparison.

In 1941 a British warship shelled the opera house, leaving a gaping hole in the building: nevertheless a performance of Puccini's *Turandot* went ahead as scheduled. Further bombing and looting left the theatre in ruins by the end of the war, and virtually no trace of the original rococo-style auditorium now survives. By the summer of 1948, however, the theatre had been partially restored, and *Aida* was given under a starlit sky. Celestina Lanfranco, Italy's first female opera-house director since Emma Carelli in Rome in the 1920s, was responsible for the theatre production of the first Italian performances of Strauss's *Capriccio*, Martinu's *Le Mystère de la Nativité* and presentation of Berg's *Wozzeck* and Shostakovich's *Katerina Ismailova*. A recent infamous production was Ken Russell's 1987 interpretation of Boito's *Mefistofele*, with the Georgian bass Paata Burchaladze in the title role.

Macerata Festival

Arena Sferisterio, Piazza Mazzini 10, 62100 Macerata

Director: Carlo Perucci
Season: Mid-July–mid-August
Productions: Approx 3, 1 new
Performances: 2–6 of each
Capacity: 6000
Ballet: 3 per season

Box Office: 1733–40735/49508
Telex: 560413
Box open: Daily 10.00a.m.–1.00p.m.; 5.00–8.00p.m.
Postal: As above.
Prices: 25000–75000 Lire

Home of a summer opera festival, the Arena Sferisterio was originally conceived as a multi-purpose entertainment centre, embracing such activities as *Sphaera* – the medieval ball-game – jousting, bull fighting and one-off state events: in 1902 the eccentric poet Orlandi launched his balloon from within the arena, and various Popes and other dignitaries have been received there. The construction, which initially included a roof, proved a long and costly business, seventy-two years elapsing between they laying of the foundation stones and the official opening in 1892.

The first opera to be given there was the Count of Macerata's production of *Aida* in 1921. This was followed at a rate of one new production a year, until 1966, when restoration temporarily called a halt to proceedings. Since then the Arena has been made into an open-air theatre accommodating six thousand people.

The Festival has meanwhile expanded to include at least three productions a year as well as ballets, concerts and recitals. The repertoire consists of large-scale Italian Romantic opera and is not dissimilar to that given at the Arena in Verona.

A set design for Verdi's 'Oberto, Conte de San Bonifacio' performed at La Scala in 1839

Teatro alla Scala
Via dei Filodrammatici 2, Milan 20121

Director: Carlo Maria Badini
Artistic Director: Riccardo Muti
Season: December–mid-July
Productions: 14, 5 new
Performances: Average of 5
Capacity: 3,600
Ballet: 4 per season

Box Office: (02) 809120
Telex: 335328
Box open: Daily 10.00a.m.–1.00p.m. (not Mon). On days of performance 5.30p.m.–10.00p.m.
Postal: Ufficio Biglietteria, via dei Filodrammatici 2, Milan. Tickets may be reserved when request is accompanied by postal money order

Recordings: All major operas by Donizetti, Bellini, Verdi and Puccini; Medea and Cavalleria Rusticana, Pagliacci

Opera established itself in Milan some time after most other major centres in Italy, largely because of the severe moral restrictions imposed on the city by the then Archbishop Carlo Borromeo. In 1598 the Teatro Regio Ducale was built for special occasions and sporadic operatic use, but it was not until the mid-eighteenth century that Milan ventured away from instrumental to vocal music, a move partly inspired by the Milanese opera composer Lapugnani (1706–81) who introduced foreign works including those of the young Gluck. In 1770 Mozart visited Milan to give concerts, returning at the end of the year to direct his own *Mitridate, Re di Ponto*, which was warmly received. The following year he gave his *Ascanio in Alba*, for the occasion of the wedding of the Austrian Archduke Ferdinand and Princess Maria Ricciarda Beatrice of Modena (at which Hasse's *Ruggiero* was the main operatic event) and in 1772 the première of Mozart's *Lucio Silla*, all at the Regio Ducale.

In February 1776 the theatre was destroyed by fire. The box holders then took it upon themselves to appeal directly to Maria Theresa, Empress of Austria and Duchess of Milan, for permission to build on the site of the church of Santa Maria della Scala, named after Regina della Scala, wife of a powerful member of the Visconti family. The whole project cost them over one and a half million lire and many important families have maintained private ownership of boxes to this day. The completed theatre, designed by Piermarini, opened on August 3, 1778 with Salieri's *L'Europa Riconosciuta* with sets by Galliari and containing two ballets.

The Teatro alla Scala thereafter became the most important opera house in the country and at the same time the kernal of social and political life in northern Italy. The house was considered by one devotee as 'a well heated, well-lit establishment, where one can be quite certain of meeting people on almost any evening of the week . . . a most invaluable institution for any city'. Gambling came to play an important part in the history of La Scala, as it was the only place in Milan where the activity was permitted; the profits generated helped finance operatic productions. As to behaviour inside the auditorium, Stendhal gave the following report:

'The Teatro alla Scala can hold three thousand five hundred spectators with the greatest of ease and comfort . . . and there are, if I remember rightly, twenty-two boxes, each seating three people in front, in a position to watch the state; but, except at premières, there are never more than two people occupying these seats; the escorted lady and her recognized gallant and servitor, while the remainder of the box, or rather salon may contain anything up to nine or ten persons, who are perpetually coming and going all the evening; or, during subsequent performances, only while one or other of the memorable passages is being performed. Anyone who wants to concentrate on watching the opera right through goes and sits in the pit'.

The political events associated with La Scala revolved round the comings and going of occupying forces. Thus there were festivities to commemorate the coronation of the Emperor Joseph II (1793) and more to celebrate departure of his forces. Napoleonic rule was welcomed with a performance of a tragedy-ballet, and the Royal Box was divided into six smaller boxes, reserved for what Napoleon called the 'liberated people.' With the return of the Austrians in 1815 there were spontaneous demonstrations against the occupation in and around La Scala, although it cannot be denied that their presence in Milan contributed much, at least financially, to a burgeoning cultural life.

From 1812, the year of the première of Rossini's *La Pietra del Paragone*, important operas were given first performances at La Scala and helped to establish the theatre's reputation. These included Rossini's *Il Turco in Italia* (1814) and *La Gazza Ladra* (1817) Meyerbeer's *Margherita d'Angio* (1820), Mercadante's *Elisa e Claudio* (1821) and Donizetti's *Lucrezia Borgia* (1833). In 1826 the impressario and ex-waiter Domenico Barbaja left San Carlo in Naples to take over as manager, commissioning Bellini's *Il Pirata* (1827), *La Straniera* (1829) and *Norma* (1831). His successor Bartolomeo Merelli, disturbed by the vacuum caused by the death of Bellini and Rossini's retirement, accepted the young Verdi's first surviving opera *Oberto, Conte di San Bonifacio* for a performance in 1839, the success of which hastened the commissioning of three further operas, *Un Giorno di Regno* (1840), *Nabucco* (1842) and *I Lombardi alla prima Crociata* (1843).

Un Giorno di Regno survived only one performance and jokes were made about the aptness of its title. However *Nabucco* was an unqualified success and not just a musical one. By his setting of the captive Hebrews chorus, *Va, Pensiero*, Verdi had dramatized what the Italians themselves felt as an oppressed and captive people. Merelli's response was to hand Verdi a blank cheque for whatever the composer considered to be a suitable amount for another opera. For *I Lombardi*, encouraged by Guiseppina Streponi, his future wife, he asked for 'the Norma tariff' – the amount Bellini had asked for Norma: 6,800 Francs and within seven months the work was completed. The new opera immediately fell foul of the censors and during the first performance had to suffer the presence of the police who were instructed to prevent the repetition of arias that might incite the public.

Verdi's relationship with La Scala worsened during the period of the first production of *Giovanni D'arco* (1845), which he considered like many others there to have been mounted sloppily and on the cheap. He later developed a cagey relationship with the Milanese critics who accused him of not knowing how to write for singers and trying to emulate Wagner. Verdi consequently boycotted the theatre and Merelli was forced to revive the lesser known works of Bellini and Donizetti, although Verdi's operas remained at the centre of the repertoire. In 1879 Verdi returned to La Scala to conduct a

The Teatro alla Scala, Milan

special benefit performance of his Requiem for victims of the terrible floods that had afflicted Italy. He was later persuaded to write again for the house and went on to produce *Otello* (1887) and *Falstaff* (1893), perhaps his two greatest operas.

La Scala's finest epochs were those under the direction of Arturo Toscanini, and his administrator Guilio Gatti-Casazza. Toscanini ruled the theatre in a domineering fashion but with such vision and self-sacrifice that people were inspired to obey his every whim. During the first two periods of his régime (1898–1903) and 1906–8 (he stormed out after refusing to allow an encore during *Un Ballo in Maschera*) he gave the first performances in Italy of Tchaikovsky's *Eugene Onegin* (1900), Strauss's *Salome* (1906), *Elektra* (1908) and Debussy's *Pelléas and Mélisande* (1908), and maintained regular performances of Wagner at La Scala. Between 1909–15 Toscanini conducted opera at the New York Met., but returned to take over again at La Scala in 1921, a year after the theatre had become self-governing. He then formed an orchestra of one hundred players, choosing each player individually, and a chorus of one hundred and twenty and toured Italy, the U.S.A. and Canada while the stage and auditorium were being reconstructed. Finally La Scala re-opened on December 26th 1921 with Verdi's *Falstaff*, followed by *Parsifal*.

It was a truly golden age of singing, with Lauri-Volpi, Pertile, Pinza, Cigna and Gigli all present in Milan at approximately the same time and all forced to surrender to the indefatigable demands of the maestro. However, in 1929 Toscanini finally left La Scala as director owing to a series of quarrels with the Fascists (Mussolini wanted the Fascist anthem to be played before every performance), and Victor de Sabata took over for the thirty-first and thirty-second seasons, continuing some of Toscanini's policies and sustaining interest in Wagner.

The theatre was almost destroyed by allied bombing in 1943 but was restored by May 1946 and today looks virtually the same as it always has with a capacity of three thousand six hundred (six tiers four of them boxes) with a colour scheme of red, cream, gold and maroon, gently lit by a twenty-foot chandelier. The orchestra at La Scala, due to Toscanini's posthumous influence is one of the best in Italy and musical standards have been maintained by a series of great conductors the likes of which certainly no other house in the country has been privileged.

It was at this time (1946) that Ghiringhelli, a disciple of Toscanini's came to La Scala as a Souvrintendente (General Manager) to supervise the rebuilding of the house. He also installed a system of ticket sales that charged Milan's rich citizens plenty on first nights in order to sell cheaper seats for the workers. An independently rich man who paid all his own expenses and never took a salary, he acted as guardian of La Scala until 1972, believing the opera had a 'soul' that could enrich the lives of all Milanese people.

Between 1952 and 1958 the presence of Maria Callas in the company led to the revivals of forgotten works like Cherubini's *Medea* (1953) and Donizetti's *Anna Bolena* (1957) as well as the famous Visconti productions of *La Traviata* (1955), *La Sonnambula* (1955) and Spontini's *La Vestale* (1954). Her rivalry with Renata Tebaldi forced the latter off the Scala stage in 1953 to which she never returned.

Shortly after the rebuilding of La Scala, Ghiringhelli added a smaller theatre the *Piccolo Scala*, with a capacity of six hundred. By 1953 it had become the theatre for revivals of seventeenth and eighteenth century and important modern stage pieces, from

Scarlatti's *Mitridate Eupatore*, to Stravinsky's *L'Histoire du Soldat*. Ghiringhelli was succeeded by Paolo Grassi in 1972 who appointed Massimo Bogianckino as artistic director and Claudio Abbado as chief conductor. Several important commissions were instigated during this period including Berio's *La Vera Storia* (1985) and Stockhausen's *Donnerstag* (1981) and *Samstag* (1984) from his cycle *Licht*. Also under Abbado's musical direction La Scala organized special performances for trade unions and factory workers in an attempt to bring opera to those who were unable to afford to go to the house itself – the result of this was that some outstanding performances with great singers were given in warehouses and canteens. Abbado's collaboration with the Italian producer Georgio Strehler resulted in outstanding productions of *Lohengrin* in 1985 and a *Simon Boccanegra* (1986) which toured Europe to great critical acclaim. His successor from 1980, Riccardo Muti, has so far directed an outstanding production of *Nabucco* with Dmitrova and his recent *Alceste* with Rosalind Plowright has revived interest in Gluck, a composer who has never been popular in Italy.

Premières at La Scala are still grand occasions of almost unparalleled exhibitionism. Despite professing absolute devotion to the institution, audiences at La Scala, while never so rude as at Parma's Teatro Regio, have often been noted for their lack of concentration during unfamiliar operas, showing how little things have changed since Stendhal's day. A recent performance of Hindemith's *Mathis der Maler* caused great bitterness when an uninterrupted drone of conversation drowned out a great deal of fine singing.

Teatro San Carlo, Naples
Piazza Trieste e Trento, Via Vittorio Emanuelle III

Artistic Director: Francesco Canessa
Season: December–end June
Productions: 7, 2 new
Performances: 6–9
Capacity: 3,500
Ballet: 3 per season

Box Office: (81) 7972412/7972370
Box open: Tues–Sun 10.00a.m.–1.00p.m.,
4.30p.m.–beginning of performances
Postal: As above at Biglietteria de San Carlo
Prices: 15,000–100,000 Lire

Although evidence suggests that operatic troupes were active in Naples from 1640, the first recorded performance was of Cirillo's *L'orentia Regina di Egito* at the Teatro San Bartolomeo in 1654. The opera was imported from Venice by the then Viceroy of Naples, the Count d'Onate, who maintained a steady stream of productions for the next three decades. However, it took Naples no less than fifty years to supplant its rival and build for this purpose two more theatres, the Teatro dei Fiorentini and the Teatro Nuovo.

It wasn't until the very end of the seventeenth and first decade of the eighteenth centuries that opera began to flourish in Naples, largely as a result of the arrival of Alessandro Scarlatti in 1684. Bringing a style of production superior to that of his predecessors, he inspired most of the group of composers we now refer to as the Neapolitan School, including Porpora, Mancini and Feo. By the middle of the eighteenth century *opera buffa* had reached a point of great sophistication at the hands of Pergolesi, Jomelli, Galuppi and Paisello, all resident Neapolitans.

The most important operatic development to happen in Naples was the rise of Metastasian drama, which adopted Renaissance classical ideals. The idiom which came to be known as *opera seria* represented a new and simplified form with clear differentiation between aria and recitative within a clearly defined dramatic-musical structure. The subjects always tended to be mythological or classical with emotions expressed in a formalized and ordered manner. The greatest operas in this genre are considered to be Scarlatti's *Mitridate Eupatore* (1707) and *L'Olympia Vendicata* (1686) and Porpora's *Flavio Anicio Olibrio* (1711).

In Naples public taste was slow to change and *opera seria* became increasingly rigid in structure. Various visitors to Naples during the eighteenth century commented on this: Mozart, for instance, wrote to his sister complaining about a performance of Jomelli's *Armida Abandonata*, as being 'too serious and old-fashioned for the theatre'. As a reaction to this, short musical entertainments were inserted in many *opere serie* to provide some sort of comic relief. The subjects revolved around comic daily life, cuckolds, and adultry and used many characters from Commedia dell'Arte.

The Teatro San Carlo opened on November 4th, 1737 with Sarro's *Achille in Sciro*, to a libretto by Metastasio. It was built in only two hundred and seventy days to commemorate the city's independence under Charles III, the Bourbon king of Naples, construction of the house being part of his larger plan to enrich and beautify the city. The building contractor and first impressario Angelo Carasale was imprisoned soon after its completion, having failed to satisfy the royal auditor as to how the one hundred

The Teatro San Carlo, Naples

thousand ducats it had cost to construct were spent. In 1768 San Carlo was redecorated to celebrate the marriage of Ferdinand IV to Marie Caroline, daughter of Marie Theresa and boxes were added to the first four tiers and over the stage. An Englishman Samuel Sharp commented on 'the amazing extent of the stage, with the prodigious circumference of the boxes and the height of the ceiling producing a marvellous effect on the mind'. The arrival of Mrs Billington, the English prima donna, to sing for the King in 1794, and later at San Carlo in Bianchi's *Inez de Castro,* caused a sensation and the opera house developed a reputation as a singers' theatre. Stendhal wrote in 1825 that the greatest composers of the day were Neopolitans and that the city was the 'only capital in Italy' and 'the very fount and birthplace of fine singing'. Another reputation which it still holds is an audience notorious for being among the most badly behaved in Italy.

The most prominent man in Naples in the first half of the nineteenth century was the impressario Domenico Barbaja, a man of extraordinary abilities who began life as a waiter, invented *capuccino* and ran gaming halls in the foyers of several theatres including La Scala. Barbaja belonged to the new breed of impressario, the cunning businessman as opposed to the dignified nobleman, and he had a genius for opera management. In 1815 he brought Rossini to Naples under contract to write two operas a year, and he went on to play a decisive role in the careers of Bellini, Donizetti and the singers Giuditta Pasta and Isabella Colbran. The latter created the lead female roles in most of Rossini's operas for Naples, including *Otello* (1816), *Armida* (1817), *Mosè in*

Egitto (1818) and *La Donna del Lago* (1819) and having been Barbaja's mistress, left him in 1815 to marry Rossini.

One year later San Carlo like so many other opera houses, went up in flames. It re-opened on January 12th 1817, having been rebuilt for twice the original amount of money with an enlarged stage and auditorium. Stendhal compared the new San Carlo favourably with La Scala, considering it 'better suited to listening to music'. The auditorium was for him 'a symphony in silver' and the new ceiling 'a faultless mirror of that taste in art prescribed by the French School'.

Bellini was commissioned by Barbaja to write his second opera *Bianca e Gernando* (1826), Donizetti gave the première of *Lucia di Lammermoor* at San Carlo (1835) and later on Verdi brought *Oberto* (1839), *Alzira* (1845), and *Luisa Miller* (1849) to the theatre. However, Verdi's problems with censors, particularly over *Un Ballo in Maschera* (which he eventually withdrew) made him feel bitter towards the Bourbon authorities and in 1870 he refused an invitation to succeed Mercadante as head of the Conservatory there.

The period following the turn of the century was fairly unremarkable and further censorship was imposed during the Mussolini era. After the war the theatre was restored by the British Army who ran the house for three years, thanks largely to the efforts of Brigadier Cripps and Captain Peter Francis. These two men, together with the impresario Pasquale di Costanzo, enlarged the repertoire to include *verismo* opera, more non-Italian nineteenth-century opera and some Italian premières of modern works. These included the first revival of *Wozzeck* in Italy as well as Hindemith *(Neues vom Tage)*, Prokofiev *(The Love of Three Oranges)* and Schönberg *(Moses und Aaron)*.

One recent radical production which shocked this rather old-fashioned establishment was the film director Lina Wertmuller's *Carmen* with choreography by the New York dancer Trisha Brown, which was staged in 1986.

Teatro Massimo, Palermo

Piazza G. Verdi, 90138 Palermo

Director: Ubaldo Mirabelli
Musical Director: Girolamo Arrigo
Season: Jan–June; July–August; the company performs in the Teatro di Villa Castelnuovo
Productions: 7
Performances: 14 of each
Capacity: 1800
Ballet: 2 per season

Box Office: (091) 584334/581512
Box open: Daily during season: 10a.m.–1p.m., 3.00p.m.–7.00p.m.
Postal: As above
Prices: 50000–160000 Lire

In the nineteenth century opera in Palermo was performed first in the Real Teatro Carolino (constructed 1809 – no longer extant) and later in the Teatro Politeama Garibaldi (constructed 1874), but neither was large enough to accommodate opera on the grandest scale. The story of how the Teatro Massimo came into being has a distinctively Sicilian flavour.

In 1863 the Palermo architect G. B. F. Basile published an article proposing the construction of a theatre which would be 'truly worthy of this rich and populous city'. The fairest way to choose an architect for the task, he suggested, was to hold a competition. This idea was approved by the city authorities, thirty-five competing designs were submitted and put on display, and a panel of judges – headed by Gottfried Semper of Dresden fame – was convened. In 1869 the winner was at last announced – G. B. F. Basile. This outcome caused such a prolonged and heated exchange of views that Basile could not start work for over five years; and once started, he was sacked because his cupola cost more than he had estimated. There followed several more years of intense discussion, during which not a brick was laid, before Basile was reinstated. In 1897 the Teatro Massimo was finally inaugurated with *Falstaff*, but its originator never lived to see the occasion.

In the first season the twenty-four-year-old Caruso appeared in *La Gioconda* – the start of an admirable tradition at the Massimo of engaging great performers before they have become internationally famous. The early years were strongly influenced by the indigenous conductor Gino Marinuzzi, and the repertoire increasingly reflected his personal predilections. These were perhaps unusual for a Sicilian – the 1914 season included *Lohengrin*, *Parsifal*, and *Salomé*. During the next two decades the theatre went into a general decline, before being granted the status of an autonomous institution in 1936. Franco Alfano briefly took over the direction of the theatre in 1940, and initiated a policy of performing works by Sicilian composers, such as Pietro Ferro's *Persefone*. This was to become a recurring, if minor, theme in the Massimo's programming, although it must be admitted that none of these native works has established itself elsewhere. The war years left the Sicilians with an insatiable appetite for opera, which the Massimo strove to satisfy with the Italian classics sung by Beniamino Gigli, Maria Caniglia, and Mariano Stabile. In 1949 Maria Callas came to sing Brünnhilde in *Die Walküre*, returning in 1951 for *Norma*.

During the fifties the Massimo was in the forefront of the *bel canto* revival, with the first performance this century of *I Capuleti e i Montecchi* (1954), conducted by Vittorio

Gui. Other 'firsts' have included *Beatrice di Tenda*, *La Straniera*, and *Elisabetta Regina d'Inghilterra*. Joan Sutherland's performance of *Lucia* in 1960 is still a talking point and a yardstick in Palermo, just as her Covent Garden appearance the previous year continues to be in London.

The practice of employing young talent rather than well-known stars is not motivated entirely by artistic altruism: Palermo's remoteness from other musical centres, and the Massimo's policy of giving fourteen performances of every opera, make it difficult to lure the most famous performers to the island for such a long stay. The results of this enforced talent-scouting have been impressive, to say the least – Carlo Maria Giulini, Riccardo Muti, and Claudio Abbado all conducted at the theatre very early in their careers. But famous directors are apparently not averse to working in Sicily – Luchino Visconti, Franco Zeffirelli, and Peter Hall all staged productions in Palermo after their international reputations had been established.

In 1974 the Teatro Massimo was declared unsafe and closed for urgent repairs and restoration; the company moved its activities – and its prolific ballet company – to the confined spaces of the Teatro Politeama Garibaldi, and has remained there ever since. It is hoped that the Massimo will re-open in 1988.

During July and August the company performs in the open-air Teatro di Verdura di Villa Castelnuovo, which sounds like vegetables but in this context means lush foliage. It was inaugurated in 1957 with *Otello*, sung by Mario Del Monaco. And every year hundreds of performances – ranging from a few instrumentalists to full-scale operas – are given in churches, courtyards, and school halls all over the island. Tours further afield have included the 1972 Edinburgh Festival *(Attila, La Straniera, and Elisabetta Regina d'Inghilterra)* and the 1963 Verdi celebrations at Busseto *(Otello and Il Trovatore)*.

The main characteristics of the company's repertoire are its belcanto revivals, a continuing – if intermittent – commitment to German music (there was a complete *Ring* in 1970/71), and in general a much more cosmopolitan range than is to be found in most of Italy's opera houses.

Teatro Regio, Parma
Via Garibaldi 16, Parma

Director: Francesco Quintavalla
Season: January-end April
Productions: 7, 2 new
Performances: Varies
Capacity: 1,200

Box Office: (521) 795690
Box open: Daily 10.00a.m.–1.00p.m.;
4.30p.m.–7.00p.m. open on all days when
there are performances
Postal: As above
Prices: 20–55,000 Lire
Special shows: for senior citizens

The city of Parma was given to the Farnese family in 1545 by Pope Paul III, and within fifty years had become an important musical centre. In 1618 Duke Ranuccio Farnese, one of the great patrons of the Arts during the Italian Renaissance commissioned Gian Battista Aleotti to build the Teatro Farnese on the first floor of the Palazzo della Pilotta. Constructed entirely of wood, the building is, with the Teatro Olympico in Vicenza, one of the two oldest and most beautiful theatres in Italy, and is designed strictly according to classical principles. It opened in 1628 with an intermedio (a musical interlude to a dramatic entertainment) by Monteverdi, entitled *Mercurio e Marte*, for the occasion of Edoardo Farnese's marriage to Margherita de Medici. Monteverdi also provided another opera for the city, *Gli Ampri di Diana e di Endimione*, one of twelve that were lost during the seige of Mantua, where he resided at court. The Farnese continued to flourish until 1732, after which time the theatre was abandoned for almost two centuries. It was unfortunately damaged during the Second World War but was sumptuously rebuilt during the fifties.

Several other theatres were erected in Parma in the seventeenth century, including the Teatro Ducale (predecessor of the present Teatro Regio) which opened in 1688 with *Taseo in Atene* by Giannettini with sets designed by Bibiena. During this period Parma managed to attract leading singers including Cuzzoni, Bordoni and the castrato Farinelli. Others were reported to be reluctant to come, as by 1680 the Parma public was already notorious for being the rudest in Italy and sometimes went so far as to arrest performers who didn't suit them.

After the fall of Napoleon, his second wife, the Empress Marie Louise, refused to accompany him into exile and became benefactress of Parma. In 1821 considering the Teatro Ducale to be inadequate, she commissioned the architect Nicola Bettoli to design the exterior and Paolo Toschi and Gian Battista Borghese the interior, which like La Scala was to be decorated in white, gold and red velvet. The auditorium is, however, smaller than its model, seating one thousand five hundred with some one hundred and twelve boxes, each with an ante-room. It has one of the best equipped and most spacious stages in Italy, and it has the unique feature of dressing rooms on the stage. The magnificent ceiling and drop curtain with its allegory of the Triumph of Paris were both painted by Borghese. The theatre opened on May 16 1829 with Bellini's Zaire: it was not a great success, largely because the board of directors and people of Parma had wanted a Rossini première, but failed to secure his services: Bellini, it seems, was not by that stage famous enough for this most demanding of audiences.

During the latter part of the century, Parma enjoyed its greatest triumphs largely because of its proximity to Verdi's birthplace (Roncole, near Bussetto) and the privilege it enjoyed of having the composer supervise certain productions. It has produced twenty-three of Verdi's total output of twenty-six operas and is the home of the Institute of Verdi studies, founded in 1959. *Vespri Siciliani* received its first performance in Italy at the Regio, although much to Verdi's displeasure the censor insisted on changing the location from Palermo to Portugal and the title to *Giovanna di Guzman*.

Opera continues to flourish at the Regio, albeit with a somewhat limited repertoire, and the audience still continues its policy of intolerance towards mediocrity. At a recent 150th anniversary performance of *La Traviata* at the Teatro Regio, on December 27th, 1979, the heckling of Violetta and her tenor was so loud that the Souvrintendente was forced to announce at a suitable point during the opera: 'the performance is suspended, given that Miss Nunziato, seeing the direction the evening has taken, no longer has the tranquillity or serenity to conclude it'. After the show, during which the conductor was begged to speed things up or put down his baton and retire, the perplexed Miss Nunziato said 'I can't imagine how this happened'.

A caricature of the castrato Farinelli by P.L. Ghezzi

Rossini Opera Festival, Pesaro

via Rossini 37, 61100 Pesaro

Director: Gianfranco Mariotti
Season: August–September
Productions: 2, both new
Performances: 4 of each
Capacity: Teatro Communale G. Rossini 914;
Auditorium Pedrotti 800.

Box Office: 0721/33184
Telex: 560216 PP PS I 'attn. Rossini Opera
Festival'
Box open: 10.00a.m.–12.00p.m.
Postal: Rossini Opera Festival, Servizio
Prenotazioni, via Rossini 37, 61100 Pesaro
Credit Cards: Bankamerica card/Visa
Prices: 10,000–250,000 Lire

Recordings: La Donna del Lago; Il Viaggio a Reims (DG)

Rossini was born in Pesaro in 1792 and in 1818 the Teatro Nuovo opened with his *La Gazza Ladra*, with the composer himself accompanying the recitatives from the harpsichord. The theatre was designed by Pietro Ghinelli and primarily built as a charitable project, providing work for the unemployed and indigent. In 1854 it was closed for a year and renovated, reopening as the Teatro Rossini. Since then it has been the scene of many Rossini festivals and individual events commemorating the composer. After Rossini's death in 1869, for instance, a series of performances called *Pompe Funebri Rossiniani* featured *Semiramide*, *Otello* and the *Stabat Mater*, with Teresa Stolz, Verdi's favourite soprano, as soprano soloist. The first performances of Mascagni's *Zanetto* in 1896, and Zandonai's *La Via della Finestra* in 1919 were also given here.

The Teatro Rossini closed again for renovation in 1967, reopening in 1980. Since then a small but increasingly important and admired Rossini Festival takes place every August and September. This has attracted singers of the calibre of Marilyn Horne and conductors like Claudio Abbado, and has staged some significant revivals of rarely heard Rossini operas, such as *Il Viaggio a Reims* and *Bianca e Faliero*. The festival is held in two theatres, the Teatro Comunale G. Rossini, with a capacity of nine hundred and fourteen, and the Auditorium Pedrotti, with a capacity of eight hundred.

A caricature of Rossini by A. Gill

Baths of Caracalla, Rome

Viale Terme di Caracalla, Rome

Director: Alberto Antignani
Season: July–August
Productions: 2
Performances: 8 of each
Capacity: 6,000
Ballet: 1 or 2 per year

Box Office: (396) 5758300
Box open: Tues–Sun 9.30a.m.–6.30p.m.
Postal: Ufficio Biglietteria Piazza Beniamino Gigli, 00185 Rome
Prices: 15,000–40,000 Lire

A small opera festival was set up in the Roman Baths in 1937 for the purpose of using the available space for large-scale productions. The Baths were built by Caracalla in AD 212 eclipsing in size and magnificence all previous constructions of this type, and though most of the space is occupied by the stage and production facilities, there is still enough room to seat six thousand people. Not surprisingly their most famous production is *Aida*, featuring a triumphal envoy by Radamès on a horse-drawn chariot. The festival's production of *Un Ballo in Maschera* was affectionally parodied in Bertolucci's film *La Luna*.

An average of two major operas are given there during July and August of each year, using resources borrowed from Rome's Teatro dell'Opera. Recently a production of *Turandot* was directed by the composer Sylvano Bussotti.

The Teatro dell'Opera, Rome

Teatro dell'Opera, Rome

Via Firenze 63, Rome 00184

Director: Alberto Antignani
Season: November–end May
Productions: 11, 3 new
Performances: Varies
Capacity: 2,200
Ballet: 2 per season

Box Office: (396) 46 17 55
Box open: Mon–Fri 9.30a.m.–1.00p.m.;
3.00p.m.–7.00p.m.
Postal: Ufficio Biglietteria, Piazza Beniamino
Gigli, 00185 Rome
Prices: 10,000–40,000 Lire

*Recordings: La Traviata (EMI), Un Ballo in Maschera (Decca),
La Bohème (EMI), Madame Butterfly (EMI)*

The first operatic productions in Rome were, as in Florence, ostentatious private entertainments for the rich and powerful. Agazzari's *Eumelio* (1606) may have been the earliest, followed soon after by specially written works by Rossi and Marazzoli. The city's most powerful family, the Barberini, were prolific entertainers: they gave a series of spectacles either in the new palace at the Quattro Fontana, or in the old Barberini Palace itself, whose great hall had been inaugurated in 1632 with a performance of Landi's opera *Il S. Alessio* for which a libretto had been provided by the future Pope Clement IX. The last opera to be given there, Marazzoli's *La Vita Humana, overo il trionfo della pieta* (1656) welcomed Queen Christina of Sweden to Rome. Until her death in 1689 there were frequent musical events in her palace (now the Corsini Palace), given by musicians such as Alessandro Scarlatti and Corelli. The first public opera house in Rome – built by a member of her court, Count Giacomo D'Alibert – opened in 1761 with Stradella's *Lesbo e Ceffea*.

Other opera houses sprang up around the beginning of the eighteenth century for public performance, and were used largely by visiting companies for *opera seria*. These included the Teatro Valle and Teatro Caprinaca, both described by the French writer Stendhal as 'cramped and inadequate'. By 1731 a suitable theatre came into existence: Duke Giuseppe Sforza Cesarini commissioned the architect Theodalli to build the still extant Teatro Argentina specifically with opera in mind. It premièred some important operas during the nineteenth century, including Rossini's *Barber of Seville* (1816) and Verdi's, *I Due Foscari* (1844) and *La Battaglia di Legnano* (1849), and is still used today as a house for small-scale productions.

In 1851 the builder Domenico Costanzi settled in Rome, where, having constructed a number of hotels he put forward a plan for a new opera house, both as a monument to himself and as a symbol of Roman civic pride. It was designed by Achille Sfondrini and opened on 27th November 1880 to Rossini's *Semiramide*: the performance was interrupted during the first act for the Royal March as King Umberto and his wife had arrived late. In 1888 the publisher Sonzogno became the theatre's director and immediately started a competition for the composition of a one-act opera. The winner for the second year, Mascagni's *Cavalleria Rusticana* (1890) initiated the *verismo* style of opera that proved so popular in the last decade of the nineteenth century and the opening years of the twentieth. Mascagni, along with Leoncavallo, Zandonai, Puccini and Giordano, attempted to depict ordinary life, albeit emotionally heightened, as opposed to historical or mythological subjects which he considered were alienating the public. He remained a firm favourite with Calvé and de Luca at the Costanzi with premières spanning thirty years *(L'Amico Fritz, Iris, Il Piccolo Marat)*. Subsequently other important productions of Rossini, Donizetti and Verdi put Rome with Milan and Naples at the forefront of operatic centres. Verdi was invited to Rome for its first performance of *Otello* but stubbornly refused to go: 'Why should I come to Rome to exhibit myself' was the old man's gruff reply. For *Falstaff*, however he was persuaded (by Boito) to go and was pleased with its success. That night as he was preparing to retire at the hotel opposite the Opatanzi House, he was serenaded by the opera's orchestra playing several of his overtures.

Under the direction of Costanzi's son, the opera house approved the introduction of lighter entertainment – including operetta and equestrian circuses. Then in 1936 it was acquired by the city of Rome, closed for two years, and opened again as the Reggio Teatro dell'Opera with a performance of Boito's *Nerone* (subsequently the word Reggio was dropped). During the thirties when the chief conductor was Tullio Serafin, Mussolini attempted to turn Rome into Italy's principal opera house and ordered the production of the *Ring* in Italian with almost exclusively Italian singers as part of a drive to entice artists back to their native country. Although Rome never outshone Milan, several singers – the sopranos Muzio and Caniglia and tenors Gigli and Lauri-Volpi – succumbed to pressure and returned to sing there. In 1943 The Teatro Costanzi gave the Italian première of Berg's *Wozzeck*, surprisingly perhaps, giving the Nazis' total ban on Berg's music.

Since Mussolini's fall there have been several significant new productions of modern operas (Hindemith's *Mathis der Maler*, Britten's *Rape of Lucretia*) and producers like Visconti and De Filippo have collaborated with conductors of the calibre of Giulini and Mehta. In 1958 Maria Callas walked out of a performance of *Norma*, given in honour of the President of Italy and caused considerable consternation. She had apparently caught a cold while rehearsing in the unheated theatre earlier in the day – an excuse which didn't satisfy the audience: one member stood up to shout: 'Go back to Milan – you cost us a million Lire!' Massimo Bogianckino was artistic director between 1963–8, during which time the theatre produced some of its best opera. He was succeeded by a series of musical directors that included Mario Zafred, Gioachino Tomasi, Gianluigi Gelmetti, and now Gustav Kuhn.

Despite being one of the most comfortable theatres in Italy, the Teatro Costanzi has one of the least attractive auditoria. It was described by Romana as being in a '*stile indefinibile*,' with its pseudo-moorish arches making up the tiers and a nineteenth-century neo-Gothic amphitheatre. The exterior was altered considerably during the Mussolini era, and now bears the unmistakable stamp of the Fascist style.

There have been recent attempts to catch up on modern repertoire with the commissioning of Philip Glass's opera *CIVIL WarS* in 1984, which was produced by Robert Wilson. There have also been some interesting revivals instigated by the new general director Alberto Antignani, including Spontini's *Agnes von Hohenstaufen* and Cherubini's *Démophoon*, but this has not really altered the fact that Rome is no longer considered to be a major centre of opera, despite its fine tradition.

Festival of Two Worlds, Spoleto

Via del Duomo 7, Spoleto

Director: Gian Carlo Menotti
Season: 2–3 weeks late June–early July
Productions: 3 new
Performances: 7 or 8 of each
Capacity: Teatro Nuovo 900; Teatro Caio Melisso 500
Ballet: 2 or 3 visiting companies

Box Office: (0473) 40265 (Spoleto); (06) 6798664
Box open: Daily 10.00a.m.–1.00p.m., 4.00p.m.–7.00p.m.
Postal: From beginning of May to Via Margherita 17, 00187 Rome. Cheque or money order to correct amount plus 8%
Prices: 10,000–170,000 Lire

The beautiful Umbrian town of Spoleto is the home of the Festival of Two Worlds, founded by the American composer, Gian Carlo Menotti in 1958. It was Menotti's intention to provide a stage for rising talent from Europe and America, at the same time involving local people in the festival's varied productions. The Teatro Nuovo, opened in 1864, and Teatro Caio Melisso, dating from 1667, provide perfect locations for major events, although most of the entertainments take place in open air in the Piazza del Duomo and San Niccolo Cloister.

Thomas Schippers was musical director until 1970, and was succeeded by Christopher Keene. Important operatic events, many produced by Menotti himself, include *Carmen* in 1962 with Shirley Verrett and George Shirley, *Don Giovanni* in 1967, and a rare revival of Donizetti's *Il Furioso all'isola di San Domingo* in 1967. Luchino Visconti, who admired Menotti's earlier operas, collaborated with Schippers on Donizetti's *Duca d'Alba* in 1959, *Salome* in 1961, and Puccini's *Manon Lescaut* in 1973.

The various performance sites are used for ballet, chamber music, theatrical events and folk singing. Gian Carlo Menotti has made Spoleto Festival as personal as Britten did at Aldeburgh. He has recently opened festivals in Charleston, Virginia and Melbourne, Australia, which will further his democratic ideals in other parts of the world. The 1986 festival opened with Menotti's *Saint of Bleecker Street*, and the highlight of the 1987 festival was the production of *Parsifal* with the emerging American *heldentenor* Pell. An interesting revival, *Montezuma* by Graun, court composer to Frederick the Great, was also staged.

A shift of emphasis to more radical productions of opera was initiated in 1974 with Roman Polanski's controversial interpretation of Berg's *Lulu*.

Teatro Regio, Turin
Piazza Castello 215, Turin

Director: Ezio Zefferi
Season: November–end June
Productions: 7, 4 new
Performances: 8 to 14 of each
Capacity: 1,800
Ballet: 2

Box Office: (39 11) 549126
Box open: Daily (except Mon) 10.00a.m.–
1.00p.m., 3.30p.m.–7.00p.m.
Postal: As above to Botteghino del Teatro
Prices: 26,000–120,000 Lire
Concessions: Discount for senior citizens and
students who live in city

The first opera to be performed in Turin was *Zalizura* by Sigismondo d'India which was given in 1611 in the Court Theatre of the Royal Palace. The New Teatro Regio was designed by Benedetto Alfieri, first architect to Carlo Emmanuele III and Andrea di Castellamonte, who had both sought advice from Galli Bibiena at the Teatro Farnese in Parma. It opened in December of that year with Feo's *Arsace* with the castrato Carestini in the title role and went on to stage a series of operas by Venetian and Neopolitan composers, including Jommelli, Traetta, Galuppi, Piccinni and Cimarosa. In the latter part of the eighteenth century it opened its doors to works by foreign composers, commissioning J.C. Bach's *Artaserse* (1761) and producing opera by Johann Hasse (1699 to 1783), Gluck's *Poro*, Nicolai's *Il Templaro* and Meyerbeer's *Semiramide*. During this period B. and F. Galiari worked for the theatre as scenery designers.

As La Scala assumed greater prominence towards the middle of the nineteenth century, the Regio's importance was dimmed temporarily. In 1865 Carlo Pedrotti was brought in to restore morale, and during his fifteen years the theatre became one of the leading operatic institutions in Italy, rivalled only by its neighbour in Milan. Pedrotti directed every production and although he gave particular prominence to the works of Verdi, he is most famous for his 1877 production of *Lohengrin*, the first in Italy, that according to the impressario Depanis, 'awakened Italy to the genius of Wagner'. From then on Turin became the Wagnerian capital of Italy, encouraged by conductors as talented as Fritz Busch and the great Arturo Toscanini who was music director in 1895 to 1898 and 1905 to 1906. Under his regime Catalani's *Loreley*, and Puccini's *Manon Lescaut* and *La Bohème* had their world premières at the Regio in 1890, 1893 and 1896.

Wear and tear of the theatre forced its closure for four years at the beginning of this century. After its re-opening in 1906 Strauss came to conduct the first Italian performance of *Salome*. With Toscanini's departure for La Scala in Milan and the Teatro Costanzi in Rome, artistic standards fell. Little of any note happened at the Regio except for the 1925 Rossini revival under Vittorio Gui which set a precedent for the rest of Italy.

On the night of the 8th February, 1936 the theatre was completely destroyed by fire and performances had to continue at the Teatro Vittorio Emmanuelle and the Teatro della Moda. The New Regio was a long time in reconstruction, the eventual designs by Carlo Mollino and Marcello Zavalani Rossi, were not approved until 1963. The theatre re-opened in 1973 with a controversial production of Verdi's *I Vespri Siciliani* with Maria Callas and Giuseppe di Stefano.

Teatro La Fenice, Venice

Campo San Fantin 30124, Venice

Director: Lamberto Trezzini
Artistic Director: Italo Gomez
Season: December–May; Summer Festival
Productions: 8, 3 new
Performances: Varies
Capacity: 1,500
Ballet: 5

Box Office: (41) 5210161
Telex: 215647 1
Box open: Daily 9.30a.m.–12.30p.m., 4.00–6.00p.m.
Postal: As above
Prices: 1st night 20,000–85,000 Lire; other nights 14,000–70,000 Lire

In 1637 Venice became the first city in the world to have a public opera house. Originally a private theatre built by the Tron family, the Teatro San Cassiano had burned down in 1629 but on its rebuilding, the family decided to open its doors to the public (with a performance of Manelli's *Andromeda*) and end the monopoly on opera enjoyed by aristrocratic families. The house relied on the selling of subscriptions for public support, and such was its success that various rival companies quickly arose to exploit the proliferating interest in this art form. The Teatro San Cassiano remained active until 1800 and gave the first performance of Monteverdi's *Il Ritorno d'Ulisse in Patria* (1641) as well as several of Cavalli's forty operas. By the middle of the eighteenth century about three hundred and fifty operas had been produced in seven different opera houses, three for *opera seria* and four for *opera buffa*. These houses were owned by the Venetian nobility including the Vedramin, Grimani, and Marcelli families and administrated by impresarios.

With the gradual decline of the Venetian empire throughout the eighteenth century, there was also a decline in musical activity, and the high salaries demanded by a burgeoning group of self-important singers caused some houses to close. The most important of those that remained profitable, the San Benedetto, re-named the Teatro Gallo after one of its impresarios, burned down in 1774 and was replaced by the Teatro La Fenice (the phoenix), which was to become the largest and most important opera house in Venice. A legal battle between managers of the old theatre and the family who owned the land on which it stood delayed the building for some time, and a new site had to be found. A newly-formed society, made up of a syndicate of Venetian patricians, citizens and merchants chose the architect Gianantonio Selva to present a design, and work commenced in May 1790, the completion taking two years. Architects of opera houses have traditionally been unpopular and Selva was by no means exempted: his inscription SOCIETAS on the theatre's façade was wickedly satirized by the Venetians as standing for Sine Ordine Cum Irregularis Erexit Theatrum Antonius Selva (without methods and with irregularities Antonius Selva built this theatre).

The theatre has dimensions loosely based on the Théâtre de l'Odéon in Paris, its small and intimate auditorium seating only one thousand five hundred. The Venetian audience at that time was considered sophisticated and made up in Stendhal's words of 'the most philosophic of men'. But Stendhal also went on to describe the city as a whole as 'sinking slowly into degredation' and its people as 'slowly dying of boredom'.

La Fenice opened on May 16 with Paisiello's *I Giuochi d'Agrigento* and continued to be the scene of many important premières, including Rossini's *Tancredi* (1813), Bellini's *I Capuleti e i Montecchi* (1830) and Donizetti's *Belisario* (1836).

However, Donizetti had a notorious string of failures at La Fenice for which he partly blamed the inhabitants of the city, which he considered 'cool'. On the last occasion he was asked to write a new work he demanded thirty thousand francs, an exhorbitant sum for that time, but he did not get a reply from the management.

Although the collapse of the Republic was imminent, the city continued to enjoy its operatic festivities: tunes from popular operas were sung in squares, on gondolas and even in the law courts, and extravagant fees for visiting singers were still paid. During the 1830s the great soprano Maria Malibran appeared many times as Desdemona, Rosina, Norma and Cenerentola, and a theatre was named in her honour.

In 1836 La Fenice had to be rebuilt after a fire which had begun during a rehearsal of *Lucia di Lammermoor* wrecked most of the interior. The new theatre, designed by the Meduna brothers at a cost of two hundred and twelve thousand lire, displayed the beautifully decorated interior which we still see today. Opinions at the time were laudatory – Mary Shelley described the auditorium as a 'resplendent and glittering array of blue, cream and gold' – but one hundred and twenty years later, in 1951, Vera Stravinsky was criticizing the theatre's chairs as 'badly in need of deodorants' and as uncomfortable as 'European railroad compartments'.

Five Verdi operas were premièred at La Fenice, causing a swelling of patriotic feeling amongst Venetians and leading to the direct censorship of his works by the occupying Austrian forces. These were *Ernani* (1844), *Attila* (1846), *Rigoletto* (1851), *La Traviata* (1853) and *Simon Boccanegra* (1857). *La Traviata* which was set in modern costume, initially proved unpopular: the impresario Gallo later redressed the opera to the period 1700 and completely won over its audience.

La Fenice has continued to give premières of important works during recent years: Stravinsky's *Rake's Progress* (1951), Britten's *The Turn of the Screw* (1954), Nono's *Intolleranza* (1961), and since 1968 it has put together important revivals of neglected Italian operas such as Verdi's *Il Corsaro* and Spontini's *Fernand Cortez*.

Recent revivals include Cimarosa's *Il Matrimonio Segreto* (1986) and Verdi's *Stiffelio* with Rosalind Plowright (1985). La Fenice has gained a reputation for specializing in less popular but interesting repertoire. It can always guarantee to fill its house with the constant flow of tourists through the city, many of whom are keen to visit this beautiful theatre which must surely be the only opera house in the world that can be approached by canal.

Ente Lirico Arena di Verona

Piazza Bra 28, 37100 Verona

Director: Renzo Giacchieri
Musical Director: Aldo Rocchi
Season: July–August
Productions: 2–3
Performances: 12 of each
Capacity: 20,000
Ballet: 1 per season

Box Office: (45) 23520/22265/3867
Telex: 480569
Box open: Mon–Fri 9.00a.m.–12.20p.m.;
3.00–5.30p.m.; Sat 9.00a.m.–12.20p.m.
Postal: As above. Enclose correct sum of
money in postal order or bank draught
Prices: 15000–130000 Lire

There was no important theatrical activity in Verona until 1732 when a new theatre, the Teatro Filarmonico was inaugurated with the pastoral play *La fida ninfa* by Scippione Maffei, with music by Antonio Vivaldi. Designed by Francesco Galli-Bibiena, the greatest Baroque architect of Italian opera houses, it burned down in 1749 but re-opened five years later with Hasse's *Alessandro nell'Indie* and Perez's *Lucio Vero*. It was in this theatre that the fourteen-year-old Mozart performed in 1770 on his first trip to Italy. Several important operas were premiered at the Filarmonico in the latter half of the eighteenth century including Traetta's *Olimpiade* (1758) and Cimarosa's *Giumio Bruto* (1781) and the theatre remained active until 1945 when it was destroyed by bombs.

In 1856 and 1859 the famous Roman Arena, situated in the heart of the city, had been used to stage performances of works by Rossini and Donizetti. This practice was discontinued until 1913 when the entrepreneurial tenor Giovanni Zenatello, his future wife Maria Gay and the impresario Ottone Rovato set up a series of open-air performances of Romantic Italian opera. Advice was sought from the conductor Tulio Serafin and the acoustics of the arena, which dates back to the second half of the first century, were found to be excellent.

For the opening night *Aida* was staged before an audience that included Puccini, Illica, Zandonai, Mascagni and Pizzetti. With the exception of the war years, this Festival has been presenting an average of two or three operas each summer, as well as at least one ballet and several concerts; an estimated seven hundred performances of fifty different operas. With an amphitheatre that can hold twenty thousand people comfortably and a stage suitable for three thousand, the majority of the operas performed there are grand spectacles such as *La Gioconda*, *Mefistofele*, *Turandot* and *Tosca*, although more intimate works such as *Manon* or *La Traviata* do appear. The festival attracts most of Italy's leading singers and some international stars: Maria Callas, Placido Domingo and Richard Tucker all made their Italian debuts there. Tradition calls for the public to light small candles during the overture, which, if as many as ten thousand are lit at one time, can create an extraordinary atmosphere. The whole place has an almost nineteenth-century feel to it, with various items on sale and the audience talking throughout the performance. It is a place to go for fun rather than for serious concentration.

Opéra de Monte Carlo

Salle Garnier, Place du Casino, Monte Carlo, Monaco 98000

Musical Director: John Mordler
Season: January–March
Productions: 4, 2 new
Capacity: 500
Ballet: Many visiting companies

Box Office: (93) 50 69 31/50 76 54
Telex: (42) 469760
Box open: Daily (except Mon) 10.00a.m.–12.30p.m., 2.30p.m.–5.00p.m.
Postal: As above
Prices: 90–320 F
Concessions: Only for groups at dress rehearsal

*Recordings: Fra Diavolo (EMI),
Pénélope (Erato), Pelléas et Mélisande (Erato), Lakmé (Decca)*

One opera house that has never suffered financial embarrassment is Monte Carlo. After the province of Monaco was freed from Sardinian sovereignty in 1861, the inhabitants were quick to realize that the beautiful scenery and climate had financial potential. Luxurious hotels were built in quick succession, and to provide entertainment, a casino was constructed in 1862, a concert hall in 1872 and finally a Grand Opera House in 1878. The architect engaged to design the theatre was Charles Garnier, who had previously built the Opéra in Paris. Indeed the Monte Carlo theatre is, in effect, a smaller replica of that original, in a similar Second Empire style. It is lavishly decorated; a multi-coloured spectacle and a feast for the eyes, reflecting a little society bent on extravagant pleasures.

The opening concert in 1879 featured both music and drama, with the tenor Joseph Capoul and Marie Miolan-Carvalho, creator of Marguerite in Gounod's *Faust,* and a spoken monologue delivered by Sarah Bernhardt. From then on the policy implemented by the *bon viveur* director Jules Cohen was to engage the top singers. Among them were Galli-Marie (the first Carmen), Fauré, Jean de Reszke, Tamagno, Melba, Caruso, and Mary Garden. Adelina Patti was paid the astonishing sum of fifteen thousand francs for playing Violetta in *La Traviata.*

The house's most notable artistic director, Raoul Gunsbourg, lasted in the post from 1890 until 1950. His policies were adventurous, and resulted in some important world premières including a new stage version of Berlioz's *La Damnation de Faust* (1893), Franck's *Hulda* in (1894), Massenet's *Le Jongleur de Nôtre Dame* in (1902) and *Don Quichotte* (1910), Puccini's *La Rondine* in (1917) and Ravel's *L'Enfant et les sortilèges* (1925). During this period Monte Carlo was considered a testing-ground for Paris, and its repertoire broadly resembled that of the Opéra Comique. In 1909 it attempted Wagner's *Ring,* but only with enormous cuts designed to keep the residents of Monte Carlo happy.

The latter part of Gunsbourg's tenure was less interesting from the point of view of premières and the house settled down to become a fairly routine establishment that provided standard repertoire opera in an unexciting fashion. Ballet became a more prominent feature when the house established a collaboration with Diaghilev's *Ballet Russe,* its most notable success being the creation of *Le Spectre de la Rose* in 1911, designed by Picasso and Derain. Since then the house has invited the most important companies to perform there. The Monaco Philharmonic have performed at the opera since its creation in 1870. In 1986 John Mordler, an American, was appointed as the new musical director his first great success being *Des Rosenkavalier*.

Tickets for the opera at Monte Carlo are surprisingly cheap at half the price of the Paris opera; a reflection perhaps of the amount given by the various benefactors that the establishment has seduced. Nevertheless, opera-going remains a glamorous past-time of somewhat exclusive and 'dressy' audiences.

The Opéra de Monte Carlo (photo: Roger-Viollet)

Amsterdam Opera House

Waterlooplein 22, 1001 PG Amsterdam

Director: Jan van Vlimen
Artistic Director: Juus Mostart
Season: September–June
Productions: 9 new
Performances: 8–12 of each
Capacity: 1,594

Box Office: (20) 551 811
Telex: 13108 NEDOP NL
Box open: Mon–Sat 10.00a.m.–6.00p.m.;
Sun 12.00a.m.–6.00p.m.
Postal: As above
Prices: f17.50–f65

The first opera performed in Amsterdam was probably *Il Combattimento di Errole e Torbione in il giardino di Compayne* by R.S. Nottucci, given by an Italian company in 1680 to open the new theatre completed in the same year. When this house burned down in 1770, operatic events were divided between the Stadsschouwburg and the Théâtre Français, where one could hear the works of Grétry and Méhul as well as the ever-popular Gluck.

In 1882 the Austrian baritone Angelo Neumann came with his troupe to introduce his famous *Ring* cycle in the Palaus voor Volksvlijt, precipitating an explosion of interest in Wagner. A Wagner Society was created the following year and after a successful performance of *Lohengrin* by a local company with imported lead singers, *Tannhäuser* and all the other major works duly followed.

Although there had been various indigenous attempts to form stable companies in Holland since the 1880s, it seems incredible that a permanent company was not founded until 1941, during the German occupation. From this grew the Nederlandsche Opera which gave performances in Dutch at the Stadsschouwburg until 1964 when the reorganized company became the Nieuwe Nederlandse Opera. As Amsterdam was until very recently bereft of a theatre large enough to handle major productions of opera, it had to make do with the available space the city had to offer and under its director Maurice Huismann, who was simultaneously Intendant at the Théâtre de la Monnaie in Brussels, the company toured all over Europe, Israel and Mexico. During the 1970s it gained a small reputation for Baroque opera and a few important producers were associated with it, namely Harry Kupfer, David Pountney, Lotfi Mansouri and its chief producer from 1973, Götz Friedrich. During 1973 Michael Gielen replaced Huismann as general director but became increasingly frustrated by the lack of proper facilities and the struggles with bureaucrats over plans for a new house.

The quest for a purpose-built opera house goes back to the time of the Wagner Society and the Dutch conductor Mengelberg, who directed the Concertgebouw Orchestra between 1895 and 1941. In 1929 a plan submitted by J. F. Staal was turned down by the city council and frustrated by an extraordinary series of postponements, financial and administrative struggles as well as the period of occupation, so that the final go-ahead for the realization of this particular dream was not given until 1968. Part of the problem was finding a suitable site; Mengelberg had vetoed the idea of an opera house opposite his beloved Concertgebouw, and a possible position on the Frederiksplein was taken by the powerful Bank of Netherlands. Eventually the idea to build the house in the same complex as the planned city hall on the Waterlooplein was put forward by its architect, the Austrian Wilhelm Holzbauer, who later conceived the two buildings as a single entity. There followed the usual political arguments that accompany the building of an opera house. The daily newspapers and various individuals like the composer Peter Schat protested loudly but to no avail, and by 1982 Holzbauer, assisted by Cees Dam commenced what they hoped would be 'a large form, an image, in a word an objet d'art'.

The new Town Hall Music Theatre opened on 23rd September, 1986 with a varied programme that included a one-act opera *Ithaka* by the Dutch composer Otto Ketting. The new Intendant Van Vlijmen decided on a repertoire based on Monteverdi, Mozart, Wagner, Verdi and early twentieth-century works (including those of Prokofiev, Schreker, Schönberg and Zemlinsky) with a different production team for each type of opera. Expensive stars can occasionally be hired but in general young talent is encouraged. There are also visiting companies particularly for the Holland Festival and some of these have already included The Hamburg Opera with Zemlinsky's *Die Kreiderkries* and Harry Kupfer's Komische Oper's *Boris Godunov*. A Mozart cycle recently began and a highlight of the company's 1987/88 season was Dario Fo's production of *The Barber of Seville*.

The opera house, which is picturesquely situated on the Amstel river has a rather plain exterior which makes no attempt to allude to any indigenous style. The auditorium is, however, more satisfying, with a colour scheme of warm dark red and purple, two hovering semi-circular tiers and a complicated lighting system emanating from hundreds of different points on the ceiling, designed by Peter Strycken.

Since acquiring the New Opera House, Amsterdam hosts all Holland Festival events, and recent visiting companies have included Hamburg, the National Opera of Belgium, Teatro Communale di Bologna, and the Teatro Liceu de Barcelona.

The Town Hall Music Theatre, Amsterdam

Den Norske Opera, Oslo

Storgt 23, 184 Oslo 1

Director: Bjorn Simensen
Season: End Aug–24 June
Productions: 20, 4 new
Performances: Approx. 7 of each
Capacity: 1,051
Ballet: 7 per season

Box Office: 02 42 94 75
Box open: Mon–Fri 10.00a.m.–6.00p.m.; Sat 10.00a.m.–2.00p.m.
Postal: As above
Prices: 45K–170K
Cards: VISA, MasterCard, Diners, American Express
Concessions: 50% discount for senior citizens 2 hours before performance

Opera first came to Oslo in the late eighteenth century, when King Frederik V of Denmark brought with him on his tour of the capital an Italian company, conducted by Gluck. In the early nineteenth century tours were given by the Mingotti company. From 1837 touring companies travelled to the Christiana Theatre from Italy, Denmark and Sweden. Notable performances in these early years were *Faust* and *Carmen* in 1890, Haarkous's *Fra Gamble Dage* in 1894 and Olsen's *Lajla* in 1908. In 1918 opera performances moved to the National Theatre, but after just twenty-six productions and three years major economic problems forced its closure. Although there was not another theatre devoted to opera until 1950, performances continued in other venues in the city.

The new theatre, opened in 1950, was the Norsk Operaselskap, founded by Jonas and Gunnar Brunvoll with Istvan Pajor as musical director; it was financially supported by the City of Oslo. In 1957 it became Den Norske Opera, with the Opera Foundation, the government and the city, as joint shareholders. Kirsten Flagstad was newly appointed administrator, and the opening season in 1959 began with *Tiefland,* the opera in which she had made her début in Oslo in 1913. Until 1933 she had only sung in Scandinavia, but her first visits to the US launched her as the greatest Wagner soprano of her day with her superbly projected and powerful voice. Due to ill-health Flagstad retired in 1960, to be replaced by Odd Gruner-Hegge, and by 1969 the company had established a repertoire of forty operas and seven operettas.

After Hegge, Lars Runsten became general administrator in 1969, to be succeeded by Gunnar Brunvoll in 1973, although Runsten remained as artistic director. In 1975 Martin Turrovsky was appointed music director and he has continued to raise standards significantly.

Den Norske Opera continues to expand and to stage contemporary Norwegian works, with guest appearances by foreign singers, conductors and producers.

Teatro Nacional de San Carlos, Lisbon

Rua Serpa Pinto 9, 1200 Lisbon, Portugal

Director: José Serra Formigal
Artistic Director: Joáo de Freitas Branco
Season: September–July
Productions: 10, 6 new
Performances: 4–6 of each
Capacity: 1,148

Box Office: (3511) 368408/368664
Telex: 84083623/4
Box open: Mon–Fri 1.00p.m.–5.00p.m.
Postal: As above
Prices: 275–1,800 Escudos

Opera was heard regularly in Lisbon in the Royal Opera di Tejo and the Theatre d'Ajunda in the eighteenth century until 1792 when a new opera house was built. It was designed by Jose and Costa da Silva and was modelled on the San Carlo opera house in Naples. Also named the San Carlos, it is a house noted for its numerous boxes (a hundred and twenty arranged in five tiers), its oval-shaped auditorium and excellent accoustics.

It was opened in 1793, a period when Italian opera had become the predominant genre (although, of course, compositions from France and Germany were not totally absent). The dominant Italian composers at that time, and since then, have included Cimarosa, Paisiello, Guglielmo, Donizetti, Bellini, Rossini and Verdi. Italian singers and players have also tended to dominate, taking leading parts in favour of other nationalities.

After the turn of the century fewer operas were performed here, and these mainly by touring companies. The Coliseu dos Recreios became the most popular venue until 1940 when San Carlos was reopened to Rui Coelho's *Dom Joao IV*. From 1946 the state took charge of the opera house, this leading to the celebrated production of *La Traviata* in 1958 with Maria Callas and Alfredo Krauss. The 1974 revolution resulted in major policy changes at San Carlos, and since 1981 it has had its own resident company. The result has been a much more balanced operatic outlook, the classics now sharing equal billing with contemporary works.

At the end of the 1980/81 season the then general manager João Peres was replaced by José Serra Formigal, a Lisbon lawyer and former director of the Portuguese Opera Company. This appointment marked the end of a bitter dispute that had divided the operatic world in Portugal. On one side of the schism were those who desired high standards of production. On the other were those who valued vocal qualities above all else. José Serra Formigal has always represented the latter faction and has invited a number of formerly important singers to San Carlos to coach resident singers. These include Caniglia, Stignani, and Gigli.

Peres' achievement during his seven-year tenure was the creation of an opera company of Portuguese singers and the production of more than eight light Portuguese operas, including two premières. In addition he also considerably expanded the twentieth century repertoire (Lisbon was one of the first cities to see the complete *Lulu*) and radically improved the standard of orchestral playing and choral singing. His successor may, on the other hand, be considered successful in developing the artistry of soloists within the company.

Gran Teatre del Liceu, Barcelona

Barcelona, Saint Pau – 1 bis

Director: Dr Luis Portabella
Season: November–June
Productions: 15, 3 new
Performances: 4 of each
Capacity: 3,000
Ballet: 3 or 4

Box Office: (03) 318 9277
Box open: Mon–Fri 11.00a.m.–2.00p.m.;
4.30p.m.–beginning of performance; Sat
9.00a.m.–1.00p.m.
Postal: Gran Teatre del Liceu Dept. de
Taquilles, carrer Saint Pau, 1 – baixos, 08001
Barcelona
Prices: 400–6,600 Pesetas

Opera was first staged in Barcelona at the Teatro della Santa Cruz, which opened in 1708 with Caldara's *Il Piu Bel Nome*. This was the only house in Barcelona until the rival Teatro Montésion opened its doors in 1838; as a gesture of one-up-manship the Santa Cruz changed its name to the Teatro Principal. During the following period, when Catalonia was ruled by the learned Archduke Charles of Austria, various Italian companies visited the city, including that of the great castrato Farinelli who, in 1750, brought Cimarosa and the popular intermezzo *La Serva Padrona* by Pergolesi. In 1798 Mozart's *Così fan Tutte* was given at the Teatro Montésion, eight years after its première in Vienna, and during the middle of the nineteenth century audiences in both theatres became familiar with Paisiello, Rossini and Mercadante (who was composer in residence at the Montésion for several years) as well as works by the Catalans Baguer, Sors and Rovira.

By this time Barcelona already had a population of almost two hundred thousand. The city was rapidly expanding due to the establishment of a cotton industry and the manufacture of cloth. The growing bourgeoisie demanded a more important seat for opera and the Auxiliary Building Company was formed to oversee the project. This got under way when three Barcelona noblemen, Joaquim de Gispert, Manuel Gibert and Manuel Girona managed to obtain the freehold of a monastery, previously the Colegio de Trinitarios Descalzos, which was situated at the junction of the Rambla and the Calle de San Pablo. It was financed by freeholders in the company, loans from interested persons and the sale of permanent season tickets. Miquel Garriga i Roca, the architect who conceived the plan, and his successor José Oriol Mestres, created a building in high Renaissance style with a seating capacity of three thousand five hundred. The Teatro Liceo opened in 1847 with performances given by two different companies, one dramatic, the other operatic, but for reasons unexplained the operatic company did not stage an opera. The first person to direct the new Opera was the composer Maria Oboils, who was an enthusiastic supporter of Rossini and Mercadante, and who made sure that the Italian repertoire, as well as some of his own works *Iditta di Belcourt* (1874), eclipsed everything else.

There grew to be a constant and sometimes ferocious rivalry between the Teatro Principal and the Liceu, which in some ways resembled that between Covent Garden and Her Majesty's Theatre in London. Two factions arose which represented the differing aims of the theatres; the Cruzados, being elderly and noble in birth tended to be reactionary in thought and still shared the tastes of the Ancien Regime. The bourgeois Liceistes, on the other hand favoured more progressive ideas and were eager for premières of new works by Verdi or Weber.

Disaster struck in 1861 when practically the whole of the stage and auditorium was destroyed by fire. The building was not insured and one hundred shares were issued to raise funds to rebuild the theatre (at a cost of one million pesetas), with the descendents of the shareholders still having a permanent right to individual ownership of a seat. Josep Mestres returned to supervise the work and certain improvements were made to the auditorium, which became more sumptuous, to the stage machinery and to the pit.

The Liceu was officially re-opened on 26th April with Bellini's *I Puritani* and for the first season eleven operas were given. Verdi and the French composer Flotow were invited to view the new theatre and an agreement was made by the managers of the Liceu and the Teatro Real in Madrid to share productions.

In the latter half of the nineteenth century, the Liceu expanded its repertoire in a successful attempt to become the leading opera house in Spain. During the 1860's French Romantic opera was introduced, with the premières of important works by Meyerbeer, Gounod's *Faust*, and, later on, Bizet's *Carmen*. After successful perform-ances of Weber's *Die Freischütz*, Wagner's *Lohengrin* appeared in 1882, to be sung four years later in Catalan by the greatest Spanish Wagnerian tenor Francesco Vinas. The Liceu is obliged by its 1862 charter to use the Catalan language in producing opera and to commission at least one new Spanish work a year. The first opera in Catalan, Goula's *A La Voretta del Mar* was given there in 1881 and extracts from Falla's *Atlantida* were heard there in 1961 before its première at La Scala, Milan.

After the turn of the century the new Graner administration championed Puccini with three important premières (*Tosca, Madame Butterfly, La Fanciulla del West*) and Strauss with *Salome, Intermezzo and Arabella*. In 1921 Bruno Walter conducted *Der Rosenkava-lier* and Klemperer conducted the complete *Ring* while during the following year there was a marked insistence on Russian music, until then practically unknown in the Liceu's repertoire: Tchaikovsky's *Queen of Spades* and Borodin's *Prince Igor* were both staged.

During the Civil War the last performance before Franco's entrance into Barecelona took place in January 1939. There was little indigenous activity during the war years, although the sympathy with fascism led to frequent visits from companies and orchestras from Nazi Germany: Furtwängler, Knappertsbusch and Schmidt-Isserstedt all appeared at the Liceu with the Berlin Philharmonic and a company from Frankfurt-am-main brought Mozart festivals between 1941 and 1943.

Since the war the theatre has firmly established itself as the leading opera house in the Mediterranean outside Italy, with a broad repertoire, interpreted by leading singers. The soprano Montserrat Caballe made her debut at the Liceu in Strauss's *Arabella* in 1962 and has since become a key figure there, her repertoire being in excess of thirty operas. Caballe was 'discovered' while working in a handkerchief factory, poor but ambitious to sing. Her training was paid for by a rich Barcelona family on condition that she sang at the Liceu every season.

Bilbao Festival of Opera
Teatro Arriaga, Bilbao

Director: Eugenio Solano
Artistic Director: Diego Monjo
Season: End August–end September
Productions: 6
Performances: 2 of each
Capacity: 1,700
Ballet: 3 or 4 outside opera season

Box Office: (351 4) 415 5490
Box open: Mon–Sat 11.00a.m.–1.00p.m.,
5.00–9.00p.m.
Postal: ABAO, Rodriguez Arias 3, 1 Bilbao 8
Prices: 1,950–6,800 Pesetas
Concessions: Reductions for subscriptions

Located in the Basque province of northern Spain, the city of Bilbao has played host to an annual opera festival since 1953 and is highly regarded for its all star casts rather than for exciting productions. It originally tended to rely almost totally on other companies for help; the sets invariably came from Madrid and the chorus from Barcelona. With the formation of the ABAO (Associacion Bilbaina Amigos dela Opera) in 1954 and the advent of the Orchestra Sinfonica de Bilbao, the festival rapidly became a more home-grown product with only the sets and costumes imported.

The ABAO's first production was *Tosca* with three Verdi operas following in an ambitious first season of eight productions. The concentration on French and Italian opera has continued to this day, with only the occasional Slavic work such as *Boris* or Spanish repertory like *Mirentxu* being performed, and virtually no productions of Zarzuela. The festival intends to tackle German repertoire, beginning in 1988.

Some of the highlights of the Festival since its launch have been the Simionato *Carmen* of 1954, the Del Monaco *Otello* two years, a Callas recital in 1959 and Mirella Freni's touching portrayal of Mimi in *La Bohème*. The major European interpreters of Italian and French opera continued to be frequent visitors including Tebaldi, Alfredo Kraus, Glossop, Carreras, Caballé, Berganza, Aragall, Raimondi, Chiara, Domingo and Pavarotti. There have been no resident conductors but Rafael Frübeck de Burgos conducted for a time during the 1970s.

In 1987 the festival moved into the restored Teatro Arriaga. The new management are at pains to point out that a new era has begun and from now on there will also be completely original productions.

Teatro Lirico Nacional La Zarzuela, Madrid

Los Madrazo 11, 6a Planta 28014 Madrid

Director: José Antonio Campos Borrego
Season: January–July
Productions: 8, 2 new
Performances: 5 of each. Zarzuela is staged during autumn with approx. 50 performances per production
Capacity: 1140
Ballet: Various ballet performances in December

Box Office: (1) 429 8216
Box open: Daily 11.30a.m.–1.30p.m.; 5.00–8.00p.m.
Postal: One month in advance to Calle Jovellanos, 4, Madrid
Information: Obtainable from TLNLZ, Los Madrazo, 11, 6° 28014 Madrid

Various operas were put on in Spain's capital from the early eighteenth century although these were exclusively for royalty. Most were given by visiting Italian troupes – Philip V invited the castrato Farinelli to Madrid to cure him of his melancholia – and any attempt to create an indigenous form of opera was suppressed, forcing a number of Spanish composers, Soler and Terradellas for instance, to write works in Italian. This situation substantially changed during the early part of the following century when the vogue was for Spanish opera and a rivalry emerged between *zarzuela* (the Spanish equivalent of *opera buffa*) and *opera serioso* (*opera seria*) as well as between the theatres that produced those genres, the Teatro del Instituto and the Teatro del Liceu.

In 1859 the Teatro Lirico Nacional La Zarzuela became the principal house for opera. Nowadays, it is Spain's second house after the Teatro Liceu in Barcelona. After a period of being overshadowed by its rival, La Zarzuela now gives around ten productions a year under the musical direction of Miguel Angel Gomes Martinez and can provide high standards and attract important names. Regulars at La Zarzuela recently have included Domingo, Caballe, Kraus, Carreras, Toczyska, Raimondi and Baltsa.

There are ambitious plans to turn Madrid, once again, into Spain's primary venue for opera when the company move into the newly-restored Teatro Real in 1990. From that time productions will be shared with La Zarzuela in a similar relationship to that which exists between the Opéra and the Opéra Comique in Paris, with the Zarzuela giving lighter works and *zarzuelas* themselves.

The opening night is expected to be a glamorous event, featuring the most famous Spanish singers in a production of *La Bohème*, to be televised worldwide. Campos has promised much, including a policy of giving opera in its original language and hiring more international singers. For this purpose he has managed to increase the budget to five million pounds, most of it coming from the government.

Stora Theatre, Goteborg

Box 53 116, 40015 Göteborg, Sweden

Director: Eskil Hemberg
Season: Mid-August – mid-June
Productions: 4
Performances: 20–25 of each
Capacity: 615
Ballet: 3 per season and small ballet festival at end of May
Recordings: *Abunakenm Tuntinara*

Box Office: (31) 131300/(31) 139315; groups (31) 174745
Box open: Mon–Fri 12.00p.m.–7.30p.m., Sat–Sun (and on performance days) 12.00p.m.–6.00p.m.
Postal: As above
Prices: 50–80 crowns

Sweden's third opera house, the nineteenth-century Stora Theatre, is located in the centre of Goteborg, Sweden's second city. The New Theatre, as it was originally called, opened in 1859 with no resident company, but with the intention of accommodating touring operatic and drama companies. A fairly constant stream of German companies gave performances of Mozart operas and in 1865 an Italian production of Verdi's *Nabucco* was the first to be seen in Sweden.

From 1880, when Albert Ranft took over as administrator, the newly-named Stora Theatre diversified its repertoire to include ballet and operetta. A highly successful period ensued lasting into the 1910s, highlighted by the presence of internationally famous performers including Sarah Bernhardt and Eleanora Duse for drama, Anna Pavlova for ballet and Kristina Nilsson for opera. Furthermore, the only Swedish production of Verdi's *Les Vêpres Siciliennes* until the 1950s took place here in 1928, the same year that the Norwegian soprano Kirsten Flagstad sang her first Agathe.

A joint-stock company has administered the theatre since 1920. It has developed a style of production that stresses the importance of acting in the interpretation of operatic roles, and has also gained a considerable reputation for intimate stagings of chamber operas, including Britten's *Rape of Lucretia*, and Maxwell Davies' *Lighthouse* in 1984. The wide ranging repertoire features many Swedish operas by composers such as Lars Edlund and Bo Hulphens, as well as revivals of early Italian repertoire such as Rossini *opera buffa* and modern musicals like Bernstein's *Candide*, performed in 1985.

Attempts to enlarge the house and improve the rather dry accoustics have been made recently. The administrator since 1985 has been Eskil Hemberg who from 1987 will be the director general of Stockholm, although he will remain at Göteborg until a replacement for him can be found.

Drottningholm Court Theatre, Stockholm

Forestallningar, Box 27050, 102 51 Stockholm

Director: Per Forström
Artistic Director: Arnold Östman
Season: June–September
Productions: 3
Performances: Average 8 of each
Capacity: 454

Box Office: 08–60 82 25/08–60 82 81
Box open: Daily 9.00a.m.–3.00p.m. (April–Sept)
Postal: As above; all advance booking subject to 15 Kr fee per ticket; group bookings by post only
Prices: 50Kr–210Kr
Cards: American Express

Recordings: Così fan Tutte. Videos: Così, Magic Flute, Marriage of Figaro

A visit to Drottningholm is a journey into the past, to an age of leisure when theatrical entertainment remained the privilege of an aristocratic elite. For, uniquely among surviving theatres of the Age of Enlightenment, the little court theatre at Drottningholm – the Royal residence of Sweden's artistically-inclined Gustav III as well as his present-day descendant Carl Gustav XVI – still has its original stage machinery intact; an intricate system of pulleys, ropes and wooden drums which perform miracles of scenic transformation. The spectacle so characteristic of eighteenth-century operas – quick changes of location from the nether regions of Hades to the heights of Olympus – can be realized in seconds with the man-power of four scene-shifters, turning the central windlass which sets the whole contraption in motion.

Yet Drottningholm's survival into the twentieth century is more a matter of historical accident than brilliance of theatrical design, though Carl Fredrik Adelcrantz's achievement in creating a quite magical unity of style by the simplest and most subtle of means is by no means negligible. Commissioned by Queen Louisa Ulrika – Gustav III's mother – to replace a building which succumbed to the fiery fate of most ancient theatres – Adelcrantz conceived his theatre in its entirety as an illusion. Under candle-light the painted detail of the interior would look as 'real' as the décors on stage. The cunning perspectives of the interior deceive the eye creating the trompe l'oeil effect of the stage as an extension of the auditorium. By purely architectural and decorative means, the courtly audience could be involved in the operatic, dramatic or balletic action unfolding before its eyes.

Around the heart of the building, Adelcrantz constructed a series of antechambers, foyers, dressing rooms, and even a kitchen and dining rooms to accommodate the resident company of French actors and Italian singers employed at Drottningholm during the summer months, and to provide space for the Royal social functions which provided another raison d'être of the eighteenth-century court theatre.

With the assassination of Gustav III at a masked ball in his other opera house in the Swedish capital (the original subject of Verdi's *Un Ballo in Maschera*) all theatrical activity at the Royal residence ceased and the little theatre lay dormant for over a hundred years. The candles were extinguished, the machinery fell into disuse and the theatre was forgotten. During the winter of 1921, the doors were unlocked by the theatre historian Agne Beijer who, delighted with his enchanting and important

Drottningholm Court Theatre, Stockholm

discovery, set about restoring the building to its proper use. The value of Beijer's find cannot be underestimated since it opened new doors to the understanding of staging in the Baroque theatre, previously available only in diagrams and written descriptions. Here, in Drottningholm, was the box of magical theatre tricks dilapidated but substantially intact.

Initially, operatic activity was confined to the occasional festival performance, but after the Second World War, the Swedish State took responsibility for the theatre by creating it a national museum and appointing an artistic director to mount performances during the summer months of opera, ballets and plays appropriate to the dimensions and facilities of the stage and the atmosphere of the auditorium.

Works of the Gustavian era – by the court composer Josef Martin Kraus and Abbé Vogler – returned to the site of their creation alongside the masterpieces of the period and earlier generations. Drottningholm has embraced and championed the entire Baroque and classical repertoire, performing the pioneering works of Monteverdi, Cavalli and Orazio Vecchi, the great virtuoso *opere serie* of Handel, the noble dramas of Gluck, and the imperishable comic works of Mozart. Yet it has also unearthed and staged the theatrical creations of their lesser contemporaries: the opera-ballets of Lully and Rameau, the *drames lyrique* of Grétry and the *opere buffe* of Pergolesi, Paisiello, and Mozart's friends Haydn and Padre Martini (Martin y Soler). In recent years, the historical barriers have been advanced to contain the lyric comedies of early nineteenth-century composers, Rossini and Donizetti.

This repertoire and the intimacy of the performing styles have given Drottningholm its unique atmosphere and charm, a charm enhanced by the exquisite pastoral surroundings of the Royal Palace's rambling English Garden. A boat trip from the centre of Stockholm clinches the essentially eighteenth-century nature of the Drottningholm experience.

The circumstances of performance within the walls of the theatre underline the effect: even before the curtain has risen, a costumed and bewigged lackey calls for attention by pounding his staff on the wooden floor and the musicians, likewise garbed in eighteenth-century livery, still have the air of court retainers. In recent years, under the current artistic direction of Arnold Östman, these players have usually been practitioners of period instruments, thus harmonising the historical character of the spectacle with a scholarly, yet vital, approach to the music. Östman has been responsible for some notable Mozart revivals, mostly cast from local strength – Swedish singers have reputations for excellent schooling and musicianship – which have revealed familiar scores anew to modern listeners. The often enchanting productions make use of Drottningholm's store of interchangeable sets of scenery. Regular visitors will see the same street scenes, arcadian groves, seascapes, heavenly expanses and infernal regions in a variety of operas, but that was how they were staged in Gustav III's day. Then, the scenery was regarded as an investment which, in the twentieth century, has yielded a legacy of musical and theatrical knowledge to enrich the lives of everyone fortunate enough to experience this lovely opera house in action.

Stockholm Opera

Gustav Adolf Torg, Stockholm

Director: Eskil Hemberg
Season: September–June
Productions: 22, 5 new
Performances: Varies
Capacity: 11,000
Ballet: Average 15 per season

Box Office: (08) 24 82 40
Telex: 8105103 SWEDOP
Box open: Mon–Sat 11.00a.m.–7.30p.m.
Postal: P.O. Box 16094, Stockholm 10322
Prices: 10K–105K (more expensive if guests appear)
Concessions: Discounts for senior citizens, students, children under 16

Stockholm must be the only city whose opera began on a tennis court: it started when Gustavus III decided to create a house for the first Swedish operas and dismissed the resident French company. The Old Ball House, as it was called, opened in 1773 with *Thetis och Pelee*, based on a text by the King and set to music by Uttini, the former chief composer at Drottningholm. The same year saw a performance of Gluck's *Orphée et Euridice* before its official Paris première a year later, which provided a model for subsequent Swedish operas, encouraged by the King. The greatest of these was Naumann's *Gustav Vasa* (1876) again with a libretto by Gustavus III. In 1782 Carl Frederick Adelcrantz designed the first opera house which stood for over one hundred years. From all accounts one of the most beautiful houses in Europe, it became infamous when, in March 1792, during a masked ball, the King was assassinated by the nobleman Ankarström who disagreed with his reforms, which favoured the poorer classes: the story was used by Verdi in his opera *Un Ballo in Maschera*. The King's son threatened to tear down the building, but relented, eventually putting it to use as a temporary hospital during the war against Finland.

It was not until the reign of Charles XIII that Stockholm was revived as a centre for opera and the first great singers associated with this house began to emerge. Long-forgotten Swedish operas were given alongside imported ones with Jenny Lind and Christine Nilsson in the lead roles. In 1838, Lind, who was nicknamed the Swedish Nightingale, made her debut as Agathe in Weber's *Die Freischütz* at the age of seventeen and amazed audiences by the purity and range of her voice. During this period she befriended the composer Adolf Lindblad, singing his songs and treating him and his wife as surrogate parents. When the composer declared his love for her and suggested a *ménage à trois*, she felt she had to leave Stockholm and went to Paris to study with Manuel Garcia, only occasionally returning to her native country. One of these occasions was the coronation of Oscar I in 1844, for which she sang extracts from Bellini's *La Sonnambula* and *Norma*.

Many of the Swedish composers who wrote prolifically during the nineteenth century have been forgotten, with the possible exception of Rangström, whose work is considerably more interesting than that of, for instance, Stenhammer and Hállen. A revival in Swedish composition occurred this century initiated by the composer Rosenberg *(Reson till Amerik)*, 1932 and *Marionette*, 1939) and was continued by Blomdahl and Back.

A portrait of Jenny Lind by L. Asher (photo: Mansell Collection)

The new opera house opened in 1898 with parts of Berwald's *Estrella de Soria*: Hallén's *Waldmarsskatten* performed a year later was the first opera specially written for the new building. The house is considered an adequate showcase for an exceptional company, but Anderberg's design is generally unremarkable. Humble in appearance, it does not dominate the city to the same extent as other great houses do; Vienna or Paris for instance. The opera has always been subsidized by the state, except for a brief period when an attempt was made to withdraw funding altogether with the familiar argument that taxpayer's money should not be required to support the tastes of the rich. For a while Conrad Nordqvist, the chief conductor, attempted to run the opera on a private basis but resigned, demoralized within two years. He was succeeded by Axel Buren and subsequently the state subsidy was restored. During the twenties and thirties Armas Jarnfëlt attempted to end the dominance of Swedish and French opera by creating an atmosphere of eclecticism and experimentation. This trend was officially established by Göran Gentele, who succeeded the Wagnerian singer Set Svanholm as director in 1963 and created twenty-four new productions for the company. His renowned *Un Ballo in Maschera*, which controversially portrayed Gustavus III as a homosexual, was seen in Edinburgh in 1959 and London in 1960 and put the Stockholm Opera firmly on the map for its productions. An important contribution was made by Harald Andre, whose innovatory design and lighting techniques created a style peculiar to the house.

The Swedes have a long Wagner tradition which goes back to the first *Ring* there in 1907: a long line of fine Wagner singers apart from Svanholm have included Birgit Nilsson, Berit Lindholm and Helge Brilioth. Other important singers to have begun their careers with this company include Elisabeth Söderström, Jussi Björling and Nicolai Gedda.

In 1973 the Stockholm Opera celebrated its two hundredth anniversary with Werle's *Tintomara* and in 1978, Ligeti was commissioned to write a new opera for the house which turned out to be the highly successful *Le Grand Macabre*.

Despite the fact that Stockholm is not quite on the international circuit of opera houses on account of its northerly location, it has remained a house of prodigious activity and is highly respected for its continuing high standards and adventurousness aided by a plethora of fine home-grown singers. The most recent of these to be widely recognized include, Hagan Haggegard, Anne Sofie von Otter and Marian Häggander.

Grand Théâtre de Genève
11 Boulevard du Théâtre, 1211 Genève 11

Director: Hughes Gall
Season: September–June
Productions: 8, 4 new
Performances: 7 of each
Capacity: 1,488
Ballet: 1 or 2 per season

Box Office: (22) 21 23 11
Telex: 421 132 GTG CH
Box open: Mon–Fri 10.00a.m.–7.00p.m.; Sat 10.00a.m.–5.00p.m.
Postal: Bureau de location du Grand Théâtre, Place Neuve
Prices: 14–68 SF

Geneva has an excellent musical tradition. Famous musicians, including Mozart, visited the city in the eighteenth century, when Grétry wrote his opera *Isabelle et George* here, and in the twentieth century the composers Ernest Bloch, Frank Martin and Henri Gagnebin settled at the foot of the Swiss Alps. Geneva also has several choirs, chamber orchestras, a company devoted to first performances, a first-rate performers' competition, and a symphony orchestra, L'Orchestre de la Suisse Romande, attracting attention through its creator and previous conductor, the late Ernest Ansermet. Given this distinguished musical background, and a population which is one of the wealthiest per capita income groups in Europe, it's hardly surprising to learn that the opera house is a sumptuous piece of architecture, designed for the grand social occasion. The Grand Théâtre is in the heart of the city's cultural section, adjoining the art museum and music conservatory, close to the university, cathedral and city walls. The foyer is an impressive spectacle, with its painted tableaux ceiling and chandeliers. On the opening night in 1879, the building was patriotically inaugurated to the tune of Rossini's *William Tell*. Since then it has been thoroughly modernised following a fire in 1951 which closed the building for eleven years. Now there is a mobile rear stage, and two extra side pieces for additional space which enable the theatre to bring in productions from larger houses, including Paris, the Coliseum, La Scala and Turin. The orchestra pit has also been modernized, now consisting of three lifts which can either provide extra stage frontage or vary the amount of room required by the players.

Geneva is a wealthy city, pumping seven million pounds worth of subscriptions into the opera each year. It remains faithful to its conservative clientèle, providing a diet of Bellini, Strauss and Offenbach, and some revivals of early opera. At least once a year, other companies are brought in. In 1965 Peter Hall's *Marriage of Figaro* with a number of English singers, was staged, and the Pesaro Festival's production of Rossini's *Il Turco in Italia* came in 1985.

The enormous subscriptions are channelled into funding ten new lavish productions a year, and hiring acclaimed performers such as Ruggero Raimondi, Katia Ricciarelli and Hermann Prey, Robert Lloyd, Anne Sofie von Otter, Anne Howells, Valerie Masterson and Siegfried Jerusalem. Some of the important producers to have worked at Geneva in recent years include Pier-Luigi Pizzi with *Khovanschinia* in 1982, Ken Russell with *L'Italiana in Algeri* in 1983, Andrei Serban with *The Love of Three Oranges* in 1984 and Elijah Moshinsky with *I Vespri Siciliani* in 1985.

Zurich Stadttheater

Falkenstrasse 1, CH-8008 Zurich

Director: Rolf Waeikert
Artistic Director: Christoph Groszer
Season: September–June
Productions: 20, 10 new
Performances: Varies
Capacity: 1,000
Ballet: 3 per season

Box Office: (1) 251 6920/1
Telex: 815988 OHZ CH
Box open: Mon–Sat 10.00a.m.–6.30p.m.,
Sun 10.00a.m.–12.00p.m.
Postal: As above
Prices: 17–89 SF
Concessions: 16 SF 1 hour before
performance; Sun p.m. 50% for senior citizens

The Zurich opera house, originally called the Stadttheater but known from 1964 as Opernhaus, was built in 1891, by the Viennese architects Fellner and Helmer after the old Aktientheatre had burnt down. The city's fine opera reputation is founded on its longstanding devotion to innovation, and its hiring of great conductors and composers, such as Wagner, Bulow, Busoni, Furtwängler, Hindemith, and Richard Strauss.

Notable first productions include the first authorised stage performance outside Bayreuth of *Parsifal* in 1913, Berg's *Lulu* in 1937, Hindemith's *Mathis der Maler* in 1938 and the new version of his *Cardillac* in 1952. In 1945 Gershwin's *Porgy and Bess* was given its first European showing, and in 1957 Schönberg's *Moses und Aron* was premièred under the baton of Hans Rosbaud, musical director from 1955 to 1958.

From 1937 to 1956 Hans Zimmerman ran the theatre, specialising in Strauss and Wagner. He hired Knappertsbusch and Furtwängler and a cast of first-rate singers. In the 1960's premières included Martinû's *The Greek Passion*, Mussorgsky's *Boris Godunov* and Klebe's *Ein Wahrer Held*.

From 1975 to 1986 the Zurich opera was directed by Claus Helmut Drese. It was his idea to enact a cycle of Monteverdi operas for which the conductor Nikolas Harnoncourt and the producer Jean-Pierre Ponnelle would collaborate. Harnoncourt's particular touch was to give early opera a tinge of authenticity by using the instruments used at the time of composition. The series was so successful that plans were made for a Mozart cycle, beginning with *Die Entführung*. During the last two years of Drese's reign, the opera house was renovated and reopened to Wagner's *Die Meistersinger* in 1984. There was also a specially commissioned new work for the same season, Rudolf Kelterborn's *Der Kirschgarten*. During that time performances were put on at the sporting stadium, where a suitable choice was, not surprisingly, *Aida* and also at a smaller theatre which catered for chamber opera.

Since Drese's departure for Vienna, Christof Groszer has been the Intendant and the emphasis on early opera continues with productions of Handel and Scarlatti. Producers over the years have included Götz Friedrich with *Eugene Onegin*, Otto Schenk with *Die Fledermaus,* and Yuri Lyubimov with *Jenûfa*. Drese returns in 1988 to direct *Die Walküre* as part of a new *Ring* cycle. There have been several important singers on the Zurich stage recently, including Edita Gruberova, Maria Chiara, Gwyneth Jones, Ilona Tokody and Siegfried Jerusalem.

EASTERN EUROPE

The interior of the Komische Oper, East Berlin

National State Opera Theatre, Sofia

Dondukov Boulevard 58, Sofia

Director: Name not available
Season: September–June
Productions: 16, 4 new
Performances: Varies
Capacity: 1,200
Ballet: Varies

Box Office: (359 2) 88 43 65
Box open: Daily 9.00a.m.–7.30p.m.
Postal: Information from the Public Relations Office at above address
Prices: 1–5 Leva
Concessions: Some reduction for collective purchase from the Public Relations Office

Western art forms were first introduced to Bulgaria by visiting troupes after the country was liberated from Turkish rule in 1878. By 1890 a proper company had been formed to give occasional seasons of opera. This proved frustrating for all those involved and many singers and composers left to study in countries such as Italy, Austria and Russia. Two of these, the composers Emanuil Manolov and Konstantin Mihailov-Stoyan, returned from Moscow in 1886 with the intention of creating an indigenous style of writing based on the country's rich tradition of folk music and choral singing. Manolov's *Siromakhkinya* (The Poor Woman) performed in 1900 was the first attempt at Bulgarian opera. During the next decade various imitators sprang up, the most celebrated being the 'maestro', Georgy Atanasov. In operas like *Borislav* in 1911, *Gergana* in 1917, and *Tsveta* in 1925, Atanasov applied first-hand knowledge of the *verismo* style, acquired as a pupil of Pietro Mascagni, to historic and nationalistic librettos.

A permanent company was formed in 1921, organized by Moysey Zlatin and Atanosov. The former was responsible for the advent of a Bulgarian style of operetta, a function he shared with the composer Karastoyanov. In 1940 he conducted the first performance of Stoyanov's *Salammbo*, an important work because of its stylistic modernity; the composer was an ex-pupil of Franz Schmidt.

A new theatre was erected after the existing State Opera House had been destroyed during World War II. Since 1966 the company has travelled extensively throughout Europe and has produced many excellent singers who have become leading interpreters. These include Boris Christoff, Nicolai Ghiaurov, Raina Kabaivanska, Anna Tomowa-Sintow, Ghena Dmitrova and Nicolai Ghiuselev. With its enormous chorus and vast theatre, the company can mount spectacular, if old-fashioned, productions at the rate of about two hundred and forty performances a year. The British soprano Rosalind Plowright won a prize at Sofia which launched her international career, and she gave some distinguished performances in the house itself. The Palace of Culture, which can seat five thousand people, shows opera during a May/June Festival.

Slovak National Theatre
Gorkého 2–4, Bratislava 81586

Director: Marián Jurík
Musical Director: Oudrey Lenárd
Season: Sept–June
Productions: 15, 5 new
Performances: Approx 10 of each
Capacity: 611

Box Office: (7) 333083
Box open: Daily 10a.m.–5p.m., Sat and Sun 10.00a.m.–12.00p.m.
Postal: CEDOK Příkapy 6, Prague 1
Prices: Approx 25–30 crowns for ordinary performances, higher for Sept–Oct festival

An opera company was founded in Bratislava in 1920, made up entirely of Czech personnel with a repertoire of Czech and Italian works sung exclusively in Czech. The emergence of Slovakian elements was a gradual process: the first Slovak singer appeared in 1924 and the first opera two years later, both inspired by the leadership of the Slovak Oskar Nedbal (1923–31) who raised standards considerably and toured the company several times abroad.

The declaration of an autonomous Slovak state in 1945 led to the Czechs leaving and finally the company took on a Slovak character, translating most classic operas into Slovak and introducing the works of many composers from the region, such as Suchoň, Cikker, and Moyzes.

The theatre used by the opera company, the Slovak National Theatre, was constructed in 1886. It is in a neo-Renaissance style and bears a familial resemblance to the Smetana and Janáček Theatres, all of them reflecting the bourgeois prosperity of the Austro-Hungarian empire. The building, which was thoroughly refurbished in 1975, is shared by the opera and ballet companies.

The Slovak National Theatre, Bratislava

Janáček Opera House, Brno

Dvorakova 11, Brno 1

Director: Dr Jiři Majer
Musical Director: Dr Jiři Pinkas
Season: Sept-June
Productions: 25, 5 new
Performances: Approx 5 of each
Capacity: 1317

Box Office: (Brno) 26311, or 27421
Box open: Daily 10.00a.m.–5.00p.m.,
Sunday 10.00a.m.–12.00p.m.
Postal: Cedok Prikapy 6, CS 11000 Prague 1
Prices: Approx. 14–28 KCS, more during
Brno Music Festival

The first opera company to be resident in Brno, Janáček's birthplace, dates back to 1584 and the opening there of the first permanent Czech theatre, the National Theatre, which occurred only one year after the opening of the National Theatre in Prague. Designed by the architects Fellner and Helmer, who were responsible for forty-eight similar houses in Central and Eastern Europe, it was the first central European theatre to be equipped with electric lighting, and opened ceremoniously with a production of Goethe's drama *Egmont*.

For the first ten years it was called the Provisional Theatre and then, after renovation, it became the Stadttheater; as the city was under German control, it offered performances exclusively in German until the end of the First World War. The subsequent formation of an independent Czechoslovakia was marked by the development of a repertoire of Czech operas: as well as important works by Smetana, Dvořák and Fibich, the premières of most of Janáček's operas have taken place there – from *Jenufa* in 1904 to *From the House of the Dead* in 1930.

Considered by many the most progressive operatic institution in the country, the company has given many first performances of contemporary Czech works including those of Martinu, Novák, Cikker, Mašlík and Ostrcil and has introduced operas by Shostakovich and Henze. Since the 1960s the company has increased the number of Italian works in its repertoire, although most of them are sung in Czech. In 1965 it was moved into the Janáček Opera House, the first and largest theatre to be built in Czechoslovakia since the war. The original relatively experimental design for the building was considerably watered down by various state authorities with a final result that has a civic coldness about it. Acoustically, however, the house excels, and the modern lighting equipment and stage machinery have contributed further to its reputation for experiment and forward-thinking.

The National Theatre, Prague
Narodni Trida 2, Praha 1

Director: Prof Jiři Panner
Season: Sept–June
Productions: 42, approx 6–7 new
Performances: 1–4 of each
Capacity: 950

Box Office: (2) 205364
Telex: 2144 111
Box open: Mon–Fri 10a.m.–5p.m.; Sat–Sun 10.00a.m.–12.00a.m.
Postal: PO. Box 865, CS 11230 Prague 1. Via the agency CEDOK, Prikopy 6, CS 11000 Prague 1. Or box office for current and following week
Prices: Approx 20–70 KCS, prices higher during spring music festival. Advance booking recommended as most operas are sold out 2 months ahead of opening performance

Recordings: All the major works of Janáček, Dvořák and Smetana and Martinu's Greek Passion, all on Supraphon.

The struggle for a National Theatre in the Czech capital occupied the citizens of Prague for nearly four decades before they could take their seats for the first performance there of Smetana's patriotic opera *Libuse* on 11th June 1881. The idea of a theatre devoted exclusively to works in the Czech vernacular was mooted as early as 1844 when a committee was formed to inaugurate the great project, and the following year, the authorities of the Bohemian Estates – the regional government, owners of the first public theatre in Prague, now called the Tyl – consented to the establishment of a fund, the money to be raised through the sale of shares in the future theatre. The building was to occupy a prime site on the banks of the Vltva.

During the succeeding decade due to prevarication, hesitation and indecision, no progress was made beyond vague conceptions of a building in the prevalent Italian 'loggia' style – consisting of boxes rather than galleries – with an overoptimistic capacity of two and a half thousand. By 1854 it had become clear that specific plans would have to be drawn up, but the competition for the design of the building produced indifferent results and the project was eventually shelved in 1858 in favour of a Provisional Theatre, described by the committee chief, Frantisek Rieger, as a very modest theatre for a young and weak people. Completed in less than six months by the architect Ignac Ullmann, the Provisional gave the first performances of Smetana's operas, the *Bran denburgers in Bohemia* (1866) and *The Bartered Bride* (1866), *Dalibor* (1868), *The Two Widows* (1874), *The Kiss* (1876) and *The Secret* (1878). Despite considerable opposition from music critics in Prague, Smetana won the appointment of conductor at the theatre from 1866 until 1874, by which time his deafness had advanced to a point where he could no longer fulfil his musical duties.

Hardly had the Provisional Theatre opened its doors – on the 18th November 1862 – than the committee turned its attention to the problem of a permanent national theatre. They approached the Professor of Architecture at Prague's Technical College, Josef Zitek, directly, and by 1867 his contract was signed and sealed. Within the year the foundation stone had been laid, and by the end of 1868 the foundations were already in place.

Yet it took another thirteen years of delays, as costs mounted far beyond the originally envisaged budget, before Zitek's building could be shown to the public, and when it did open on the 11th June 1881 it stood for just over two months and only twelve public performances before a fire consumed the stage, auditorium and cuppola on the 12th August. The shell of Zitek's theatre survived, but he was blamed for the catastrophe and forced to cede his place to his pupil and disciple Josef Schulz. Under Schulz's direction the outlines of Zitek's design were retained, in particular the imposing, arched facade with its Corinthian pillars over the porch, surmounted by statues of Apollo and the nine Muses, and its twin Victories in horse-drawn chariots dominating the towers which flank the frontage. Zitek's original conception had made brilliant use of a limited site, though he had cramped the stage facilities in order to safeguard the foyers and reception rooms. These, in their present state, are extraordinarily ornate and beautiful, painted with classical allegories and scenes from Czech history. Schulz also reduced the theatre's capacity from one thousand eight hundred to about half that number, enhancing the intimacy of the resplendent auditorium. He also cleverly incorporated the Provisional Theatre into his new building in order to improve backstage facilities.

The completed theatre finally opened on the 18th November 1883, again with a performance of Smetana's *Libuse*. The artistic director of the National Theatre Association – including the Estates Theatre for spoken drama – was František Subert who extended the international repertoire of the house – *Carmen* and *Aida* were given their first performances in 1884 – while encouraging native Czech composers. Zdenek Fibich's *The Bride of Messina* had its world première on the 24th March of the same year. In 1886, however, critical voices in the press unleashed a campaign against him for his neglect of Smetana's works and he responded in December of that year with a brilliant production of *Dalibor*. Up until 1900, when Subert was succeeded by the composer Karel Kovařovic – adapter of Janáček's orchestrations – and Jaroslav Kvapil – librettist of Dvořák's *Rusalka* – he enriched the already flourishing Czech operatic heritage with a series of new works: Dvořák's *The Jacobin* in 1889, Fibich's *The Wooing of Pelops* in 1889, the same composer's *Tempest* in 1895 with the famous Czech soprano Ruzena Maturová as Miranda, his *Sarka* in 1897, Josef Foerster's *Eva* and Dvořák's *The Devil and Kate* in 1899. Earlier that year the great Bohemian tenor Karel Burian – Richard Strauss's first Herod in *Salomé* – sang at the National Theatre for the first time.

Under Kovařovic and Kvapil, the tradition established by Subert continued. In the first year of the twentieth century, Kovařovic conducted the first performance of *Rusalka* with Maturová in the title role. It was followed by the great Czech composer's last stagework, *Armida*, in 1904. By this time Emma Destinnová – soon to find fame in Europe and America as Emmy Destinn – had made her bow at the National Theatre, but she failed to win a contract returning in 1908 as a guest. Kovařovic began to introduce Wagner's music-dramas into the repertory: *Lohengrin* in 1907 with Maturova as Ortrud, *Parsifal* in 1914, *Das Rheingold* in 1915, and *Die Walküre* in 1916 with the dramatic soprano Gabriela Horvatova as Kundry, Freia and Brünnhilde. On the 26th May 1916, the Moravian composer Leos Janáček received belated recognition in Prague with the first production at the National Theatre of his internationally acclaimed *Jenufa*, conducted by Kovařovic – who 'improved' Janáček's orchestration – and starring Horvatova as Kostelnicka, Kamila Ungrova as Jenufa and Vilem Zitek as the mayor.

Janáčeck's next opera, *The Excursions of Mr. Brouček*, had its world première at the National Theatre in 1920, the only one of his operas to be inaugurated there. Otakar Ostrčil conducted the work and later, as director of opera, championed his other important stage works in Prague. During his era, the first Czech production of Alban Berg's *Wozzeck* in 1926, only a year after the Berlin première, caused a riot among conservative members of the audience and the production was withdrawn after only two performances.

Ten years later, the great Czech conductor Václav Talich took on the reins of the opera company, inaugurating his regime with a new production of *Rusalka* in June 1936. He was also responsible for the first performance of Bohuslav Martinů's *Julietta* in March 1938. A year later Czechoslovakia fell to the invading German forces and within months the Czech theatre reverted to German language performances.

Within weeks of the liberation from Nazi Germany, the National Theatre re-opened, yet again, with *Libuse* now sung by Marie Podvalova. In June 1945, the Estates Theatre reverted to Czech language performances and then in 1948, the New German Theatre, by now renamed the Smetana, was incorporated into the administration of the theatre, providing an intermediate auditorium for medium scale work and operettas. With the influx of a new opera company, the innovative productions and design of Václav Kaslik and Josef Svoboda revitalised the Czech and international repertories. Kaslik's celebrated staging of *The Cunning Little Vixen* conducted by Václav Neumann and starring Rudolf Asmus as the Forester resulted in an historic recording, one of the first Janáček operas to become widely available on record in the West. Svoboda has produced opera for the National Theatre since 1948 and is famous in the West for his stagings of *Die Frau ohne Schatten, Pelléas et Mélisande* and 'the' *Ring,* which make extensive use of gauzes, complex lighting and staircases. Martinu's later operas also joined the repertory. *Mirandolina* was given its world première in 1959 and *The Greek Passion* was performed in Prague almost a decade after the composer's death and its first performance in Zurich.

Today, it is this rich heritage of native opera – the works of Smetana, Fibich, Dvořák, Janáček and Martinů – which the National Theatre safeguards in authentic performances by an ensemble of resident singers and outstanding conductors. Bohumil Gregor, Václav Neumann, and today Zdenek Kosler have continued the long line of great Czech *maestri* and they have nurtured some great singers: the tenors Beno Blachut, Vilem Pribl and Petr Dvorsky, the sopranos Nadezhda Kniplova, Ludmila Dvořákova and Gabriela Beňačková, one of today's outstanding dramatic voices, who inaugurated the refurbished theatre – closed since 1977 – in 1983, its centenary year, as Smetana's *Libuse.* Also in 1983, much needed rehearsal rooms and workshops were built alongside the theatre, as well as a new theatre – the Nová Scéna (the New Stage) – intended for experimental works. The seating here can be adjusted to create theatre in the round and an apron stage.

Tyl Theatre
Prague

The Tyl Theatre is currently cleared for renovation, although there are plans for a re-opening in 1991. As it is part of the National Theatre, Prague the same booking information applies.

Of all surviving eighteenth-century theatres still in use as opera houses, the Tyl in Prague has the most illustrious early connections, since it was here in 1787 and 1791 that Mozart conducted his *Don Giovanni* and *La Clemenza di Tito* for the first time. Only the old Residenztheater built by François Cuvilliés in Munich can match this distinction. The foundation stone for the first theatre on the site between Prague's vegetable and fruit markets (in the Zeltnergasse) was laid on the 6th June 1781 – the year of *Idomeneo's* first performance in Munich – and by September of the same year the shell of the building had already been erected. The design had been commissioned from the architect Anton Haffenecher by the enlightened aristocrat Count Franz-Anton von Nostitz-Rieneck, who gave the theatre its first, rather cumbersome name: the Gräflich Nostitz'sche Nationaltheater. It was the first theatre of its kind in Prague, dedicated to the sister arts of German drama and Italian Opera. It opened, less than two years after commencement of construction, on the 21st April 1783 with a performance of Lessing's *Emilia Galotti*.

For its day, Haffenecher's theatre had an unusually large, not to say gigantic, capacity of one thousand four hundred, though the seating space must have been inordinately cramped since, over the years after a number of reconstructions, it has been reduced by almost one half. Today, there are eight hundred and twenty or so seats (only seven hundred and twenty-six for sale) and this despite the addition of a further tier during the nineteenth century. It is hard to ascertain otherwise how the building differs from Haffenecher's original since none of the architect's plan drawings nor those of the decorative artist, Johann Jacob Jahn have survived, but early prints suggest only minor external alterations. The theatre remains an elegant example of the classical baroque in architecture, inspired with its Corinthian pillars, its friezes and tympana by the temples of Ancient Greece and Rome. The internal layout follows the traditional patterns of eighteenth-century auditoria, a horse-shoe form of (originally four, now five) golden galleries surmounted by a splendid circular ceiling, repainted in the style of the mid-nineteenth century, with a central chandelier. In common with so many theatres of this period – the house 'Unter den Linden' in Berlin springs to mind – the building contains ample space for non-theatrical recreation in salons and refreshment rooms.

This then was the setting of Mozart's triumphant *Don Giovanni* première in 1787. Already in 1786 the Italian opera company managed by Pasquale Bondini – impresario at the theatre since 1784 – had performed his *Marriage of Figaro* to tumultuous popular acclaim only months after the first performance at Vienna's Burgtheater. On his arrival in Prague for the *Don Giovanni* rehearsals, Mozart noted and reported to his friend Gottfried von Jaquin that 'here they talk of nothing but *Figaro*. Nothing is played, sung or whistled but *Figaro*. No opera is drawing like *Figaro*. His new opera was performed for the first time on the 29th October 1787 with the twenty-one-year-old bass, Luigi Bassi in the title-role, Teresa Saporiti and Caterina Micelli as the *donne*, Anna and Elvira, and Bondini's wife as Zerlina. Four years later, at the end of his life, Mozart returned to the Nostitz National Theatre, for the first performance of his final *opera seria*, *La Clemenza di Tito*, commissioned for the coronation of the Emperor Leopold II as King of Bohemia. The occasion is reputed to have been dismissed by the (Italian-born) Empress as 'una porcheria tedescha ('German pig-swill'), though Mozart's faithful Prague audiences subsequently appear to have recognised the opera's grandiose, if somewhat stilted, musical qualities. After Mozart's death in 1791, *The Magic Flute* was taken into the opera troupe's repertory and proved a resounding success with the public.

The dominance of Italian opera in the theatre was shortlived. By 1814, the popular taste for opera in the German vernacular had been endorsed by the appointment of Carl Maria von Weber as first conductor and opera manager, a post he retained from 1813 to 1816 during which period he conducted the Prague première of Beethoven's *Fidelio*. He returned in 1822 to conduct performances of his own opera, *Der Frieschütz*, already introduced in 1821, the year of its première at Berlin's Schauspielhaus. Earlier, in 1818, the theatre had been visited by the Italian prima donna, Angelica Catalani, the soprano who, with a keen appreciation of the power of publicity, styled herself as 'the world's foremost songstress'.

As the nineteenth century proceeded, changes in the European social order affected the nature of the theatre. With the rise of Romanticism came a movement towards artistic nationalism as the Bohemian public demanded plays and operas in their own Czech language. Performances in German continued at the theatre – now called the Ständetheater, renamed again in 1861 as the Bohemian Landestheater – but works were often translated into the national tongue. In 1824, *Don Giovanni* was sung there for the first time in Czech and two years later the first Czech opera, by the composer František Škroup, had its première production.

From 1846 to 1851, the theatre was lead by the manager and playwright, Josef Kajetan Tyl, 'the soul of the Czech theatre' as the historian František Cerny has called him. During his administration, Czech-language performances – predominantly of spoken drama – became the norm (these included the local première of Verdi's *Nabucco* in 1849) yet, little more than ten years after his death the German language regained its supremacy. Angelo Neumann was Intendant from 1885 until 1910 and, during his first two seasons Gustav Mahler conducted in the pit.

The vicissitudes of Czechoslovakia in the present century have been reflected in the modern history of the theatre. Annexed during the twenties to the National Theatre as a third auditorium for small-scale operatic work and drama – the Smetana Theatre, its second auditorium presents medium-scale opera – it fell victim to the German invaders in 1938, when a German ensemble was introduced, performing plays until the closure of all the Third Reich's theatres in 1944. With the foundation of the Czech socialist republic in 1948, the theatre was renamed after Tyl and in the 1970s the auditorium once again resounded to Mozart's operas, performed in the original language by artists of the National Theatre. The operatic repertoire now embraces eighteenth-century comedies by other composers in productions, not 'authentic' perhaps by today's standards, but nonetheless important since the Tyl remains one of very few theatres of its period still in general use. It is currently closed for renovation, and there are plans for a re-opening in 1991.

The Tyl Theatre, Prague (photo: BBC Hulton Picture Library)

Smetana Theatre

Vitězného února, Prague 1

Director: Jiří Pauer
Season: September–June
Productions: 24, 6 new
Performances: Approx. 10 of each
Capacity: 1044

Box Office: (2) 269746
Box open: Mon–Fri 10.00a.m.–5.00p.m.;
Sun 10.00a.m.–12.00p.m.
Postal: Cedok, Příkapi 6, CS 11000 Prague 1
Prices: 12–40 Kcs; higher during spring
festival

Prague's third opera house, the Smetana Theatre is now part of the larger establishment of the National Theatre, but during the period when the main house was undergoing reconstruction and the little Tyl theatre would only occasionally put on a mini-production, the Smetana was the only venue for a broad-based opera repertoire. It has since kept an independent identity and has been congratulated for developing its own house style during the seventies and the early part of this decade. Built between 1885–87 by the city's German minority in response to the cultural challenge represented by the Czech National Theatre, it was originally called the Neues Deutsches Theater. Designed by the Viennese architects Fellner and Helmer who were prolific builders of opera houses of this type, its style is essentially Neo-Renaissance with an auditorium that is light and spacious and painted red, cream and gold. There is an elaborately painted ceiling that is quite captivating especially during dull productions, and sculpted decorations on the roof by the Viennese painter Friedl.

The first season began in 1888 with an important event – the visit of Angelo Neumann's touring company for a performance of *Die Meistersinger*. The ex-baritone turned impressario succeeded in taking Wagner to the masses by forming this group for the express purpose of giving Wagner and travelling to all the major centres of Europe including St. Petersburg. This began an important tradition of German-language opera directed by an impressive list of musical directors, including Gustav Mahler (1885), Otto Klemperer (1907–10), Alexander Zemlinsky (1911–1927; the champion of Schönberg he premiered *Erwartung* in this theatre in 1924) and George Szell (1929–36).

At the end of the Second World War, the house changed its name to the 'Great Opera House of the 5th of May', then to the Grand Theatre and finally to its present name. From 1973 when the house re-opened after an extensive period of restoration, the company have alternated between Slavic and German repertoire with less emphasis on Italian and French works. Dvořák, Smetana, Tchaikovsky, Mussorgsky, Wagner and Mozart are the principal beneficiaries of this opera house.

Komische Oper, East Berlin

Behrenstrasse 55–57, Postfach 1311, Berlin 1086

Director: Prof. Werner Rackwitz
Artistic Director: Harry Kupfer
Season: September–July
Productions: 13, 3 or 4 new
Performances: Varies
Capacity: 1,120
Ballets: 14 per season

Box Office: (2) 220276/2292555
Box open: Daily 12.00p.m.–6.00p.m.; 1 hour before performance
Postal: Alexanderplatz 5, Rieseburo der DDR
Prices: 2–20 Mks

With the Deutsche Oper in West Berlin and the Staatsoper in the East, the Komische Oper is the third important operatic centre in Berlin. It opened in 1947 when the occupying Soviet authorities surrendered the old Metropol Theatre (used for operetta and revue), to the ex-actor and producer Walter Felsenstein (1901–75). Situated parallel to the Unter den Linden, it was reconstructed in 1966 to accommodate new rehearsal studios, storage rooms, and offices. The auditorium which was built in the nineteenth century, is neo-rococo in style, but it is now surrounded by staircases, foyers and corridors in a grimmer and more austere modernist vein.

No other opera house has perhaps ever been so completely governed by the personality and intentions of one man as was the Komische Oper under Felsenstein. Influenced by the methods and ideas of Stanislavsky, Marxism, and Brecht, he created a unique form of operatic production, where the quest for the essential dramatic truth superseded all other considerations. The extraordinary subtlety and force of the results depended largely on the enormously long rehearsal periods on which Felsenstein insisted. He achieved a totally integrated ensemble and made actors out of singers. For the lover of bel canto or pure vocalism, the Komische Oper has never had much to offer: the orchestra is second-rate, the conductors of little significance, and international stars are never invited. But for those who appreciate opera staged by incisive theatrical intelligences, it has offered some incomparably rich experiences.

Felsenstein's productions ranged from the tragic to the whimsical and even frivolous: he opened the Komische Oper with *Die Fledermaus*, and later successes included Britten's *A Midsummer Night's Dream* (1961), Offenbach's *Tales of Hoffmann* (1958), *The Magic Flute* (1954), *Otello* (1959), and *Carmen* (1972).

After Felsenstein's death in 1975, Joachim Herz and Götz Friedrich continued to maintain his production techniques and standards. They also introduced modern operas such as Henze's *Der Junge Lord*, Reimann's *Lear* and Gershwin's *Porgy and Bess* into the repertoire. An adventurous repertoire continues to be the Komische Oper's policy under the present director Harry Kupfer who has invited westerners to produce opera there. David Pountney and his designer David Fielding staged an eccentric *Iolanthe* in 1984 with Gilbert's highly idiomatic texts translated into German. Since then a Mozart cycle begun with, *Entführung* and has continued with *Così* (1984), *The Magic Flute* (1985) and *Figaro* (1986), all produced by Kupfer himself with the stress being put on characterization. Singers in the present company include Werner Enders, Eva-Maria Bundschuh and Friederike Wulff-Apelt.

Deutsche Staatsoper, East Berlin

Unter den Linden 7, East Berlin

Director: Gunther Rinkiis
Season: September–July
Productions: 20, 5 new
Performances: Varies
Capacity: 1452
Ballet: 4 or 5 per season

Box Office: 20 54 556
Box open: Weekdays 12.00–6.30p.m.,
Sundays and hols 4.00–6.00p.m.
Postal: Via agency Zentraker Besucherdierist
der Berliner Buhnen
Prices: 2–16 Marks

Unter den Linden, the great boulevard through the heart of old Berlin once enjoyed the fame of the Champs Elysees, Piccadilly, and Fifth Avenue. Today it comes to an abrupt halt at the Brandenburg Gate in the Berlin Wall. Too few visitors find their way here, in the Russian sector, to the magnificently restored opera house 'under the lime trees'.

Home of East Germany's premier opera company, the present building is the fourth on the site, and has retained in outline and detail the proportions of von Knobelsdorff's original theatre commissioned by Frederick the Great, and swiftly erected between 1741 and 1743. It opened even before its lavish rococo interior had been completed, with a new work by its first Kapellmeister, Carl Heinrich Graun, *Cesare e Cleopatra*. This was followed by a setting of Metastasio's *La Clemenza di Tito* with music by the Dresden composer Johann Adolf Hasse. A contemporary report relates 'in its conception, such an excess of splendour and order reigns that I was quite dazzled when I first saw opera performed in the house: it was called Cleopatra e Cesare (sic)'. Sets and costumes for the two opening productions are said to have come to 210,000 thalers and the daily bill for candles to 3,000, huge sums when compared to an average weekly wage of one silver thaler.

As the building's classical facade suggests, Frederick intended to create a temple for the lyric arts. The influence of Palladio can be seen in the imposing colonnaded portico surmounted by a bas relief above which stand Apollo flanked by Thalia and Melpomene, the muses of comedy and tragedy.

Yet, though the architectural splendour was universally admired, it was some time before it attracted the musicians who could establish it as an important musical centre. Neither Graun nor his successor, Johann Friedrich Reichardt, could rival Hasse's company in Dresden, which had earlier benefitted from the presence of Handel's prima donna, Faustina Bordoni, Hasse's wife. Not until the emergence of Gertrud Mara, the first internationally celebrated German prima donna, in 1771, could Berlin boast an artist of major renown.

The early nineteenth century saw a fruitful association with the Berlin architect and painter Karl Freidrich Schinkel whose theatre designs, especially those for the famous *Magic Flute* of the 18 January, 1816, have passed into the annals of operatic history. In 1821 the first performance of Carl Maria von Weber's *Der Freischütz* took place at Schinkel's superb new Schauspielhaus, razed to the ground during the Second World War but now rebuilt as East Berlin's principal concert hall.

At about this time Gasparo Spontini, the Italian composer of the Parisian Grand Operas *La Vestale* and *Fernand Cortez*, took over the musical direction, remaining in office until 1841. Just over a year after Giacomo Meyerbeer and Felix Mendelssohn were appointed jointly to take responsibility for the house's repertoire, it burnt down, on the night of August 18th, 1843, after a performance by a visiting Hanoverian theatre company. By September 1st rebuilding had already started, closely following von Knobeldorff's original designs, and the theatre reopened on December 7th, 1844 with Meyerbeer's *Ein Feldlager in Schleisien*. Other highlights of the period included the Berlin première of Richard Wagner's *Rienzi*, conducted by the composer himself on October 24th, 1847, and the first performance of Otto Nicolai's *The Merry Wives of Windsor* in March 1849, only months before his premature death.

In the three succeeding decades, under Botho von Hulsen, the 'opera circus' favoured the Italian and French operas, and Verdi's works took precedence over those of his exact contemporary, Wagner. However, between 1888 and 1898 Joseph Sucher, Felix Weingartner, Karl Muck and Richard Strauss mounted the podium to restore the primacy of German works.

The great years of operatic activity here were those between 1918 and the early 1930s when Berlin collected and nurtured an ensemble of the finest German singers, including Frida Leider, Tiana Lemnitz, Lotte Lehmann, Richard Tauber, Max Lorenz, and Alexander Kipnis, under the direction of Max von Schillings the composer of the now-forgotten *Mona Lisa* and Erich Kleiber, who conducted the world première of Alban Berg's *Wozzeck* on 14 December, 1924.

The rise of Nazism drove many of Berlin's stars into exile, including Kleiber and Otto Klemperer, who had joined the conducting staff after the closure of his own opera company the Kroll Oper, one of Europe's most progressive companies in repertoire and staging. Freidelind Wagner, the composer's granddaughter, wrote of a moving performance of *The Magic Flute* given in the presence of Hitler: 'Leo Blech conducted and Alexander Kipnis sang Sarastro. Both of them Jews. As we entered the Intendant's box, I became aware of an air of tension, and felt as nervous as the artists. In the box opposite, I saw Otto Klemperer sitting, his face betraying his great anxiety. When the lights went out and Blech took his place on the podium, the public gave him an ovation such as I have never heard before or since in this otherwise complacent theatre . . . At this moment at least, an assembly of Germans had courage to make plain their sympathy for a Jew.'

Well before the outbreak of war, most of the Jews, Kipnis and Tauber among them, had fled from Berlin. Under the administration of Heinz Tietjen, the opera house took care to tread a careful path and succeeded in not offending Goering who was directly responsible for the artistic policies of the house. Only Wilhelm Fürtwangler, albeit reluctantly, and Herbert von Karajan remained to safeguard the musical standards of the theatre. It was bombed in 1941, but quickly rebuilt and reopened with a famous performance of *Die Meistersinger* conducted by Fürtwängler. Less than two years later Goering closed all principal theatres of the Reich and in early 1945 the building again fell victim to a bomb. During the decade during which it was reconstructed the Deutsche Staatsoper reaffirmed the traditions of the ensemble but, sadly, without many of the great German singers. After Kleiber's refusal to take on the musical direction in 1955, ostensibly because the original inscription had been replaced with the words Deutsche Staatsoper over the colonnade, Franz Konwitschny remoulded the company, though many of the best singers chose to go to the West after the building of the Wall in 1961 and to the other Berlin opera house, the Deutsche Oper, on the site of the old City Opera in Charlottenburg.

Today the Deutsche Staatsoper presents a wide repertory of predominantly German works, from Mozart and Weber to Beethoven, Wagner, Strauss and some contemporary East German composers. Some of these can be seen in the radical productions of Ruth Berghaus and Harry Kupfer, now chief producer at East Berlin's more theatre-conscious Komische Oper. At the Staatsoper, productions tend to be more conservative and the singing varies, with a stronger contingent of men – Theo Adam and Peter Schreier are resident stars – than women. Though some dramatic roles have become difficult to cast from ensemble strength, the house can still mount performances of high musical quality. The repertory includes some rarities which certainly justify the detour into East Berlin: Pfitzner's *Palestrina*, Schreker's *Der Schmied von Gent*, and the works of Paul Dessau, commissioned for the theatre, *Die Verurteilung des Lukullus* and *Einstein*. Among the many interesting productions here, Kupfer's *Salome* with Josephine Barstow stands out as the best of East Germany's special brand of music theatre.

Even though it can be hard to obtain advance information about the Staatsoper's programme, it is publicised in the West Berlin newspapers, and it is usually possible to buy the extremely reasonably priced tickets the day of the performance, especially if the opera is not one of the great Strauss or Wagner works.

The Deutsche Staatsoper, East Berlin (photo: BBC Hulton Picture Library)

Dresden Semper Oper

8010 Dresden, Theaterplatz 2

Director: Dr. Gerd Schönfelder
Musical Director: Joachim Herz
Season: September–June
Productions: 13, 7 new
Performances: Varies
Capacity: 1,200
Ballet: 4 or 5 per season

Box Office: (51) 48423 33
Box open: Mon 2.00p.m.–6.00p.m.; Tues 10.00a.m.–5.00p.m.; Wed closed; Thurs 1.00p.m.–5.00p.m.; Fri 1.00p.m.–3.00p.m.
Postal: P.O. Box PS 450
Prices: 75M for tourist; 6M–18M for East Germans; some tickets available 1 hour before performance

Many important names are connected with opera in Dresden. The kapellmeister Heinrich Schütz, the four-hundredth anniversary of whose birth was celebrated in 1985, was one of the earliest composers to make an impact: his opera *Daphne* (1627) was the first to be written in the German language, countering the contemporary predilection for Italian opera.

But German opera developed slowly: when the Grosses Opernhaus at the King's Castle, opened to the public in 1770, it was for the performance of German *singspiel* written by composers such as Hiller and Benda. In 1813 the city was briefly inhabited by the celebrated novelist, critic, composer and conductor E. T. A. Hoffmann, who arrived as musical director of a local opera troupe. Hoffmann's idealistic vision of German opera as a self-contained work of art, in which all elements merge into one another and are variously absorbed, anticipate the ideas of Richard Wagner. Hoffman's contemporary, the official court composer Carl Maria von Weber purposefully continued the struggle for German musical autonomy by encouraging performances of Mozart, Beethoven and Gluck operas. He also introduced the inhabitants of Dresden to his own works *Der Freischütz* and *Euryanthe* in the early 1820s. Based on German folklore, *Der Freischütz* remains the most frequently performed opera in Dresden, having been staged there over one thousand two hundred times.

With Weber's early death in 1826, it might have seemed that the cause of German opera was lost. However, within two decades, a true successor appeared from Leipzig with a highly successful opera: Richard Wagner's *Rienzi* was given in 1842 at the new Royal Saxon Opera House designed by Gottfried Semper. Taking up a position as kapellmeister the following year, Wagner was then in a position to produce the premières of his *Flying Dutchman* (1843) and *Tannhäuser* (1845), while at the same time working on *Lohengrin*, and the librettos for the *Ring* and *Die Meistersinger*. His conducting, notably of Gluck, Weber (whom he once described as 'the greatest man alive') and Beethoven, was considered exemplary. But his days at Dresden were numbered: obsessed with the idea of unifying the fragmented states of Germany into a single republic, he became involved in revolutionary activity and was hounded out of the country after the failure of the 1849 uprising in the city.

With Wagner's departure, Dresden's operatic life went swiftly into a decline, exacerbated by the partial destruction of the Semper opera house by fire in 1869. A temporary wooden structure served for a few years, until the opening of the rebuilt opera house in 1878 heralded a second great era. The conductor Ernest von Schuch became the guiding light of the house; he was general director from 1889 and 1914. Under his regime the later works of Wagner and Verdi were championed, and an impressive tradition of presenting the premières of Strauss operas was initiated with *Feuersnot* in 1901 – continuing with *Salome* (1905), *Elektra* (1909) and *Der Rosenkavalier* (1911). In all, during Schuch's forty-two-year association with Dresden, fifty-one world premières and one hundred and seventeen other operas were added to the repertory.

In 1914 Schuch was succeeded by Fritz Reiner, who in turn gave way in 1922 to Fritz Busch. Important premières in the ensuing years included Busoni's *Doktor Faust* and Hindemith's *Cardillac* (both 1925), Weill's *Der Protagonist* (1926), as well as Strauss's *Intermezzo* (1924) and *Die Aegyptische Helena* (1928).

The staging of Strauss's *Die Schweigsame Frau* in 1935 however was frustrated after only four performances: the Nazis banned the piece, objecting to the librettist Stefan Zweig's Jewish origins. By this time the musical director was Karl Böhm, and the company included an impressive array of singers, such as Meta Seinemeyer, Richard Tauber, Max Lorenz, Paul Schoeffler and Gottlob Frick.

In 1945, the opera house was again destroyed, this time by the Allies' saturation bombing. The company managed to survive, performing in halls and theatres before moving into the Schauspielhaus in 1948. Despite the obvious difficulties of such a position, the company managed to maintain high standards under a further succession of distinguished musical directors – Joseph Keilberth, Rudolf Kempe, Lovro von Matacic and Kurt Sanderling. Three great singers of recent years nurtured by Dresden are the tenors, Peter Schreier, Rainer Goldberg and the baritone Olaf Bauer.

In 1975 plans were announced for the reconstruction of the Semper opera house, after various architectural plans came to light, allowing for its exact reproduction down to the finest details. For the opening night in 1985, the General Administrator Gerd Schönfelder chose Dresden's 'signature' opera *Der Freischütz*, with a cast including Theo Adam, a long-term star of the company and now also one of its directors. The new director of productions is Joachim Herz, famous for his work at the Komische Oper in East Berlin and productions at the English and Welsh National Operas.

Dresden has a summer festival which features many visiting companies from all over Europe, including those from Lodz, Kiev, Leipzig, Rome and Warsaw, making it a particularly worthwhile event for those interested in what is happening musically in Eastern Europe. Visiting ballet companies have recently included the Royal Ballet from London, the Kirov company and the Pina Bausch Dance Theatre from Wuppertal. Demand for tickets is intense, and they will usually only be issued to those with hotel reservations.

Hungarian State Theatre, Budapest
1373 Budapest VI, Nepkoztalsasag utja 22

Director: E Petrovics
Artistic Director: M. Szilagyi
Season: Mid Sept–mid June
Productions: 22, 4 new
Performances: 3 of each
Capacity: 1,261, with 82 removable seats
Ballet: 14 per season

Box Office: (361) 312 550
Box open: 10a.m. to the beginning of performance (except lunch 2.00–2.30p.m.)
Postal: Postafiok 503
Prices: 10–120 FTS (more expensive when finest singers are performing). Season tickets for students
Advance Booking: Tickets can be reserved through the official tourist office IBUSZ at double rates

Recordings: Der König von Saba, Nerone,
Tosca, Medea (all HUNGARATON)

As one of the two capitals of the former Austro-Hungarian Empire, Budapest has enjoyed the status of a great musical centre for centuries. In the realm of opera, however, Hungary has established native traditions only comparatively recently, from the mid-1830's to be precise. Until that time most public theatrical activity had been in the language of the Imperial masters: the German Theatre opened in Pest in 1812 to the music of Beethoven – his overture and incidental music to *King Stephen* – but only much later did opera, predominantly of the Italian variety, become a regular element of public entertainment in the city.

With the foundation of the National Theatre in 1837, work in the vernacular became the norm. establishing a local operatic tradition which has persisted by and large until the present day. The National Theatre specialized in work of a popular nature – folksy plays enlivened with national music – but eventually, under the direction of the Hungarian conductor and composer, Ferenc Erkel, also the composer of the Hungarian national anthem, 'classical' operas gradually took hold of the public imagination. Erkel himself conducted the first Hungarian performances of Rossini's *Barber of Seville* in this theatre before the world premières of his own operas, *Bánk Bán* and *Hunyadi László* and the early works of Verdi and Wagner.

In 1873 the city held a competition for the designs of a grand opera house which was won by the Hungarian architect Miklós Ybl whose plans were realized between 1875 and 1884. The house remains one of the most important examples of late nineteenth century Hungarian architecture, a temple of opera and ballet to rival the imperial theatres of Vienna, Paris and Berlin. Ybl's exterior is characteristic of its age, bulky yet ornately decorated. Before the façade, the covered porch shelters a carriage-way above which, on either side, two of the four relevant Muses – Erato, Thalia, Terpsichore and Melpomene – stand watch. On the upper balustrade statues of the great opera composers look down on the square. Over the years the originals deteriorated to the point where it was deemed necessary to replace them with new models: Monteverdi, Scarlatti, Gluck, Mozart, Rossini, Donizetti, Wagner, Verdi, Gounod, Bizet and the nationalist composers Glinka, Musorgsky, Moniuszko and Smetana, all of them seen through the eyes of modern Hungarian sculptors.

The lavishly decorated interiors of the recently renovated building evoke the typically social atmosphere of the nineteenth-century opera house. The spacious foyers and imposing staircases are adorned with classical reliefs, mosaics and murals, frescoes on mythological themes and allegorical paintings. But the focal point of the building is the magnificent gold and maroon auditorium in the customary horse-shoe layout. An unusual feature of Ybl's design is the terracing of the tiers with each level slightly recessed to give an impression of the interior rising towards the beautiful round ceiling painted by Károly Lotz surmounted by a chandelier.

The opera house opened on September 27th 1884, not with Erkel's new opera *King Stephen*, which was not completed in time, but with a hybrid programme consisting of the overture to Erkel's earlier *Hunyadi László* and the first acts of both *Bánk Bán* and Wagner's *Lohengrin*, performed three days later in its entirety. From its beginnings, the Hungarian State Opera modelled its operations on the well-worn lines of the German repertoire system, playing up to forty-five operas and ballets during the inaugural season and singing opera only in the vernacular. Even guest artists were required to learn their roles in Hungarian.

Later, around the turn of the century the rules relaxed to accommodate performances by international stars: Budapest heard the great *coloratura*, Marcella Sembrich as Lucia, Rosina and Violetta, Lilli Lehmann as Norma and Beethoven's Leonore. In 1907 Caruso sang Radames there and other famous singers included Emma Calve, Emmy Destinn, Selma Kurz, Luisa Tettrazini, Mattia Battistini, Alessandro Bonco, Adam Didur, Riccardo Stracciari and Titta Ruffo.

Erkel presided over the musical performances from the opening of the theatre until 1888 when he was succeeded as director by the young Gustav Mahler. As he was to later in Vienna, Mahler supervised great improvements in the standard of preparation and production, insisting on the value of the ensemble. During his reign at the State Opera, he expanded the Wagner repertoire to include the first Hungarian productions of *Das Rheingold* and *Die Walküre*, but he left Budapest in 1891 as a result of a disagreement with the Intendant Count Zichy before he could mount a complete production of the *Ring*.

After Mahler's departure, the house fell into temporary decline but with the appointment of Arthur Nikisch, future chief conductor of the Berlin Philharmonic Orchestra, the fortunes of the opera revived. The years of the Nikisch regime saw important visits by famous foreign composers: Massenet and Delibes conducted their own operas, Puccini came to supervise the Hungarian première of his *Manon Lescaut* – as he did later those of *Madame Butterfly* and *La Fanciulla del West* – and Mascagni achieved a personal success with his *Cavalleria Rusticana* which secured a lasting place for his works in the repertoire of the Hungarian State Theatre.

Although native works have always occupied a special position in the theatre's programme even to this day, only one can be said to have passed into the international repertoire: Bartók's unique duodrama *Bluebeard's Castle* of 1918 which marks perhaps the pinnacle of the State Theatre's creative achievement in the field of opera. Ironically, Bartók's theatre works – including the two ballets *The Miraculous Mandarin* and *The Wooden Prince* – have found more congenial homes in the world's concert halls than its opera houses. Great Hungarian works were not, however, the only musical highlights of

The Hungarian State Theatre, Budapest (photo: Mansell Collection)

the inter-war period. Alongside the resident ensemble international star singers and conductors continued to appear: Maria Caniglia, Gina Cigna, Maria Jeritza, Ebe Stignani Beniamino Gigli Alexander Kipnis, Giacomo Lauri-Volpi, Aureliano Pertile, Friedrich Schorr and Richard Tauber walked the boards while Sir Thomas Beecham, Wilhelm Furtwängler, Erich Kleiber and Fritz Reiner mounted the podium. Richard Strauss came to conduct performances of his own operas.

After the Second World War – the house had been closed by the Nazis like so many of the Reich's great theatres on 23rd December 1944 – Otto Klemperer ushered in another golden age along the lines of the Mahler era. Reaffirming the ensemble ethic, he directed – both in the pit and on stage – memorable performances of Mozart, Beethoven and Wagner, some of which have survived in radio recordings now available commercially. Like his great mentor, Klemperer proved a controversial director. A tape exists of a *Lohengrin* performance he conducted in which he is heard to rebuke the audience ('Impudence! Impudence') for applauding the tenor after 'In fernem Land' and drowning Wagner's music!

Since 1951, the opera company has also had the use of the smaller Municipal Theatre – now Erkel Theatre – for medium-scale works. During the sixties the international repertory of the house was substantially extended to include, alongside the Romantic Italian French, German and Russian works, both of Alban Berg's operas, Kurt Weill's *Mahagonny*, Stravinsky's *The Rake's Progress*, Gershwin's *Porgy and Bess*, the major operas of both Shostakovich and Prokofiev and five by Benjamin Britten.

In recent years, too, Hungary's outward-looking foreign policy has resulted in mutually beneficial exchanges of singers and conductors. Many leading Western musicians have appeared at the State Theatre which has also served as an important nursery of high quality Hungarian talent. Among the singers and conductors whose careers began in Budapest and who subsequently travelled throughout the world, the following deserve especial mention: Rosette Anday, Mária Németh, Eszther Réthy, Endre Koreh – a famous 'Viennese' Osmin – Kálmán Pataky – the tenor who appeared as Glyndebourne's first Don Ottavio as Kilomon von Pataky – Ferenc Fricsay, Antal Doráti, Georg Solti and István Kertész. Still more recently, three Hungarian sopranos have won wide international acclaim and continue to sing at the State Opera: Éva Marton, Sylvia Sass and Ilona Tokody. Enlightened artistic policies and commitment to the ensemble make the Hungarian State Theatre one of the most important sources of outstanding voices in the world today.

When buying tickets from hotels or reserving them in advance through IBUSZ, one is charged double-rates, so it is therefore worthwhile going to the box-office. There are season tickets for students for Sunday performances. More than any other opera house in the Eastern bloc The Hungarian State Opera management pays out large sums in Western currency for big names and during the past two years they have invited Pavarotti (in *Bohème*) and Domingo (in *Aida*, with Russian soprana Elena Obratszova). Although the tickets prices were more expensive, the management decided to make the tickets unavailable to tourists so Hungarian audiences could enjoy these artists.

Teatr Wielki, Warsaw

00 950 Warszawa-Place Teatralni 1

Director: Arnold Juniter
Artistic Director: Robert Satanowski
Season: September–June
Productions: 30, 6 new
Performances: Varies

Box Office: (48 22) 263288/263287 day of performance/265019 groups, subscription tickets. In person at the Teatr Wielki or at 25 Jerozlimskie Av.
Box open: Mon–Sat 9.00a.m.–7.00p.m.
Postal: As above
Prices: 100–350 Zts; most expensive for foreign companies and singers
Concessions: 33% discount for children and groups

Recordings: Major works by Moniuszko, King Roger

The Teatr Wielki, or Great Theatre, designed by Antonio Corazzi who was also responsible for several other important buildings in Warsaw, opened in 1833 with Rossini's *The Barber of Seville*. At that time the director was Karol Kurpinski, a man of enormous versatility who composed several operas (his *Jadwiga, Queen of Poland* was revived recently) and introduced to Warsaw the latest works of Rossini, Donizetti, Auber, and Weber. Under his management the opera separated itself from legitimate drama, also housed in the Wielki, and artistic standards soon rose.

The cause of Polish opera received a boost with the appearance of the rousingly nationalistic *Halka* in 1848. Its composer was Stanislaw Moniuszko (1819–72), who was director of the Wielki for thirty-nine years, and who sponsored many native works, not least his own *Stasny Dvor* (The Haunted Castle, 1865). By the turn of the century the

The Teatr Wielki as it looked before the Second World War

repertoire included operas by Gluck, Mozart, Verdi, Meyerbeer, and Tchaikovsky, as well as some Polish works by Paderewski and Wieniawski. An important early twentieth-century Polish composer was Karol Szymanowski (1882–1937) whose powerful and haunting *King Roger* was premièred here in 1926.

During World War II the theatre was destroyed by bombing, leaving only the façade standing. At first only makeshift theatres and converted cinemas could be used for operatic activity in Warsaw, but by 1965 the Teatr Wielki had been restored.

The largest theatre in the world, it occupies an area of about twelve thousand square feet, and is situated in a huge square. Apart from Salzburg Festpielhaus it has the largest stage in Europe and an auditorium seating two thousand. The acoustics and lighting are excellent. The stage machinery is also very sophisticated in that a whole set can be moved upwards into the flies while another rises from below the stage, in a manner similar to that of the Met in New York. The building also houses a ballet-school, an opera studio and a theatre museum.

The dominating figure at Warsaw is Robert Satanowski, who between 1958 and 1960 worked with Felsenstein at the Komische Oper in East Berlin, while simultaneously studying with Herbert von Karajan. Satanowski, musical director since 1981, continues a policy that favours Italian and Slavic opera but seriously and deliberately neglects German opera; Warsaw has never given a *Ring* cycle and there has been no Strauss opera since the war.

Despite this, there has been more tolerance towards artistic experiment in Poland since the war than elsewhere in the Eastern bloc. This may be seen in the widespread popularity of the modernist music of Krzystof Penderecki. A number of foreign contemporary operas have also been staged, including Britten's *Midsummer Night's Dream*. Singers in the company who are familiar to western audiences include Zdzislawa Donat, Wieslaw Ochmann and Halina Lukomska.

The interior of the Teatr Wielki after the 1965 restoration

National Theatre, Bucharest

70 Gheorghe Gheorghiu Dej Boulevard, Bucharest

Director: Mr Bryncus
Season: September–June
Productions: 40, 6 new
Performances: Varies
Capacity: 1,100

Box Office: (400) 146980
Box open: Daily 10.00a.m.–1.00p.m.,
5.00p.m.–7.00p.m.
Postal: As above
Prices: 8–25 Lei

From the 1860s various attempts were made to set up a Rumanian opera company. Both George Stephănescu's Opera Romana and the Compania Lyrică Română lasted for just over twenty years before they were forced to close in 1901. An immensely talented man, Stephănescu translated librettos, wrote polemical articles and founded a school of singing whose pupils included Hariclea Darclée, later famous for creating the role of *Tosca*. For the next twenty years visiting Italian and German companies occupied the National Theatre, bringing some important singers such as Tetrazzini, Ruffo and Battistini and giving the first performances in Rumania of Wagner's *The Flying Dutchman* in 1909 and *Lohengrin* in 1910. During the occupation of World War I, the Dessau company visited the city several times to give Weber's *Oberon*, the major Mozart operas and the Rumanian première of Wagner's *Tristan und Isolde* in 1917.

Finally, in 1919, the Asociaţa Lirică Română provided the people of Rumania with a national opera company. The Queen of Rumania gave generously to this enterprise and under the composer Ion Nonna Otescu the company was inaugurated in 1920 with a performance of *Aida*. During the following seasons, guest stars were invited to sing with the opera, including the tenor Leo Slezak and the conductors Felix Weingartner and Nedbal. New Rumanian works started to appear, the best examples being those of Tiberiu Brediceanu, who directed the Bucharest Opera during the war, and Marţian Negrea, a pupil of Franz Schmidt. The latter's *Marin Pescarul* (1934), a fervently nationalistic work has become the most popular of all Rumanian operas.

Earthquakes and bombings wrecked the old theatre. The present building which could be described as neo-classical in style was designed by O. Diocescu, and opened in 1953 with a performance of Tchaikovsky's *The Queen of Spades*. Attempting to imitate its predecessor, the auditorium is a pleasant Rococo-style structure generously decorated with gilt, marble and chandeliers.

A high standard of singing has long been associated with the Bucharest opera as evident in the versatility and artistry of such artists as Ileana Cotrubas and Nelly Miriciou, although unfortunately for Bucharest, both have now left the country. The Rumanian government is planning to build a massive new opera house as part of a complete restructuring of the city. Meanwhile performances continue at the National Theatre complex, which includes facilities for ballet and drama. As is the case in many Eastern European countries, the best way to obtain tickets is via tour guides or through hotel receptions.

Kirov Opera House

1 Teatralnaya Ploshchad, 190000 Leningrad

Director: Maxim Eduardovich Kristin
Artistic Director: Yuri Temirkanov
Season: September–July (including White Nights Festival)
Productions: 25, 5 new
Performances: Varies
Capacity: 1,780
Ballet: 18

Box Office: 216 1211
Box open: Daily 11.00a.m.–7.00p.m.
Postal: No postal booking; further information from Intourist
Prices: Average 25 roubles for tourists Maximum of 4 roubles at box office.

Opera in the former capital of the Czarist Empire dates from the early years of the Russian Englightment; the era of Peter the Great's reforms and westernisation of a largely medieval ethnic culture in the first half of the eighteenth century. Italian operas were first performed in St. Petersburg by troupes of Italian singers in the 1720s and by the middle of the century, the first opera on a Russian text, a version of Cephalus and Procris by a now forgotten Italian composer, reached the stage of the Court Theatre. Throughout the latter half of the century, the Imperial Court became a mecca for European artists, particularly French *littérateurs* and Italian musicians. Among those who served as musical directors and composers to the Russian court were Galuppi, and Paisiello (whose once popular *Il Barbiere di Siviglia* was premiered on October 26th 1782 in St. Petersburg).

The first public theatre, the Bolshoi Kamenniy (Great Stone) Theatre, opened in 1757 and continued in use until the end of the nineteenth century. It was here that the nationalist movement began with the first performances of Glinka's *Life for the Czar* on December 9th 1836 and *Ruslan and Ludmilla* exactly six years later. By the middle of the nineteenth century, the needs of the Imperial Court Opera had far outgrown the Bolshoi Theatre. Its replacement, then the Maryinsky Theatre (known as the Kirov since 1935) witnessed the first performances of Verdi's *La Forza del Destino* – the Italian composer accepted a commission from the Court Opera only on the most generous financial terms – on November 10th 1862 with one of his favourite tenors, Enrico Tamberlik, as Alvaro; of Mussorgsky's *Boris Godunov* on November 8th 1874 – the cast included Ivan Melnikov in the title role, Vladimir Vasilyev as Pimen and Ossip Petrov as Varlaam – and the official première of *Khovanschina* in 1911, conducted by the English musical director Albert Coates and starring Fyodor Shalyapin as Ivan Khovansky; five of Rimsky-Korsakov's most popular operas – *The Maid of Pskov, May Night, The Snow Maiden, Christmas Eve,* and *The Legend of the Invisible City of Kitezh* – had their first performances between 1873 and 1907 and four of Tchaikovsky's, including *The Queen of Spades* (1890) with its St. Petersburg setting, were premièred there. During this great period of the theatre's creative productivity, the ensemble included singers such as Nikolai Figner and his wife, Medea Mei (the first Hermann and Liza) Elisaveta Lavrovskaya and Stravinsky's father, Fyodor. Later the young Shalyapin and Sobinov joined the company.

Since the Revolution and the establishment of Moscow as the capital of the Soviet

The interior of the Kirov Opera House (photo: Novosti Press Agency)

Union, the Maryinsky Theatre's reputation has receded in favour of Moscow's Bolshoi, though, like that great theatre, it is presently renowned more for its ballet than its opera company. However, the notorious scandal instigated by Stalin surrounding the first production of Shostakovitch's *Lady Macbeth of the Mtensk District* at Leningrad's Maly Theatre in 1934, in which the opera was described as 'a muddle instead of music', completely curtailed all modernist tendencies in both cities. As with all theatrical activity in the USSR today, productions rarely depart from tradition and sets tend to follow the original stage directions with a slavish opulence that can be impressive in the grandest of Russian operas.

In recent years, the artistic direction of Yuri Temirkanov, a well-known orchestral conductor in the West, has given the Kirov Opera an injection of artistic purpose with new stagings of the great Russian classics – some staged as well as conducted by Temirkanov himself – and an intake of bright young singers, including Nikolai Okhotnikov, Yuri Marusin and Irina Bogachova and Alexander Chernov, all of whom have appeared with the company in the West.

It is possible to get hold of tickets to the Kirov directly from the box office situated in the building. However, it is still advisable to use the services provided by travel companies which offer package tours which usually include tickets to at least one performance, or through Intourist offices. The best time to go to Leningrad is undoubtedly the White Nights Festival, a ten-day period of performances at the Kirov and Maly Theatres (at Irkutsk Square, 1) of opera and ballet as well as concerts.

The Kirov Opera House (photo: Novosti Press Agency)

The Bolshoi Theatre (photo: Novosti Press Agency)

Bolshoi Theatre

Ploschad Sverdlova 1, Moscow

Director: Yuri Simonov
Season: September–July
Productions: 30, 3 new
Performances: Varies
Capacity: 2,100

House Number: (7 095) 292 6534
Booking: Information from Intourist
Prices: 1 – 3.30 roubles; more for tourists

Recordings: All major works of Tchaikovsky, Glinka, Mussorgsky, Borodin, Rimsky-Korsakov and Prokofiev; Dead Souls by Schedrin; Aida, Traviata and Rigoletto

The first opera house in Russia, the Operny Dom, opened in 1742 with a performance of the Metastasian opera *La Clemenza di Tito* almost a decade after the appearance of the first visiting troupes from Italy. The history of the Bolshoi (meaning 'Grand') Theatre dates from 1776 when the Petrovsky Theatre was built by the aristocrat Prince Urusov, an opera lover who had managed to secure the rights to all theatrical performances in Moscow for ten years. He invited an English impresario and ex-acrobat Michael Maddox to assist him and opened the theatre in 1780. It was there that most of the early Russian operas were given, including works by Matinsky, Pashkevitch and Zorin. In October 1805, the Petrovsky Theatre burned to the ground during a rehearsal of the *Nymph of the Dneper* and the company was given temporary accommodation in Rossi's new 'Bolshoi' theatre in the Arbat district. It was not until 1825 that a new 'Bolshoi' theatre opened on the site of the old Petrovsky Theatre and the opera secured a permanent residence.

The core of the company before the turn of the century consisted of dancers and musicians from the best serf theatres in Moscow, those of the families Sheremet'yev, Yusupov, Stolipin and Apraksin, although there was a small body of professional musicians and a few students from the University. Operatic and dramatic troupes in the company were joined together as one body; the finest singers of the early years, such as Sokolovskaya, Sinyavskaya and Repina successfully performed in plays, and the actor Shusherin certainly sang a role in the *Miller, Magician, Deceiver and Matchmaker*.

In the decades following the liberation of serf actors in 1806, the institution of the Petrovsky Theatre took on a more democratic aspect and tended to look for guidance from leading intellectuals at the time, partly encouraged by the new, more liberal Tsar Alexander I. Besides Russian opera there was renewed interest in French Opera (Boieldieu, Grétry), a fashion for German fairy opera, and Italian *opera buffa* (Paisiello, Pergolesi, Cimarosa). The seminal figure at the Bolshoi under the Imperial period was the composer and pupil of John Field, Alexey Nikolayevich Verstovsky. Together with the playwright F. Kokoshkin he virtually ran the theatre until the end of the 1840's, raising the standards considerably, and actively contributing to the creation of a uniquely Russian operatic style. His best-known opera *The Tomb of Askold* established the trend towards the use of folk music and folk lore, creating a vocal style equivalent to song. Written in 1835, it was given over six hundred times in Russia during the nineteenth century and became the first Russian opera to be performed in the United

States (1869). Verstovsky's example was often alluded to during the extreme national-ism of the Stalin era and today he remains a hero of Soviet culture.

A new era for the Bolshoi began in 1842 with the first performance of Glinka's *Ivan Susanin*, renamed *A Life for the Tsar*, to be followed four years later by his second opera *Ruslan and Ludmilla*. This began an extended period of nationalist operas, whose subjects were realistic and at the same time intrinsically linked with Russian literature, particularly the works of Pushkin, Lermontov, Gogol and Ostrovsky.

In March 1853 a fire destroyed a large part of the interior and the house was rebuilt by Kavos, who took the opportunity to correct its acoustical faults. The new Bolshoi, as it now stands, was opened on August 20, 1856 with the capacity of two thousand. The auditorium is horse-shoe shaped with six tiers of boxes covered with rich gilding, handsome foyers and wide staircases and a predominantly red and gold scheme of decoration. As opposed to the grace and elegance of the Kirov Theatre in Leningrad, the Bolshoi has a majestic opulence.

The Bolshoi's ascendency continued into the reign of Alexander II when much was done to improve the training of composers and singers with the creation of Conserva-tories of Music in Moscow (1864) and Leningrad (1861). During the last two decades of the century the operas of Peter Tchaikovsky appeared more frequently and also those of the 'moguchaya kuckha' (mighty handful); Balakirev, Mussorgsky, Borodin, Cui and Rimsky-Korsakov. By now the company was producing singers of great calibre such as Semyonova, Lavrovskaya and Khokhlov, culminating in the famous bass Fyodor Shalyapin (1873–1938). With the inclusion of Tchaikovsky's *Eugene Onegin* and *Queen of Spades*, as well as Mussorgsky's *Boris Godunov* and Borodin's *Prince Igor*, the repertoire was augmented by several important productions. Simultaneously the ballet master Gorky was training a whole generation of dancers and succeeded in co-ordinating every aspect of production in the search for an epic style. Towards the end of the century a style evolved that still exists today in opera production. Typical features are the monumental sets with ultra-realistic painted backdrops, large crowd scenes, elaborate costumes and heavy-handed acting styles.

During the Revolution, the Bolshoi became subject to the jurisdiction of the People's Commission for Englightenment, whose aim was to induce the company to reach a broader cross-section of people. Inevitably, the political situation required the creation of operas that reflected either historical realism, Soviet style or the preoccupations of the common man. Thanks to the efforts of Boris Asafyev in defending the function of opera against charges of aristocratic association, the Bolshoi emerged largely unscathed and continued to employ the leading artists at a somewhat reduced salary. Though some singers decided to leave, many had no choice but to accept the new challenges being offered. During the revolutionary period stage directors were encouraged to attempt opera production and Stanislavsky, Nemirovitch-Danchenko and Meyerhold tried their hand at the media, managing to bring new life to old productions. During Stalin's period, innovation was discouraged and artists were subjected to iron discipline in their working methods. Many were also intimidated by a manipulative management who lived in constant fear of Stalin and were humiliated into doing operatic hackwork in provincial cities to satisfy the party's requirements. The thirties and forties were the most productive in socialist-realist operas, although some used old librettos for lack of

Fyodor Shalyapin (photo: BBC Hulton Picture Library)

imagination. Thus *Les Huguenots* became *The Decembrists* and *Tosca* became *Into Battle for the Commune*. The odd attempt by serious composers to be adventurous led to their immediate victimization by the party media, as exemplified by Pravda's giving the death-blow to Shostakovitch's *Lady Macbeth of Mtensk* (first performed in Leningrad) in the article 'Muddle instead of Music' although since the fifties a cautious evolution seems to have been taking place. In the post war years leading singers at the Bolshoi have included Obratzsova, Arkhipova, Atlantov, Vishnevskaya and Nesterenko, while some outstanding conductors have directed there, including Yevgeny Svetlanov, Yuri Simonov and Mark Ermler.

There is a box office where anyone can obtain tickets but more than any theatre in the world the Bolshoi is notoriously difficult to get into and since tickets are usually come by through corruption of one kind or another, a trip down there would hardly be advisable. For the tourists the best and only way to get into the theatre itself is through a tour package which usually includes tickets to at least one event. One should also be warned in advance that the second company do not usually perform in the Bolshoi Theatre but in the gargantuan Hall of Congresses in the Kremlin. An innocent visitor to the 'Bolshoi' can sometimes be led to this monstrous building which is usually used for party gatherings.

The theatre closed in June of 1986 for two years restoration work, and the whole company now performs in this auditorium. The Bolshoi offers a valuable experience for those wanting to hear unusual Russian works such as the *Maid of Pksov* by Rimsky-Korsakov or Rachmaninov's *Aleko*. There have also been some modern works 'commissioned' recently from composers such as Schedrin (*Dead Souls*) and Alexander Kholminov's *The Karamazov Brothers*. Under the superb musical direction of Yuri Simonov there have been recent attempts to improve productions with less old-fashioned lighting techniques and design. At the same time producers themselves appear to be getting a little more varied: the film director Sergei Bondarchuk's *Mazeppa* in 1987 and Obratszova's production of *Werther* (1986) with herself as Charlotte may signal the beginning of a more progressive era.

The Bolshoi Theatre (photo: Novosti Press Agency)

Palyashvili Theatre, Tbilisi

Rustaveli Prospekt, 25 Tbilisi

Director: Zyrab Lomidze
Musical Director: U. L. Palyashvili
Season: September–June
Productions: 14
Performances: Varies
Capacity: 1,061
Ballet: 12 per season

Box Office: 997586 or 997457 (Intourist)
Postal: Through Intourist, Rustaveli Prospekt
Prices: 6.50 Roubles for tourists, maximum 3 Roubles at box office

This opera house – now called the Palyashvili Theatre and named after a great Georgian composer Palyashvili (1871–1933) – is situated in the centre of Tbilisi, next to the Rustaveli Theatre on the main thoroughfare, the Rustaveli Prospect. It opened in 1851, to house the Italian opera companies that then regularly toured Russia and its neighbouring states. Only towards the end of the century did it begin to give Russian opera, as a sop to the summer tourists from Moscow and Leningrad.

With the composition of Meliton Balanchivadze's *Daredzan Tsviery* (1898) Georgian opera was born: stylistically it borrows from Russian opera, particularly the early nationalist type, assigning a major part to folk instruments and choruses. The subject-matter is characteristically patriotic in flavour and message. Vocal lines can be highly melismatic, and the harmonies often reflect the proximity of Turkey and its musical traditions.

Outside the Soviet Union, Georgian opera remains virtually unknown, but in Tbilisi, audiences flock to hear works by composers such as Andrey Balanchivadze (brother of the famous choreographer George Balanchine), Kvernadze, and Kiladze: Russian operas, on the other hand, often leave the house half-empty.

After the Revolution, the regional autonomy encouraged by Lenin gave added impetus to the cause of Georgian opera, and the company regularly tours the Southern Russian republics and has recently visited the Bolshoi in Moscow. Operetta and musicals have been incorporated into the repertoire: Lehar's *Frasquita* and Lerner and Loewe's *My Fair Lady*, for instance, were first heard in 1986. Internationally known singers whose careers have started in Tbilisi include the dramatic soprano Makvala Kavakshvili and the bass Paata Burchuladze, both known to Covent Garden and Met audiences.

The house itself is in a pseudo-Moorish style, with an arched auditorium in cream colours; the foyers and staircases feature multi-coloured stained-glass windows. It is possible for tourists to obtain tickets at the box office.

National Theatre, Belgrade

Francuska 3, Dositeyeva 2, 11000 Belgrade

Director: Verliner Lokay
Season: September–mid June
Productions: 40, 5 new
Performances: Varies
Capacity: Under construction

Box Office: (011) 626–566/628–640
Box open: Mon–Sat 10.00a.m.–12.00p.m.
and 1 hour before performance
Postal: As above
Prices: 4,000–18,000 Dinars

The first permanent company in Belgrade was formed by the composer Stanislav Binički. Having written the first Serbian opera *Na Uranku* in 1903, he was invited to direct the National Theatre in 1920. Previously there had only been visiting companies from Germany and Italy, often brought over by the Czech impresarios who, during the latter part of the nineteenth-century, dominated Serbian musical life.

With Binički's appointment, Serbian opera was in a position to develop. There was already a fine tradition in choral singing, and the influx of Russian refugees from the Bolshevik revolution also made a significant contribution. During the twenties and thirties Russian opera became extremely popular and was emulated by local composers in works such as Petar Krstie's *The Tyrant* (1928) and Peter Konjovic's *Kostaria* (1931), both strongly evincing the influence of Mussorgsky. Between 1924 and 1934 the opera was dominated by Stevan Hristić who founded the Belgrade Philharmonic and trained the first generation of Serbian singers. During his tenure important visiting artists, such as Shalyapin, Destinn and Journet, came to Belgrade; and the tours of certain foreign companies, notably La Scala, the Paris Opéra, and the Bolshoi set examples that helped to raise standards.

The National Theatre which currently houses the opera company was erected in 1869 but suffered badly from bombing in 1941. It was soon rebuilt, and in 1944, the newly appointed director Oskar Danton presented liberated Belgrade with its first opera, Tchaikovsky's *Eugene Onegin*.

Over the last twenty years, the repertoire has grown considerably and now includes the major operas of Puccini, Strauss, Berg and Shostakovich, as well as modern Serbian works. The company tours Europe regularly and has put out several recordings.

The National Theatre is presently undergoing reconstruction and will reopen, considerably altered, in 1988. Meanwhile opera and ballet continue in two separate theatres, the Zemun and Sava Centre. Many visiting artists have performed here including Placido Domingo in *Tosca* at the Sava Centre. There is a limited budget for the hiring of non-socialist singers.

SOUTH AMERICA

The Palacio de las Bellas Artes, Mexico (photo: Tony Morrison South American Pictures)

Teatro Colon, Buenos Aires

Cerrito 618, Buenos Aires 1309

Director: Ricardo Szwarcer
Season: 22 May–13 December
Productions: 12, 9 new
Performances: Varies
Capacity: 2,478
Ballet: 8 per season, 4 companies visiting

Box Office: 541 35 1430
Telex: 255 93 COLONAR
Box open: Daily 10.00a.m.–8.00p.m.
Postal: As above
Prices: 15–100 Austral
Cards: American Express, Diners
Concessions: Season ticket for students $5, reduction on Sundays for children

The first Teatro Colon was built in 1857, thirty-one years after the formation of the Argentine Republic, and it soon became an expression of newfound civic joy and cultural independence. After just three decades of prodigious activity, during which as many as thirty premières were given by French and Italian companies, the building had outlived its usefulness and was sold to a bank for a million pesos. With this money (£12,000), the Municipality agreed to put up a new theatre with greater capacity and a range of technical improvements. The general conception was agreed from the start: the new opera house would be Renaissance in style and inspiration would be drawn from the great opera houses of Vienna, Paris and Frankfurt.

The foundation stone was laid in 1890, but such were the vicissitudes encountered that the construction of the new building lasted for eighteen years. Initially these difficulties took the form of heated arguments between the various vested interests, but in 1903 events took a sinister turn when the principal architect Tamburini died and a year later his assistant Meano was murdered. A gloomy lull in the proceedings ensued before the Belgian Architect Julio Dormal was brought in to finish the job, seemingly against all odds.

The new house opened on the 25th May, 1908 with Verdi's *Aida*. The performance was not particularly distinguished but at least the opulent and extravagantly decorated building appears to have been a great success. It has a seating capacity of two thousand four hundred and seventy-eight and standing room for a further thousand people. During the early twentieth century, ten boxes on the same level as the stalls were used by families in mourning; they had bars so that the mourners could be partly hidden. Generally, the intimacy of the atmosphere belies the large size of the auditorium. The theatre is a perfect sound box, the stage is generous and back-stage facilities are good. Orchestral concerts are given by one of two orchestras residing in the Teatro Colon.

The first season, under the direction of Luigi Mancinelli brought a number of international singers to Buenos Aires. Boito's *Mefistofele* with the Russian bass Fyodor Chalyapin was given seven performances and in the following seasons, Titta Ruffo, Guiseppe de Luca and Rosina Storchio appeared regularly. The repertoire gradually admitted non-Italian and French operas, although it is interesting to note that pre-Romantic opera never succeeded, and even today Mozart is neglected: the first performance of *Idomineo*, for instance, did not take place until the 1970s. Spanish and Russian romantic opera appeared to fill the gap.

The seasons of 1912/3 were dominated by Toscanini, who for those two years acted as director for the theatre as a whole. Lack of adequate rehearsal time was a prevailing problem but it seemed that the maestro's infamous demands soon exerted their influence. Six years earlier he had shocked the public by abandoning a performance of *La Traviata* rather than succumb to audience pressure for an encore. He thus continued to raise standards of behaviour and performance while introducing a series of masterpieces to the house. The revolutionary *Tristan und Isolde*, earned Toscanini vilification in the press, although *Falstaff* and *Manon Lescaut* seem to have been accepted.

In 1914 Tulio Serafin conducted at the Colon for the first time and 1916 the French composer Camille Saint-Saëns arrived to conduct his own *Samson et Dalila* to mark the beginning of performances in the French language. Meanwhile, concerts were given by Richard Strauss, André Messager, Arthur Nikisch and Ernest Ansermet.

The greatest era for the Teatro Colon came after the First World War with the first performance in 1922 of Wagner's complete *Ring* under the direction of Felix Weingartner. Two years later, Mussorgsky's *Boris Godunov*, Borodin's *Prince Igor* and Tchaikovsky's *Queen of Spades* were added to the repertoire in the Russian language. When the management decided that *Elektra* was too short to constitute value for money, Richard Strauss reluctantly had to accept prologues in the form of two bad one act Italian operas, which he naturally refused to conduct.

During the 1925 season a first attempt was made to transfer the organization of the opera house to the Municipality, via an administrative board. The latter was dispensed with in 1931 and from then on the artistic directorate was appointed only by the Municipality. Since then the Teatro Colon has enjoyed the highest standards and remains the richest opera house on that continent, despite a political environment that is far from ideal. It has played host to the greatest singers, conducters, orchestras and ballet companies. The first Argentine operas appeared towards the end of the nineteenth century, in an Italianate style and usually on popular subjects. Since that time they have appeared regularly at the Teatro Colon. There has been controversy over the fact that foreign artists rather than Argentinian soloists are favoured by the opera. Recently, foreign producers have tended to favour Germans such as Robert Oswald, Ernst Prettgen and Karel Jernek, although Ana Maria Gonzáles, a local singer, has managed to achieve recognition in the house.

Teatro Municipal, Rio de Janeiro

Ave Rio Branco, Rio de Janeiro

Director: Dalah Archcar
Season: March–December
Productions: 5
Performances: 25 of each
Capacity: 2357

Box Office: (21) 224 2895
Box open: Daily during season 10.00a.m.–
10.00p.m.
Postal: As above
Prices: 150–12,000 Cruzados
Concessions: Tickets at 150 Cruzados for
students

Operatic life in Rio de Janeiro only developed when the Portuguese Court was transfered to Brazil after the Peninsular War in 1809–14. Encouraged by the Royal family, Manuel Luiz was called upon to give early examples of Portuguese opera such as the *opera buffa, L'oro non Compra Amore,* and some of the most recent Italian works by composers such as Paisiello and Cimarosa.

The first national company was formed in 1857 for the purpose of maintaining this type of repertoire, supplemented by some French *opéra-comiques* and Spanish *zarzuelas.* Meanwhile, indigenous opera was gaining popularity: the first important Brazilian opera composer Carlo Gomes, won a scholarship to study with Lauro Rossi in Italy before making a triumphant return to Brazil. His *Lo Schiavo* (1889) was given to great acclaim at the Teatro Real de San João and the earlier *O Guarani* (1870) remains one of the few Brazilian operas to have been given in European houses. For Italian opera, the company invited famous singers from across the Atlantic to join the ensemble, such as Enrico Tamberlik and Rosina Stolz.

The company moved into the new Teatro Municipal in 1909 and has remained there ever since, giving a repertoire that includes the major Italian, German, French and Russian classics. Brazilian opera has developed simultaneously and is best illustrated by the works of Hector Villa-Lobos (*Jesus, Yerma*). Other highlights of the operatic scene in Rio include an explosion of the infamous rivalry between Maria Callas and Renata Tebaldi; Tebaldi sang there in the early part of her career and was appreciated in Rio even before she had been appropriately recognized in Europe. In 1979 there was a new production of *La Traviata* by Zeffirelli with Maria Chiara and Franco Bonisolli; and a successful production in 1983 of Janáček's *Jenůfa*, the first in Brazil, has paved the way for plans for a further two productions of Janáček's operas.

In one of the most unusual situations, deep in the heart of the Amazon Jungle, the opera house at Manaus stands as a monument to the growth of the rubber industry which took place during the latter part of the last century. The decision to build it was originally a governmental one, presumably to please the nouveau riche and although the whole project may seem tainted with 'folie de grandeur', the opera house enjoyed a hey-day for more than two decades. The foundation stone was laid in 1881 but the strict demands of the architect, who asked that the building be raised several feet to give it better views of the jungle, caused long delays and it wasn't opened until 1896 – with a performance of *La Gioconda* given by the Great Italian Lirico Company. Visiting companies continued to come – for drama as well as opera – and for a while money seemed to be no object. Sarah Bernhardt's only appearance (as Phèdre) is reported to have been a major event, although one imagines anything must have broken the monotony of being in such a remote area.

The opera house stands in Sebastian Square in the centre of what is now a large town. It is obvious that the Brazilian architect was clearly aware of the current European trends, particularly Art Nouveau as seen in the finer details of the interior. In other respects this small building with a capacity of only eight hundred attempts to emulate the great Neo-Renaissance opera houses of Europe.

At the moment there are no operatic performances there, although there are plans to change this in the near future since renovation work was completed in 1986. One can, however, hear orchestral concerts and recitals.

The Opera House at Manaus (photo: Tony Morrison South American Pictures)

Teatro Municipal, Santiago

Agustinas 794, Santiago, Chile

Director: Andres Rodrigez
Season: March–December
Productions: 5, 4 new
Performances: 6 of each
Capacity: 1,420, no standing room
Ballet: 6 per season
Concerts: 12 per season

Box Office: 330752–712900
Telex: 440407 TEMUN CZ
Box open: Daily 10.00a.m.–7.00p.m.
Postal: Casilla 18, Santiago, Chile
Cards: VISA, Diners
Concessions: For students

The independence gained by Chile in 1827 completely changed the cultural life in the capital city of Santiago; there was a spectacular growth in secular music of all kinds, although by far the most popular form was opera. As in the other major centres in Latin America, the first operatic seasons, coming in Chile's case in 1830, were dominated by Rossini, Donizetti, Bellini and Mercandante and by the 1850s, when the opera was established at the Teatro de la República, there were regular seasons involving sometimes as many as sixty performances a year. In 1857 the new Teatro Municipal was inaugurated with Verdi's *Ernani* and from that time opera seasons have alternated with Zarzuelas, a Spanish form of opera dating from the seventeenth century, ballets, orchestral concerts and recitals. However, the first permanent ensembles were not established at this house until the 1950s when the Orquestra Filarmónica was founded by Juan Matteucci.

Now the Teatro Municipal gives around five productions a year and can afford to engage international stars and occasionally foreign producers. Rosalind Plowright's *Norma* and June Anderson's Violetta in *La Traviata* were highlights of the 1987 season, and with so few productions a year there is very little room in a country of conservative tastes to expand the repertoire adventurously. Most of the standard classics of Italian French and German Romantic opera, however, have graced the stage of this beautiful and ornate neo-Renaissance opera house.

Opera Nacional, Mexico City
Ave Hidalgo 1-3er, Piso, C.P. 06050 Mexico, D.F.

Director: Enrique Diemecke
Season: September–June
Productions: 8 to 10
Performances: 4 to 8 of each

Box Office: 512 50 81 Ext. 141/116
Box open: Mon–Sat 11.30a.m.–3.00p.m.,
5.00–8.30p.m.; Sun 10.30a.m.–1.00p.m.,
4.00–6.30p.m.
Postal: As above
Prices: 1,200–5,000 Pesos
Concessions: For students and senior citizens

After the Teatro Colon in Buenos Aires, the Mexico City Opera at the Palacio de las Bellas Artes is the most important in Latin America. It has recently produced some fine singers, notably the tenors Francesco Araiza and Placido Domingo, who made his debut there in Caballero's zarzuela *Gigantes y Cabezudos* in 1957. The history of the opera in the city can be traced back to the opening of the Teatro Coliseo in 1733 where *opera buffa* was regularly given by visiting Italian companies. The première in Latin America of Paisiello's *Barbiere de Siviglia* was given here in 1806.

After Mexico gained its independence in the 1820s, operatic life intensified: on the one hand Italian Romantic opera became popular through the visits of the famous Garcia Company led by the tenor Manuel Garcia which, despite being robbed of a considerable amount of money by bandits en route, succeeded in opening the 1827 season with Rossini's *Barber of Seville* with Garcia singing Almaviva. On the other hand native Mexican operas flourished, as exemplified by Paiagua's *Catalina de Guisa*, (1859), Morales's *Romeo e Julieta*, (1863) and Ortega's *Guatimotzin* (1871), which was sung at its first performance by the Mexican-born prima donna Angela Peralta and the celebrated Italian tenor Enrico Tamberlik.

In 1887 a pirated version of Verdi's *Otello* was given, orchestrated from a vocal score by a local composer: this was the first performance of the work outside Italy. At the same time the work of Wagner, Saint-Saëns and Massenet were introduced into the Italian-dominated repertoire.

After the Revolution of 1910, foreign companies feared for their safety in coming to Mexico City, although there were several bull-ring recitals by singers as important as Caruso and Ruffo to audiences of around twenty-five thousand. In 1934 the new Palacio de las Bellas Artes opened its doors to opera and the first steps were taken by Karl Alwin, Franz Steiner and William Wymetal, all Viennese refugees, to form a permanent company. The first production in 1941 was *The Magic Flute*, with both Mexican and European singers. During the war visiting conductors included Horenstein, Kleiber and Beecham and in 1950 Maria Callas made her Latin American debut there in *Aida* with the newly formed Opera Nacional.

The Mexico City Opera at the Palacio de las Belles Artes now has a standard repertoire of around ninety Italian, German and French operas as well as Spanish and Mexican zarzuelas. It is a high-paying establishment and can afford internationally renowned singers. Carreras, Domingo, Freni, Caballe, Berganza, Los Angeles and Alfredo Kraus have all appeared regularly for the company.

Opera de Caracas, Complejo 'Teresa Carreno'

Plaza Morelos, Caracas

Director: Elias Perez Borjas
Musical Director: Alfredo Rugules
Season: April–May
Productions: 4 or 5
Capacity: 1,500

Box Office: (2) 572 9446
Box open: Daily 9.30a.m.–5.30p.m.
Postal: As above
Prices: 20–500 Bolivares
Other venues: Teatro Municipal and Aula Magna (University of Central Venezuela)

In the early years of the Venezuelan Republic, at the start of the nineteenth century, there were at various times three principal theatres in Caracas, the Coliseo, the Tocotines and the Nacimientos. The repertoire was the usual mix of the familiar, such as *Otello, The Barber of Seville, Lucia di Lammermoor,* and *Il Trovatore,* and the rarely performed, including Ricci's *Crispino e la Comare,* Petrella's *Ione,* Apolloni's *L'Ebreo,* Adam's *Le Chalet,* Marchetti's *Ruy Blas* and Meyerbeer's *L'Africana.* While there was evidently a growing and lively interest in opera, and a willingness to experiment, the principal problem was the lack of a permanent operatic home. This was resolved in the late nineteenth century when Jesus Munoz built the Teatro Municipal, giving Caracas the security of an established season, and enabling it to bring in the top Venezuelan artists and many leading foreign singers.

Today, although Caracas' finances are in near chaos, which has of course had a serious effect on some recent productions, the composing side is doing well. 1973 saw the world première of the first Venezualan opera *Virginia* by Jose Angel Montero. Sponsored by President Guzmoan Blanco, it opened at the Teatro. Two years later Alexis Rago wrote El Paramo, which had its world première at the Aula Magna, (part of the local university). Rago has since written two further works, *Florian, El Infausto,* commissioned by the government and *Miranda,* commissioned by the Opera of Caracas.

While many operas are performed in the university or at the Teatro, the principal venue is now the Complejo 'Teresa Carreno', inaugurated in 1981. It has first-rate computerized facilities, and is an excellent base for a repertoire which has recently been embracing Puccini, Mascagni and Leoncavallo.

AUSTRALIA AND THE FAR EAST

Sydney Opera House

Opera of South Australia, Adelaide

Opera Theatre, Grote Street, Adelaide SA 5000

Director: Ian Johnston
Musical Director: Andrew Green
Season: March, June, August, November, December
Productions: 5, 4 new
Performances: Varies
Capacity: 1,000 (Adelaide Festival Theatre 2,000)

Box Office: (08) 212 6833 (Opera House); (08) 216 8600 (Festival)
Telex: AA 88 724 FESTAR
Box open: Daily 9.00a.m.–5.00p.m. (Opera Theatre and Festival Theatre)
Postal: As above for Opera; GPO Box 1269, Adelaide SA 5001 for Festival
Prices: $12–$35
Concessions: For students, senior citizens and unwaged

Adelaide, like every important centre in Australia was long dependent on touring companies, although there were occasional groups set up for small-scale productions of opera, usually given at Her Majesty's Theatre. By 1970 the general consensus of opinion called for a permanent home for opera and the same year the foundation stone was laid for a new Festival Theatre on the south bank of Torrens Lake. The project rapidly became oversubscribed and the new venue opened in 1973.

The smaller Victorian Opera Theatre, which has a capacity of one thousand, was refurbished in 1974, and usually houses the smaller productions, which include standard repertoire – particularly Mozart and Strauss – and regular productions of operetta.

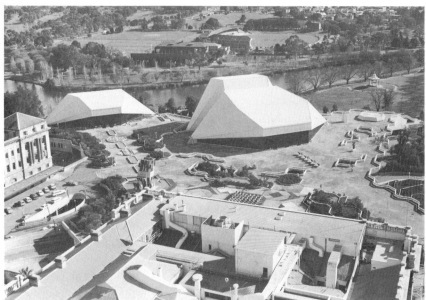

The Festival Theatre, Adelaide

A permanent company was set up the following year by the ex-Glyndebourne director Myer Fredman, who led the activities of the company for six years and introduced some important new operas.

However, it is the biennial festival at Adelaide that has generated most international interest. The event was begun in 1960 by Professor John Bishop, director of the Elder Conservatory of Music, and opened with a performance of *Salome*, given in the Theatre Royal Hindley Street, with Joan Hammond singing the title-role. Bishop, a man of enormous vision, directed the festival for almost ten years and mounted some important productions of modern repertoire using the available resources which, since 1974, have included the South Australian Opera. Bishop also invited guest singers and producers and pioneered productions of works by Janáček, Weill and Shostakovich.

Since his death there has been a series of different directors for the festival which now takes place in the Festival Theatre. Anthony Steele led the festival for most of the seventies, and returned for the 1984 and 1986 seasons. Lord Harewood will direct in 1988, when he plans to put on the first performance of Prokofiev's *The Fiery Angel* with Josephine Barstow. Clifford Hocking is lined up to direct the 1990 festival. Notable festival productions have included the 1980 *Death in Venice* directed by Jim Sharman (the director of the *Rocky Horror Show*) and choreographed by Ian Spink, *The Makropoulos Case* in 1982, and the 1986 première of Richard Neale's *Voss*.

Victoria State Opera

State Theatre, Victorian Arts Centre,
100 St Kilda Rd., Melbourne, Victoria 30 04

Director: Kevin Mackenzie-Forbes
Musical Director: Richard Divall
Season: July–August, November–December
Productions: 6, 5 new
Capacity: 1,984

Box Office: (3) 8211 11500
Telex: VICART 39414 or 151916
Box open: Daily 9.00a.m.–9.00p.m.
Postal: As above
Cards: All major cards accepted
Concessions: senior citizens, students, unwaged
Other booking procedures: BASS outlets
tel: 03 11 500

Until very recently the State of Victoria was without a permanent opera company, having depended for many years on small short-lived enterprises and visits from foreign companies touring Australia. These included the Melba-Williamson troupe set up by the famous Melbourne-born *prima donna* Nellie Melba; the Quinlan Company, which in 1912 produced the *Ring;* and the Gonsalez company. During the latter part of the nineteenth century operatic activity was prodigious; sometimes as many as eighty performances were given each year.

The First World War put an end to all this, creating a situation that lasted well beyond the next World War. Finally, in 1950, a skeletal company was put together calling itself, rather grandly, the National Theatre Opera Company of Melbourne. It merged only two years later with the Sydney company giving birth to the Australian Opera. The first season was launched in 1956 and the company toured to all the major East Coast cities. Melbourne was fortunate enough to have an old theatre, The Princess, which may not have been ideal for those involved in the production of opera but satisfied the public's desire for an old-fashioned milieu.

Despite its federal title, the Australian Opera became increasingly a New South Wales, Sydney-based affair, and the inhabitants of Victoria began to want their own company. This came to fruition in 1977 when the Victoria State Opera was created. Today the company performs at the State Theatre built in 1984 to surpass Sydney as the most technically efficient opera house in Australia. Under the musical directorship of Richard Divall, the company has had a series of successes and is considered to be the most progressive house in Australia. Divall's personal magnetism has had a lot to do with this but there has been a healthy spirit of competition with Sydney, fuelled by a certain resentment over the large difference in subsidy both companies receive. Without sufficient funds to hire internationally famous singers, the opera nonetheless continues to encourage young talent and manages to host a number of interesting productions. The company also presents one or two productions at the Spoleto Festival in Melbourne, which was set up by the founder of the original festival in Italy, the American composer Gian Carlo Menotti. One recent production for Spoleto which aroused great interest was Ken Russell's *Madame Butterfly.*

Sydney Opera House

Bennelong Point, Box 4274, Sydney 2001

Director: Donald McDonald
Musical Director: Moffatt Oxenbould
Season: June–August; January–March
Productions: 19, 4 new
Performances: Approx 14 of each
Capacity: 1547
Touring venues: The Queensland Performing Arts Centre, Brisbane; Canberra Theatre, Canberra; The Adelaide Festival Centre, Adelaide; The Victoria Arts Centre, Melbourne

Box Office: (02) 2 0588
Telex: 25525
Box open: Daily 9.30a.m. to start of performance
Postal: Ticket Services, Australian, P.O. Box 291, Strawberry Hills, NSW 2021
Prices: $10–$60
Concessions: Senior citizens and children under 17

Until the opening of the Sydney Opera House in 1973, Australia's claim to fame, operatically speaking, was the export of its finest singers. Since the great Melbourne-born soprano Nellie Melba first graced a European stage in 1887, there has been a steady stream of Australian-born Australian-trained artists who felt compelled to leave their country because of lack of opportunity at home. So, while people like John Brownlee, Florence Austral, Joan Hammond, Marie Collier and, of course, Joan Sutherland were rapidly making their names abroad, at home precious little was happening.

The situation changed radically in 1956 when the two main troupes in the country, the New South Wales Opera and the National Opera Theatre of Melbourne merged to form the first national company, the Australian Opera. Launched by the Elizabethan Theatre Trust, it was originally intended to be a touring company. It began its first season in Adelaide under the directorship of Hugh Hunt, and gave a four-week season of Mozart before touring the other major cities – but it became increasingly Sydney based. Joan Sutherland's return to Australia in 1965 with her own Sutherland-Williamson company (whose members included the young Luciano Pavarotti) and her performances in *Lucia di Lammermoor* and *L'elisir d'amore* did much to encourage opera production in the country and from that time onwards Sutherland and her husband Richard Bonynge were inextricably linked with the activities of the Australian Opera.

The history of the opera house itself is exceptional. The problems with its construction were so complex that the whole project took fourteen years to complete, at the enormous cost of one hundred and two million Australian dollars. It all began in 1954 when the head of New South Wales, J.J. Cahill, announced the plan and the setting up of a competition for the design. The winner was the Dane Jörn Utzon, a little-known radical architect who claimed to be influenced by the style of the ancient Maya temples in Mexico. Although his plans were barely more than diagrams when they were submitted, the jury were impressed by the originality of his conception which seemed bound to take not only Australia but the whole world by storm. There were various exceptional features – the broken roof formed by four enormous prefabricated shells; the radical method of moving scenery on and off stage by vertical lifts; and the huge storage space available below the stage, which adequately solved the problem of narrow width created by the side by side placing of the two auditoria.

By 1966 the project was on the verge of collapse as a series of rows between Utzon and the new minister for Public Works led to the architect resigning with the words 'it is not I, but the Sydney Opera House that created all the enormous difficulties'. Yet again another opera house had fallen victim of politics, this time with the election of a more conservative and reactionary administration. As it stands today, the exterior is the work of Utzon and the interior the work of a group of local architects brought in to finish the job. The feeble acoustics of the largest theatre prompted another crisis and the decision had to be taken to exchange the functions of the two halls: the concert hall became the opera house and vice-versa. As if this wasn't enough, the area that was to accommodate Utzon's fascinating scene-lifting machinery was now designated as a recording hall.

The opening of the Opera House by the Queen on October 20th, 1973 was greeted with slight incredulity and enormous relief; eight days later the first opera was given – Prokofiev's *War and Peace,* produced by Sam Wannamaker and directed by British conductor Edward Downes who stayed with the company until 1976.

After almost a decade of relative stability, the Australian Opera has recently been dogged by a series of administrative and financial problems, at the centre of which is the long-standing and controversial reign of Richard Bonynge, musical director from 1976–85. The house is very company-orientated with few big names brought in as guests, Dame Joan Sutherland having been the biggest box-office draw for almost two decades. Those international singers who have appeared at Sydney include Elizabeth Connell, Leona Mitchell, Rita Hunter and Jessye Norman while the native-born artists taking starring roles include Isobel Buchanan, Yvonne Kenny, Marilyn Richardson, and Rosamund Illing. A more common import to Sydney is that of producers, including Michael Hampe, Elijah Moshinsky, John Copley and David Pountney, some of whom have been associated with the Australian conductor Charles Mackerras, who has returned regularly to Sydney from the U.K.

The repertoire of the house is extremely conservative although it does include the occasional commissioned work by an Australian composer – Richard Meal's *Voss,* 1986, is one example. It continues to show an inclination towards the sort of repertoire introduced during the Bonynge regime – Italian Romantic opera and Mozart. Towards the late seventies it tended to branch out more, with Sutherland doing her first *Dialogues of the Carmelites* and we have yet to see how things will develop in future.

Dissatisfaction with the building continues unabated and there are now plans to build another opera house as a standard home for opera and turn the present theatre, which is in every way too small, into a concert hall.

The concert hall of the Sydney Opera House

The Nissai Theatre, Tokyo

1-1-1 Yurako-Cho, Chiyoda-Ku, Tokyo

Capacity: 1350
Season: Throughout the year
Ballet: Visiting companies

Box Office: 81 3 5033111
Box open: Daily 10.00a.m.–6.00p.m.
Prices: 15,000–25,000 Yen

There is a rich operatic life in Japan's capital; a number of important companies have emerged since Western opera was first introduced to Japan by the tenor Jujiwara in 1933. Despite the almost total lack of support from the state, the Fujiwara Company and the more recently formed Tokyo Chamber Opera Group have been successful enterprises, although the most prodigious and active remains the Nikikai Company (established in 1952), which now boasts a far-reaching repertoire of western classics, centred round the works of Mozart, Wagner and Puccini.

Japanese operas have flourished since the war, many influenced by the European avant garde but nevertheless written in a style that is both original and traditional. These include the works of Bekku, Takat and more recently Mizumo *(Tensho Monogatari)* and Aoshima *(The Death Goddess)*.

There are several venues in Tokyo which can be used for opera; the NHK hall has accommodated many foreign companies including the Bolshoi, the Deutsche Oper and Bayreuth, smaller works are given in the Tokyo Bunka Kaikan and the Shinjuku Bunka Centre. The best equipped however remains the Nissai Theatre, (which has a capacity of one thousand three hundred and fifty), and which opened in 1964. This will remain the principal venue until the new National Theatre is completed in 1990. As recently as April 1987 a new theatre opened in the basement of the Seibu department store on the Ginza with Peter Brook's production of *Carmen*.

The general standard of singing in Japan is good and some outstanding artists have emerged recently, a few becoming familiar to Western audiences. These include William Hu, Hiroko Motomiya and Kyoko Azuma. The best way to obtain information about opera in Tokyo is through hotels and tourist offices.

China Peking Opera House

Ho Fang Jiao, Beijing

Director: Zhang Dong-Chuan
Productions: Average of 7

Box Office: 338 149
Prices: 1–2 yuan

Peking opera is the term commonly given to Chinese opera; a mixed-media genre that bears little resemblance to European operatic forms. It incorporates acting, recitation, acrobatics, dancing and mime as well as singing, making minimal use of stage props with little or no scenery. Much more depends on the subtle interpretation of traditional roles, of which there are three main types; the patriotic-hierarchical, the social-military and the colloquial. Characters are, broadly speaking, divided into *shing* (male roles), *tan* (female roles), *chou* (comedians) and *ching* (painted face roles). *Ching* uses colour symbolically, so that red means good character, yellow means intelligent, white is evil and cunning and so on. There are approximately sixteen different, extremely elaborate designs.

The highly symbolic and stylized gestures have been sophisticated over many centuries and now require a training period of at least seven years in addition to a lifetime of study and practice. The singing essentially comes in two different forms; one nervous and strained, the other relaxed, the form being chosen according to context. Movements are closely connected with these speech patterns and the actors continually dance when singing.

There are strict rules for costumes and the musical accompaniment is usually provided by up to eight Chinese instruments with the players arranged on the corner of the stage.

The development of the form was a very gradual process, as all the separate elements had to be unified. Puppet shows, acrobatics and miming had been practised since the Chou dynasty *c.* 100 B.C. but, it was not until the Manchu dynasty in the seventeenth century that opera reached its peak, having been transplanted by the Emperor to Peking, the capital city. After a while this form of opera became known as the Ching-hsi (capital play) and this is the form we know today.

In Peking itself there are at least five companies that practice the form we commonly call Peking Opera, and it is possible to hear it in the capital city throughout the year. Approximately seven operas are put on every year by the principal company, the Peking Opera, and given at the People's Theatre. This company spends about nine months in China in most of the major cities and then tours Europe and the United States for approximately two months a year. The ticket prices in Peking cost one or two yuan. The best way to obtain tickets for the opera in China is to contact an official tour operator or a representative in a tourist hotel.

Glossary

Bel Canto: A loose term describing the tradition of beautiful singing involving refined phrasing and coloratura, which supposedly emerged in Italy during the seventeenth century.

Coloratura: A form of singing in which florid ornamentation demanding remarkable technical prowess is the predominant feature.

Grand Opera: A form of opera that emerged in France during the first half of the nineteenth century. It is best illustrated by Meyerbeer's *Grand Spectacle*, in which the demands of the production, obliged to contain at least four acts, an active chorus and a ballet took precedence over musical values.

Heldentenor: A German term meaning 'heroic' tenor.

Intermezzo: A short comic interlude, normally intended as light relief between the acts of conventional *opera seria* in Italy during the seventeenth and eighteenth centuries, which emerged as a form in its own right and encouraged the development of *opera buffa*. The most famous example is Pergolesi's *La Serva Padrona* (1733).

Kapellmeister: Literally, 'chapel master', the German term for the choir master at a court chapel, although it was later used to describe the wider duties of the court composer and conductor of the resident orchestra.

Metastasian opera: Named after Pietro Metastasio (1698–1782), an eighteenth century poet employed at the Viennese court, some of whose numerous lyric dramas were set as many as sixty or seventy times by a profusion of different composers of *opera seria*. The subjects Metastasio chose were essentially classical.

Opera buffa: Italian comic opera which emerged as a separate form out of comic interludes called *intermezzi* that provided light relief between acts of *opera seria*.

Opéra comique: Musical numbers with spoken dialogue which formed an alternative to French *Grand Opera*. Although it had its origins in eighteenth-century farce and satire, it became more serious in tone in the nineteenth century. Famous examples include Boieldieu's *La Dame Blanche* and Bizet's *Carmen*.

Opera seria: The most important operatic form throughout Europe during the seventeenth and eighteenth centuries, at the centre of which was the *da capo aria*, an elaborate entertainment designed to display the virtuosity of the principal singers. The plot almost always revolved around mythological or historical subjects.

Reform opera: A term used to describe the operatic reaction to the rigidity and conventionality of *opera seria*. Instigated by Gluck, it aimed to intensify the drama with clarity of effect and simplicity of means.

Rescue opera: A term given to opera where the rescue of a hero or heroine formed the basis of the plot. It became a popular genre in France after the Revolution but was most successfully represented by Beethoven in *Fidelio*.

Singspiel: Literally, 'sung play', the forerunner of German Romantic Opera where musical numbers are interspersed with dialogue.

Tragédie Lyrique: A type of French opera seria created by Lully and his librettist Quinault; a musical version of to the genre of tragedy epitomized by Racine and Corneille.

Verismo: A term of literary criticism meaning 'true to life' describing late nineteenth century Italian literature but extended to include opera whose plot aimed to describe real life situations albeit emotionally exaggerated. Famous examples include *Cavalleria Rusticana*, *Pagliacci* and *Louise*.

Zarzuela: A Spanish form of comic opera, with spoken dialogue.

A Selective Index of Names

INDEX